JavaScript Crash Course for Beginners in 10 Hours or Less

(Book 1)

This book may be purchased in bulk for educational, business, fundraising, or sales promotional use.

ISBN:

Published by: Ekesy In-Outdoor Company

10B, Mufutau Opeifa Street, Oke-Odo, Ile-Epo B/Stop, Alimosho, Lagos, Nigeria

Email: dev@israeljoshua.com.ng

Tel: +234 803 815 4459, +234 813 2228 534

For information, please contact us @

dev@israeljoshua.com.ng

www.israeljoshua.com.ng

Call: +234 803 815 4459

Whatsapp: +234 813 2228 534

TABLE OF CONTENT

DEDICATION

I, **Israel Joshua Chukwubueze**, formerly known as **Christopher Ekene Okade**, wholeheartedly dedicate this book to the **Almighty God**, the source of my wisdom, creativity, and strength. Through every challenge, every sleepless night, and every step of the journey, His presence has been my anchor. Every line of code I write, every word I teach, and every lesson I pass on is shaped by His grace working in me and through me. To God alone be all the glory.

To my **two beautiful daughters**—you are the lights of my life. Your curiosity, laughter, and bright minds inspire me to keep learning, teaching, and creating. I write with you in mind, hoping that one day you will read these pages and see what can be achieved with belief, purpose, and determination. May your lives be filled with possibilities, confidence, and courage to build things that matter.

To my **beloved mother**, your strength and support have been the foundation of everything I've accomplished. Your prayers, encouragement, and unwavering belief in me carried me through the hardest times. You taught me the value of discipline and compassion, and I honor you with this work. You are not just my mother, but my guide and greatest blessing.

To **you**, my dear **reader**, thank you for picking up this book. Whether you are a student, a dreamer, a future developer, or someone simply eager to learn something new—you are the reason this book was written. Your desire to grow and understand JavaScript is respected and appreciated. I have taken every effort to make this journey as smooth, practical, and enjoyable as possible for you.

A Few Words to Inspire You

📌 **Bold Reminders:**

- **You don't need to know everything to start.** Just start. Learn one thing at a time. Progress is more powerful than perfection.

- **This book is your companion.** Whether you read it in one day or one hour a day, you'll find helpful guidance, real-life examples, and actionable steps to help you learn JavaScript confidently.
- **The world of technology needs your ideas.** Coding isn't just about syntax—it's about solving real problems and improving lives.

To everyone out there who has ever felt overwhelmed by code or doubted your ability to learn something technical—this book is especially for you. You're not alone. I was once where you are now. And if I can write over 500 books, teach over 500 students one-on-one, and still learn new things every day, so can you. You've got what it takes.

So, with a heart full of gratitude and hope, I offer this book as a gift of knowledge and empowerment. Learn at your pace, write your first lines of JavaScript with joy, and let this be the beginning of something great.

With deep appreciation,
Israel Joshua Chukwubueze

PREFACE

JavaScript Crash Course for Beginners in 10 Hours or Less

My name is **Israel Joshua Chukwubueze**, formerly known as **Christopher Ekene Okade**. Over the years, I have been blessed with the opportunity to wear many hats—as an author, instructor, coach, mentor, creative designer, and developer. One thing that has remained consistent in all my roles is the **passion for teaching** and **sharing knowledge** in the most practical and approachable way possible.

This book—***JavaScript Crash Course for Beginners in 10 Hours or Less***—was written to support **beginners** who are curious about programming and want a fast yet reliable way to get started. Whether you're just stepping into the world of web development or you're trying to build your first app, I've designed this book to help you understand JavaScript **without feeling overwhelmed**.

My Journey with Code and Teaching

I started writing code just like many others—curious, confused, and often stuck. I know what it feels like to search endlessly for tutorials, watch video after video, and still struggle to connect the dots. I also know what it means to finally understand something that once seemed impossible—and that moment of clarity is what I want **you** to experience through this book.

Over the years, I've taught **over 500 students in one-on-one sessions**, and written **more than 500 books** on topics ranging from self-development to design to software development. Through these experiences, I've come to learn that **the best way to teach code is not through complicated terms or abstract theory**, but through **real-life explanations**, **clear examples**, and **step-by-step guidance**.

What Makes This Book Different

Here are a few things that make this book special:

◆ **Simplicity First**
You don't need to be a genius or a math wizard to learn JavaScript. This book breaks down each concept into **easy, friendly language** with lots of **practical code samples**.

◆ **Learn Fast, Learn Smart**
You have 10 hours or less? That's enough. This book is organized into short, clear chapters that you can read and practice quickly, helping you **build confidence and skills at the same time**.

◆ **Real Examples You Can Use**
Each chapter comes with real-world code examples, so you're not just learning theory—you're writing actual JavaScript and seeing what it does.

◆ **A Friendly Voice**
Think of me as your coach. This book is written like a conversation between you and someone who genuinely wants to help you get better at JavaScript.

◆ **You're Not Alone**
Every reader matters. This book is part of my larger mission to **help everyday people become creators**, not just consumers, in the digital world. I want to **see you succeed** and build amazing things with code.

Who This Book Is For

If you're:

- A **complete beginner** who has never written a single line of JavaScript.
- Someone who tried learning JavaScript before and felt **lost or stuck**.
- A **creative person**, designer, marketer, or entrepreneur who wants to **add coding to your skillset**.
- Or someone looking for a **quick refresher** with practical insight…

Then this book was written with **you** in mind.

How to Use This Book

◆ **One Chapter at a Time**
Each chapter is short and focused. Try to practice the code as you go. Don't rush. Even if you only spend 30 minutes a day, **you'll see real progress**.

◆ **Use the Examples**
The examples are there to help you **learn by doing**. Tweak the code, break it, fix it again. That's how real developers grow.

◆ **Revisit Whenever Needed**
This book is your tool, not a one-time read. Come back to any chapter when you need a quick reminder or code example.

A Note from the Author

Writing this book was more than just a task for me—it was a way of **giving back**. I've stood where you're standing. I know the doubts, the frustration, and the moments where it all starts to make sense. JavaScript is not just a language—it's a skill that can **open doors**, **launch careers**, and **spark creativity**.

I wrote this book with **clarity**, **kindness**, and **respect for your time**. My goal is not just to help you learn JavaScript, but to help you believe that **you can do this**.

So, thank you. Thank you for choosing this book. Thank you for trusting me to guide you. And thank you for taking the first step toward a new skill that could **change your future**.

With sincerity and support,
Israel Joshua Chukwubueze

Chapter 1: Introduction to JavaScript

1.1 What is JavaScript and Why Use It?

Understanding JavaScript's Core Nature

JavaScript stands as one of the most influential programming languages in modern web development, serving as the dynamic force that transforms static HTML pages into interactive, responsive web applications. At its fundamental level, JavaScript is a high-level, interpreted programming language that enables developers to create dynamic content, control multimedia, animate images, and handle user interactions on web pages.

The language operates as a client-side scripting language, meaning it runs directly in the user's web browser without requiring server-side processing for basic functionality. This characteristic makes JavaScript incredibly powerful for creating immediate, responsive user experiences. When a user clicks a button, hovers over an element, or submits a form, JavaScript can instantly respond to these actions without needing to communicate with a remote server.

The Versatility Factor

JavaScript's versatility extends far beyond simple web page interactions. Modern JavaScript can power full-scale web applications, mobile applications through frameworks like React Native, desktop applications using Electron, and even server-side applications through Node.js. This unprecedented flexibility means that learning JavaScript opens doors to virtually every aspect of software development.

The language supports multiple programming paradigms, including procedural, object-oriented, and functional programming styles. This flexibility allows developers to choose the approach that best fits their project requirements and personal coding preferences. Whether you prefer writing functions that process data step-by-step or creating objects that encapsulate both data and behavior, JavaScript accommodates your chosen methodology.

Why JavaScript Dominates Web Development

JavaScript's dominance in web development stems from several critical factors. First, it's the only programming language that runs natively in web browsers without requiring plugins or additional software installations. This universal browser support means that JavaScript code can reach any device with a web browser, from smartphones and tablets to desktop computers and smart TVs.

The language's relatively gentle learning curve makes it accessible to newcomers while still offering advanced features for experienced developers. JavaScript's syntax borrows heavily from languages like C and Java, making it familiar to developers with experience in other programming languages. However, its dynamic nature and flexible typing system make it more forgiving for beginners who are still learning programming concepts.

Real-World Applications

JavaScript powers some of the world's most popular websites and applications. Social media platforms use JavaScript to update feeds in real-time, e-commerce sites employ it for shopping cart functionality and product filtering, and productivity applications rely on it for document editing and collaboration features. Online games, data visualization tools, and interactive educational platforms all depend heavily on JavaScript's capabilities.

The rise of Progressive Web Apps (PWAs) has further elevated JavaScript's importance. These applications blur the line between web pages and native mobile apps, offering offline functionality, push notifications, and app-like user interfaces—all powered by JavaScript technologies.

1.2 A Brief History of JavaScript

The Birth of JavaScript (1995)

JavaScript's origin story begins in 1995 at Netscape Communications Corporation, where programmer Brendan Eich faced an ambitious deadline: create a scripting language for the Netscape Navigator web browser in just ten days. This rushed development timeline would later contribute to some of JavaScript's infamous quirks and inconsistencies, but it also resulted in a language that prioritized flexibility and ease of use over rigid structure.

Initially called "Mocha," then briefly renamed "LiveScript," the language finally became "JavaScript" as part of a marketing partnership with Sun Microsystems, whose Java language was gaining popularity. Despite the name similarity, JavaScript and Java share little beyond basic syntax influences and both being programming languages.

The Browser Wars Era (1996-2004)

Following JavaScript's introduction, Microsoft developed JScript for Internet Explorer, creating their own implementation of the language. This led to compatibility issues as different browsers supported different features and syntax variations. Web developers during this period often had to write multiple versions of their code to ensure compatibility across different browsers.

The lack of standardization created significant challenges for the web development community. Simple tasks like handling user events or manipulating page elements required browser-specific code, making development time-consuming and error-prone.

Standardization Through ECMAScript (1997-Present)

Recognizing the need for standardization, Netscape submitted JavaScript to the European Computer Manufacturers Association (ECMA) International for standardization. This process resulted in ECMAScript, the official standard upon which JavaScript implementations are based.

The first ECMAScript standard (ES1) was published in 1997, followed by ES2 (1998) and ES3 (1999). ES3 remained the dominant standard for nearly a decade, providing the foundation for most JavaScript development during the early 2000s.

The Renaissance Period (2005-2015)

The introduction of Asynchronous JavaScript and XML (AJAX) in 2005 marked a turning point for JavaScript development. AJAX enabled web pages to update content dynamically without requiring full page reloads, paving the way for more sophisticated web applications.

Google's release of the V8 JavaScript engine in 2008, initially developed for the Chrome browser, dramatically improved JavaScript performance. V8's speed improvements made complex JavaScript applications practical and led to the development of Node.js, which brought JavaScript to server-side development.

The Modern Era (2015-Present)

ECMAScript 2015 (ES6) introduced revolutionary changes to JavaScript, including arrow functions, classes, modules, template literals, and destructuring assignment. This update modernized the language and made it more suitable for large-scale application development.

Since ES6, new ECMAScript versions are released annually, each adding incremental improvements and new features. This regular update cycle ensures that JavaScript continues to evolve with modern development needs while maintaining backward compatibility.

1.3 How JavaScript Works in the Browser

The Browser Environment Architecture

Understanding how JavaScript operates within web browsers requires examining the browser's internal architecture. Modern browsers consist of several key components that work together to process and execute JavaScript code: the rendering engine, the JavaScript engine, the Document Object Model (DOM), and various Web APIs.

The rendering engine handles HTML parsing and CSS styling, creating the visual representation of web pages. The JavaScript engine, such as Chrome's V8 or Firefox's SpiderMonkey, interprets and executes JavaScript code. These engines have evolved significantly over the years, implementing advanced optimization techniques like just-in-time compilation to achieve near-native performance speeds.

The Document Object Model (DOM)

The DOM serves as the bridge between JavaScript and HTML content. When a browser loads an HTML page, it constructs a DOM tree—a hierarchical representation of all page elements. JavaScript can access and manipulate this tree structure, allowing developers to dynamically modify page content, styling, and structure.

Each HTML element becomes a DOM node that JavaScript can target using various selection methods. For example, JavaScript can find elements by their ID, class name, tag type, or complex CSS selectors. Once an element is selected, JavaScript can change its content, attributes, styling, or even remove it entirely from the page.

Event-Driven Programming Model

JavaScript operates on an event-driven programming model within browsers. Events represent user interactions (clicks, key presses, mouse movements) or browser actions (page loading, window resizing). JavaScript can "listen" for these events and execute specific code in response.

This event-driven approach enables highly interactive user experiences. When a user clicks a button, JavaScript can validate form data, send requests to servers, update page content, or trigger animations. The browser's event system ensures that JavaScript code executes at the appropriate times without blocking other operations.

The JavaScript Execution Context

JavaScript code executes within specific contexts that determine variable accessibility and function behavior. The global execution context serves as the default environment where variables and functions declared outside of other functions reside. Each function call creates its own execution context with its own variable scope.

The browser maintains an execution stack (call stack) that tracks the currently executing functions. When a function calls another function, the new function's context is pushed onto the stack. When a function completes, its context is removed from the stack, and execution returns to the previous context.

Asynchronous Operations and the Event Loop

One of JavaScript's most powerful features in the browser environment is its ability to handle asynchronous operations without blocking the user interface. The event loop mechanism allows JavaScript to execute long-running tasks (like network requests or file operations) in the background while maintaining responsiveness.

When JavaScript encounters an asynchronous operation, it delegates the task to browser APIs and continues executing other code. Once the asynchronous operation completes, its callback function is added to a task queue. The event loop continuously monitors the call stack and task queue, executing queued tasks when the call stack is empty.

1.4 Setting Up Your First JavaScript Environment

Browser-Based Development Setup

The simplest way to begin JavaScript development requires nothing more than a web browser and a text editor. Every modern browser includes a JavaScript engine and developer tools that provide everything needed for basic JavaScript experimentation and learning.

To access your browser's developer tools, press F12 (Windows/Linux) or Cmd+Option+I (Mac) in most browsers. The Console tab provides an interactive JavaScript environment where you can type commands and see immediate results. This console serves as an excellent playground for testing small code snippets and learning JavaScript syntax.

`#javascript`

```javascript
// Type this directly in the browser console
console.log("Hello, JavaScript!");
console.log(2 + 3);
console.log("Current time:", new Date());
```

Creating Your First HTML File with JavaScript

Create a new file called `index.html` and save it with the following content:

#html

```html
<!DOCTYPE html>
<html lang="en">
<head>
    <meta charset="UTF-8">
    <meta name="viewport" content="width=device-width,
initial-scale=1.0">
    <title>My First JavaScript Page</title>
</head>
<body>
    <h1>Welcome to JavaScript</h1>
    <p id="demo">This text will be changed by
JavaScript</p>

    <script>
        // This JavaScript code runs when the page loads
        document.getElementById("demo").innerHTML =
"Hello from JavaScript!";
    </script>
</body>
</html>
```

Open this file in your web browser by double-clicking it or dragging it into a browser window. You'll see how JavaScript modifies the page content by changing the paragraph text.

External JavaScript Files

As your JavaScript code grows more complex, storing it in separate files becomes essential for organization and maintainability. Create a new file called `script.js`:

#javascript

```javascript
// script.js
function greetUser() {
    const userName = prompt("What's your name?");
    if (userName) {
        alert("Hello, " + userName + "! Welcome to
JavaScript!");
    }
}

function changeBackgroundColor() {
    const colors = ["#ffcccb", "#add8e6", "#90ee90",
"#ffd700", "#dda0dd"];
    const randomColor = colors[Math.floor(Math.random() *
colors.length)];
    document.body.style.backgroundColor = randomColor;
}

// Wait for the page to load before running code
document.addEventListener("DOMContentLoaded", function()
{
    console.log("Page loaded and JavaScript is ready!");
});
```

Link this external file to your HTML:

#html

```html
<!DOCTYPE html>
<html lang="en">
<head>
```

```
    <meta charset="UTF-8">
    <meta name="viewport" content="width=device-width,
initial-scale=1.0">
    <title>JavaScript with External File</title>
</head>
<body>
    <h1>JavaScript Interactive Demo</h1>
    <button onclick="greetUser()">Greet Me</button>
    <button onclick="changeBackgroundColor()">Change
Background</button>

    <!-- Link to external JavaScript file -->
    <script src="script.js"></script>
</body>
</html>
```

Text Editors and Development Tools

While any text editor can write JavaScript, using a code editor designed for programming significantly improves the development experience. Popular free options include Visual Studio Code, Atom, and Sublime Text. These editors provide syntax highlighting, error detection, code completion, and various extensions that streamline JavaScript development.

Visual Studio Code, in particular, offers excellent JavaScript support out of the box, including IntelliSense code completion, integrated debugging, and Git version control. Installing extensions like "Prettier" for code formatting and "ESLint" for error checking can further enhance your development workflow.

Browser Developer Tools Deep Dive

Modern browser developer tools offer sophisticated JavaScript debugging capabilities. The Sources tab allows you to set breakpoints in your code, step through execution line by line, and inspect variable values at runtime. The

Network tab shows all HTTP requests your JavaScript makes, helping you understand data flow in web applications.

The Performance tab can identify JavaScript performance bottlenecks, while the Application tab displays local storage, cookies, and other browser-stored data that your JavaScript might manipulate. Learning to use these tools effectively can dramatically speed up your development and debugging process.

1.5 Writing and Running Your First JavaScript Code

Understanding JavaScript Syntax Fundamentals

JavaScript syntax shares similarities with other C-style programming languages, making it familiar to developers with experience in Java, C++, or C#. However, JavaScript's dynamic nature introduces unique characteristics that distinguish it from statically typed languages.

Variables in JavaScript can be declared using `var`, `let`, or `const` keywords, each with different scoping rules and reassignment capabilities:

#javascript

```javascript
// Variable declarations
var oldStyleVariable = "This is a var declaration";
let modernVariable = "This is a let declaration";
const constantValue = "This value cannot be reassigned";

// Numbers
let age = 25;
let price = 99.99;
let temperature = -15.5;

// Strings
let firstName = "JavaScript";
let message = 'Learning JavaScript is fun!';
let templateString = `Hello, ${firstName}!`;
```

```
// Booleans
let isLearning = true;
let isComplete = false;

// Arrays
let colors = ["red", "green", "blue"];
let numbers = [1, 2, 3, 4, 5];
let mixedArray = ["text", 42, true, null];

// Objects
let person = {
    name: "John Doe",
    age: 30,
    city: "New York",
    isStudent: false
};
```

Functions: The Building Blocks of JavaScript

Functions represent reusable blocks of code that perform specific tasks. JavaScript supports multiple function declaration syntaxes, each with subtle differences in behavior:

#javascript

```
// Function declaration
function calculateArea(length, width) {
    return length * width;
}

// Function expression
```

```
const calculateVolume = function(length, width, height) {
    return length * width * height;
};

// Arrow function (ES6+)
const calculatePerimeter = (length, width) => {
    return 2 * (length + width);
};

// Shortened arrow function for simple expressions
const double = x => x * 2;

// Using the functions
console.log("Area:", calculateArea(5, 3));
console.log("Volume:", calculateVolume(5, 3, 2));
console.log("Perimeter:", calculatePerimeter(5, 3));
console.log("Double of 7:", double(7));
```

Control Structures and Logic Flow

JavaScript provides various control structures for managing program flow and implementing logic:

#javascript

```
// Conditional statements
let temperature = 75;

if (temperature > 80) {
    console.log("It's hot outside!");
} else if (temperature > 60) {
    console.log("Perfect weather!");
```

```
} else {
    console.log("It's cold outside!");
}

// Switch statement
let dayOfWeek = "Monday";

switch (dayOfWeek) {
    case "Monday":
        console.log("Start of the work week");
        break;
    case "Friday":
        console.log("TGIF!");
        break;
    case "Saturday":
    case "Sunday":
        console.log("Weekend time!");
        break;
    default:
        console.log("Just another day");
}

// Loops
// For loop
for (let i = 1; i <= 5; i++) {
    console.log("Count:", i);
}

// While loop
let countdown = 5;
while (countdown > 0) {
```

```
    console.log("Countdown:", countdown);
    countdown--;
}

// For...of loop (for arrays)
let fruits = ["apple", "banana", "orange"];
for (let fruit of fruits) {
    console.log("Fruit:", fruit);
}

// For...in loop (for objects)
let car = {brand: "Toyota", model: "Camry", year: 2022};
for (let property in car) {
    console.log(property + ":", car[property]);
}
```

Working with Arrays and Objects

Arrays and objects form the foundation of data manipulation in JavaScript:

#javascript

```
// Array methods and operations
let numbers = [1, 2, 3, 4, 5];

// Adding elements
numbers.push(6);           // Add to end
numbers.unshift(0);        // Add to beginning
console.log(numbers);      // [0, 1, 2, 3, 4, 5, 6]

// Removing elements
```

```
let lastNumber = numbers.pop();       // Remove from end
let firstNumber = numbers.shift();    // Remove from
beginning
console.log("Removed:", lastNumber, firstNumber);

// Array iteration methods
let doubled = numbers.map(num => num * 2);
let evens = numbers.filter(num => num % 2 === 0);
let sum = numbers.reduce((total, num) => total + num, 0);

console.log("Original:", numbers);
console.log("Doubled:", doubled);
console.log("Even numbers:", evens);
console.log("Sum:", sum);

// Object manipulation
let student = {
    name: "Alice Johnson",
    age: 20,
    courses: ["Math", "Science", "History"],
    gpa: 3.8
};

// Accessing properties
console.log("Student name:", student.name);
console.log("Student age:", student["age"]);

// Adding new properties
student.email = "alice@email.com";
student.graduationYear = 2024;
```

```
// Modifying existing properties
student.gpa = 3.9;
student.courses.push("Art");

console.log("Updated student:", student);

// Object methods
student.introduce = function() {
    return `Hi, I'm ${this.name} and I'm ${this.age}
years old.`;
};

console.log(student.introduce());
```

Error Handling and Debugging

Understanding how to handle errors and debug JavaScript code is crucial for effective development:

#javascript

```
// Try-catch error handling
function divideNumbers(a, b) {
    try {
        if (b === 0) {
            throw new Error("Division by zero is not
allowed");
        }
        return a / b;
    } catch (error) {
        console.error("Error occurred:", error.message);
        return null;
```

```
    } finally {
        console.log("Division operation completed");
    }
}

console.log(divideNumbers(10, 2));  // 5
console.log(divideNumbers(10, 0));  // Error handled
gracefully

// Debugging techniques
function debugExample() {
    let x = 5;
    let y = 10;

    console.log("Debug: x =", x, "y =", y);

    let result = x + y;

    // Using console methods for debugging
    console.info("Info: Calculation completed");
    console.warn("Warning: This is just a demo");
    console.error("Error: This is a sample error
message");

    return result;
}

debugExample();
```

Interactive Examples and Practice

Creating interactive examples helps solidify JavaScript concepts:

#javascript

```
// Interactive quiz function
function runQuiz() {
    const questions = [
        {
            question: "What does 'DOM' stand for?",
            options: ["Document Object Model", "Data
Object Management", "Dynamic Object Method"],
            correct: 0
        },
        {
            question: "Which keyword is used to declare
constants in JavaScript?",
            options: ["var", "let", "const"],
            correct: 2
        }
    ];

    let score = 0;

    for (let i = 0; i < questions.length; i++) {
        let q = questions[i];
        let optionsText = q.options.map((option, index)
=> `${index + 1}. ${option}`).join("\n");

        let userAnswer =
prompt(`${q.question}\n\n${optionsText}\n\nEnter your
choice (1-3):`);

        if (parseInt(userAnswer) - 1 === q.correct) {
```

```
            score++;
            alert("Correct!");
        } else {
            alert(`Incorrect. The correct answer is:
${q.options[q.correct]}`);
        }
    }

    alert(`Quiz completed! Your score:
${score}/${questions.length}`);
}

// Simple calculator function
function calculator() {
    let num1 = parseFloat(prompt("Enter first number:"));
    let operator = prompt("Enter operator (+, -, *,
/):");
    let num2 = parseFloat(prompt("Enter second
number:"));

    let result;

    switch (operator) {
        case "+":
            result = num1 + num2;
            break;
        case "-":
            result = num1 - num2;
            break;
        case "*":
            result = num1 * num2;
            break;
```

```
        case "/":
            result = num2 !== 0 ? num1 / num2 : "Error:
Division by zero";
            break;
        default:
            result = "Error: Invalid operator";
    }

    alert(`Result: ${num1} ${operator} ${num2} =
${result}`);
}

// Random number guessing game
function guessingGame() {
    const randomNumber = Math.floor(Math.random() * 100)
+ 1;
    let attempts = 0;
    let maxAttempts = 7;

    alert("I'm thinking of a number between 1 and 100.
You have 7 attempts to guess it!");

    while (attempts < maxAttempts) {
        let guess = parseInt(prompt(`Attempt ${attempts +
1}: Enter your guess:`));
        attempts++;

        if (guess === randomNumber) {
            alert(`Congratulations! You guessed it in
${attempts} attempts!`);
            return;
        } else if (guess < randomNumber) {
```

```
        alert("Too low! Try a higher number.");
    } else {
        alert("Too high! Try a lower number.");
    }
  }

  alert(`Game over! The number was ${randomNumber}.`);
}
```

Essential Tips

- **Start with browser developer tools for immediate feedback and experimentation.** The browser console provides instant results for JavaScript expressions, making it perfect for testing small code snippets and understanding how different functions work. This immediate feedback loop accelerates learning and helps build confidence with the language.
- **Focus on understanding variable scope and function behavior before moving to advanced topics.** JavaScript's flexible scoping rules can be confusing for beginners, but mastering these concepts early prevents many common bugs and misunderstandings later. Practice creating variables in different scopes and observe how they behave.
- **Practice writing functions daily, even for simple tasks.** Functions are fundamental to JavaScript programming, and regular practice helps develop good coding habits. Start with simple functions that perform basic calculations or string manipulations, then gradually increase complexity.
- **Use meaningful variable and function names that clearly describe their purpose.** Good naming conventions make code self-documenting and easier to maintain. Instead of generic names like `x` or `data`, use descriptive names like `userAge` or `calculateTotalPrice` that immediately convey the variable's purpose.
- **Learn to read error messages carefully and use them as learning opportunities.** JavaScript error messages often provide valuable information about what went wrong and where. Instead of ignoring errors, take time to understand what they mean and how to fix them, as this builds debugging skills essential for advanced development.

Actionable Strategies

- **Create a daily coding routine with 30-minute practice sessions focused on specific JavaScript concepts.** Consistency beats intensity when learning programming. Dedicate specific time each day to writing JavaScript code, alternating between learning new concepts and reinforcing previously learned material through practice exercises.
- **Build small projects immediately after learning each concept to reinforce understanding through practical application.** Theory alone doesn't create programming skills. After learning about arrays, create a simple to-do list. After understanding functions, build a basic calculator. These projects cement knowledge and provide portfolio pieces.
- **Join JavaScript communities and forums to ask questions and learn from experienced developers.** Online communities like Stack Overflow, Reddit's JavaScript forums, and Discord servers provide valuable resources for getting help and discovering best practices. Don't hesitate to ask questions, as helping others learn also reinforces your own knowledge.
- **Study and modify existing JavaScript code from open-source projects to understand different coding styles and techniques.** Reading other people's code exposes you to different approaches and solutions. Start with simple projects on GitHub, examine how they're structured, and try modifying them to add new features or fix bugs.
- **Set up a personal JavaScript playground repository where you can experiment with new concepts and save useful code snippets.** Create a dedicated space for experimentation without the pressure of building complete applications. This repository becomes a valuable reference as you encounter similar problems in future projects.
- **Focus on one JavaScript concept at a time until you achieve comfortable proficiency before moving forward.** Avoid the temptation to rush through multiple topics simultaneously. Master variables before moving to functions, understand functions before tackling objects, and build a solid foundation at each step.
- **Teach JavaScript concepts to others or write blog posts explaining what you've learned to deepen your understanding.** Teaching forces you to organize your knowledge and identify gaps in understanding. Whether explaining concepts to friends, writing blog posts, or creating tutorial videos, teaching others strengthens your own grasp of JavaScript fundamentals.

Chapter 2: JavaScript Syntax and Basics

Understanding JavaScript syntax forms the foundation of your programming journey. This chapter covers the essential building blocks that every JavaScript developer must master, from the proper use of semicolons to effective debugging techniques. By mastering these fundamentals, you'll write cleaner, more maintainable code and avoid common pitfalls that trip up beginners.

2.1 Statements and Semicolons

Understanding JavaScript Statements

A statement in JavaScript represents a complete instruction that performs an action. Think of statements as complete sentences in human language – they express a complete thought and tell the computer what to do. JavaScript statements can declare variables, assign values, call functions, or control program flow.

#javascript

```
let userName = "Alice";          // Variable declaration
statement
console.log("Hello World");      // Function call statement
if (true) { }                    // Conditional statement
for (let i = 0; i < 5; i++) { } // Loop statement
```

The Role of Semicolons

Semicolons in JavaScript serve as statement terminators, marking the end of executable statements. While JavaScript has a feature called Automatic Semicolon Insertion (ASI) that attempts to add semicolons automatically, understanding when and why to use them explicitly prevents unexpected behavior.

#javascript

```
// Explicit semicolon usage
let message = "Hello";
let count = 42;
console.log(message);

// Multiple statements on one line require semicolons
let x = 5; let y = 10; let sum = x + y;
```

Automatic Semicolon Insertion (ASI)

JavaScript's ASI feature automatically inserts semicolons in certain situations, but relying on it can lead to problematic code. The engine inserts semicolons when it encounters a line break that would otherwise cause a syntax error.

#javascript

```
// ASI will insert semicolons here
let name = "John"
let age = 25
console.log(name)

// But ASI can cause problems:
function getValue() {
    return
        42; // This becomes: return; 42; (returns
undefined!)
}

// Correct version:
function getValue() {
    return 42;
}
```

When Semicolons Are Required

Certain situations absolutely require explicit semicolons to prevent errors or unexpected behavior:

#javascript

```
// Before immediately invoked function expressions
let result = (function() { return 42; })()
(function() { console.log("This will cause an error!");
})()

// Correct version with semicolon:
let result = (function() { return 42; })();
(function() { console.log("This works fine!"); })();

// When using array or object literals at line start
let numbers = [1, 2, 3]
[0, 1].forEach(function(item) { console.log(item); })

// JavaScript interprets this as: numbers[0,
1].forEach(...)
// Correct version:
let numbers = [1, 2, 3];
[0, 1].forEach(function(item) { console.log(item); });
```

Best Practices for Semicolon Usage

Consistent semicolon usage improves code reliability and readability. Most professional JavaScript codebases use explicit semicolons to avoid ASI-related issues.

#javascript

```
// Good practice - explicit semicolons
function calculateTotal(price, tax) {
    let subtotal = price * 1.0;
    let taxAmount = subtotal * tax;
    let total = subtotal + taxAmount;
    return total;
}

let productPrice = 29.99;
let taxRate = 0.08;
let finalPrice = calculateTotal(productPrice, taxRate);
console.log("Final price: $" + finalPrice.toFixed(2));
```

2.2 Case Sensitivity and Comments

JavaScript Case Sensitivity

JavaScript distinguishes between uppercase and lowercase letters, making it a case-sensitive language. This means `userName`, `USERNAME`, and `UserName` are three completely different identifiers.

#javascript

```
// These are all different variables
let userName = "alice";
let USERNAME = "ALICE";
let UserName = "Alice";
let username = "alice123";

console.log(userName);  // "alice"
```

```
console.log(USERNAME);  // "ALICE"
console.log(UserName);  // "Alice"
console.log(username);  // "alice123"
```

Case Sensitivity in Functions and Methods

Built-in JavaScript functions and methods must be called with exact casing. Common errors occur when developers mix up the case of method names.

#javascript

```javascript
// Correct method calls
console.log("Hello World");              // Correct
document.getElementById("myDiv");         // Correct
Math.floor(4.7);                         // Correct

// Incorrect - these will cause errors
Console.Log("Hello World");              // ReferenceError
document.getElementByID("myDiv");        // TypeError
math.Floor(4.7);                         // ReferenceError
```

Naming Conventions and Case Styles

JavaScript developers follow specific naming conventions to maintain consistency and readability across codebases.

#javascript

```javascript
// camelCase for variables and functions (recommended)
let firstName = "John";
let lastName = "Doe";
let userAccountBalance = 1500.75;
```

```
function calculateMonthlyPayment(principal, rate, months)
{
    return (principal * rate) / (1 - Math.pow(1 + rate, -
months));
}

// PascalCase for constructors and classes
function BankAccount(initialBalance) {
    this.balance = initialBalance;
}

class ShoppingCart {
    constructor() {
        this.items = [];
    }
}

// UPPER_SNAKE_CASE for constants
const MAX_LOGIN_ATTEMPTS = 3;
const API_BASE_URL = "https://api.example.com";
const DEFAULT_TIMEOUT_MS = 5000;
```

Single-Line Comments

Single-line comments use two forward slashes (//) and extend to the end of the line. They're perfect for brief explanations or notes about specific lines of code.

#javascript

```
// Calculate the area of a rectangle
let width = 10;       // Width in pixels
let height = 20;      // Height in pixels
```

```
let area = width * height;  // Area formula: width × height

// Temporary code for testing
// console.log("Debug: area = " + area);

// TODO: Add input validation
function processUserInput(input) {
    return input.trim().toLowerCase();
}
```

Multi-Line Comments

Multi-line comments begin with `/*` and end with `*/`, allowing comments to span multiple lines. They're useful for longer explanations, documentation, or temporarily disabling blocks of code.

#javascript

```
/*
 * This function calculates compound interest
 * Formula: A = P(1 + r/n)^(nt)
 * Where:
 * P = principal amount
 * r = annual interest rate
 * n = number of times interest compounds per year
 * t = time in years
 */
function calculateCompoundInterest(principal, rate, compounds, years) {
    let amount = principal * Math.pow((1 + rate / compounds), compounds * years);
```

```
    return amount - principal; // Return only the
interest earned
}

/*
let debugMode = true;
if (debugMode) {
    console.log("Debug information here");
}
*/
```

Documentation Comments (JSDoc)

JSDoc comments provide structured documentation for functions, classes, and modules. They start with `/**` and use special tags to describe parameters, return values, and usage examples.

#javascript

```
/**
 * Converts temperature from Celsius to Fahrenheit
 * @param {number} celsius - Temperature in Celsius
 * @returns {number} Temperature in Fahrenheit
 * @example
 * // Convert 25°C to Fahrenheit
 * let temp = celsiusToFahrenheit(25);
 * console.log(temp); // 77
 */
function celsiusToFahrenheit(celsius) {
    return (celsius * 9/5) + 32;
}
```

```
/**
 * Represents a user account
 * @class
 */
class UserAccount {
    /**
     * Create a user account
     * @param {string} username - The user's username
     * @param {string} email - The user's email address
     */
    constructor(username, email) {
        this.username = username;
        this.email = email;
        this.createdAt = new Date();
    }
}
```

2.3 Whitespaces and Code Formatting

Understanding Whitespace in JavaScript

Whitespace in JavaScript includes spaces, tabs, and line breaks. While JavaScript ignores most whitespace for execution purposes, proper formatting dramatically improves code readability and maintainability.

#javascript

```
// Poor formatting - hard to read
let x=5;let y=10;if(x<y){console.log("x is less than
y");}else{console.log("x is greater than or equal to
y");}
```

```
// Good formatting - easy to read
let x = 5;
let y = 10;

if (x < y) {
    console.log("x is less than y");
} else {
    console.log("x is greater than or equal to y");
}
```

Indentation Standards

Consistent indentation creates visual hierarchy and makes code structure immediately apparent. The JavaScript community commonly uses either 2 or 4 spaces per indentation level.

#javascript

```
// 2-space indentation (common in many projects)
function processOrder(order) {
  if (order.items.length > 0) {
    for (let i = 0; i < order.items.length; i++) {
      let item = order.items[i];
      if (item.quantity > 0) {
        console.log(`Processing: ${item.name}`);
      }
    }
  }
}

// 4-space indentation (also widely used)
function processOrder(order) {
```

```
    if (order.items.length > 0) {
        for (let i = 0; i < order.items.length; i++) {
            let item = order.items[i];
            if (item.quantity > 0) {
                console.log(`Processing: ${item.name}`);
            }
        }
    }
}
```

Spacing Around Operators

Consistent spacing around operators improves readability and helps distinguish between different types of operations.

#javascript

```
// Good spacing practices
let sum = a + b;
let product = x * y;
let isEqual = (value === expectedValue);
let isGreater = (score > passingGrade);

// Assignment operators
let count = 0;
count += 5;
count *= 2;

// Comparison with proper spacing
if (user.age >= 18 && user.hasLicense === true) {
    console.log("User can drive");
}
```

```
// Function calls with spacing
let result = calculateTotal(price, tax, discount);
let formatted = formatCurrency(result, "USD", 2);
```

Line Length and Breaking

Keeping lines to a reasonable length (typically 80-120 characters) improves readability, especially when viewing code side-by-side or on smaller screens.

#javascript

```
// Long line - hard to read
let message = "This is a very long message that extends
beyond the recommended line length and should be broken
up for better readability";

// Better - broken into multiple lines
let message = "This is a very long message that extends
beyond " +
              "the recommended line length and should be
broken up " +
              "for better readability";

// Or using template literals
let message = `This is a very long message that extends
beyond
              the recommended line length and should be
broken up
              for better readability`;

// Function calls with many parameters
let user = createUser(
```

```
    "john.doe@example.com",
    "John",
    "Doe",
    new Date("1990-05-15"),
    "555-123-4567",
    "123 Main Street"
);
```

Object and Array Formatting

Proper formatting of objects and arrays makes complex data structures much easier to understand and modify.

#javascript

```javascript
// Simple objects - single line is fine
let point = { x: 10, y: 20 };
let colors = ["red", "green", "blue"];

// Complex objects - multi-line formatting
let userProfile = {
    id: 12345,
    username: "johndoe",
    email: "john.doe@example.com",
    profile: {
        firstName: "John",
        lastName: "Doe",
        age: 28,
        interests: ["programming", "music", "travel"]
    },
    settings: {
        theme: "dark",
```

```
        notifications: true,
        privacy: "friends-only"
    }
};

// Array of objects
let products = [
    {
        id: 1,
        name: "Laptop",
        price: 999.99,
        category: "Electronics"
    },
    {
        id: 2,
        name: "Mouse",
        price: 29.99,
        category: "Accessories"
    },
    {
        id: 3,
        name: "Keyboard",
        price: 79.99,
        category: "Accessories"
    }
];
```

Function Formatting

Consistent function formatting makes code more professional and easier to understand.

#javascript

```
// Function declarations
function calculateDistance(x1, y1, x2, y2) {
    let deltaX = x2 - x1;
    let deltaY = y2 - y1;
    return Math.sqrt(deltaX * deltaX + deltaY * deltaY);
}

// Function expressions
let multiply = function(a, b) {
    return a * b;
};

// Arrow functions
let add = (a, b) => {
    return a + b;
};

// Short arrow functions
let square = x => x * x;
let greet = name => `Hello, ${name}!`;

// Functions with complex logic
function processPayment(amount, paymentMethod,
customerInfo) {
    // Validate input parameters
    if (amount <= 0) {
        throw new Error("Amount must be greater than
zero");
    }
```

```
    if (!paymentMethod) {
        throw new Error("Payment method is required");
    }

    // Process payment logic here
    let transaction = {
        amount: amount,
        method: paymentMethod,
        customer: customerInfo,
        timestamp: new Date(),
        status: "pending"
    };

    return transaction;
}
```

2.4 The Console and Debugging with console.log()

Introduction to the Browser Console

The browser console serves as your primary debugging tool and interactive JavaScript environment. It provides immediate feedback on code execution, displays error messages, and allows real-time code testing.

#javascript

```
// Basic console output
console.log("Hello, World!");
console.log("JavaScript is running!");

// Multiple arguments
console.log("User:", "John Doe", "Age:", 25);
```

```
// Variables and expressions
let userName = "Alice";
let userAge = 30;
console.log("Welcome", userName, "you are", userAge,
"years old");
```

Different Console Methods

The console object provides various methods for different types of output, each serving specific debugging purposes.

#javascript

```
// Basic Logging
console.log("General information");

// Informational messages
console.info("This is informational");

// Warning messages
console.warn("This is a warning message");

// Error messages
console.error("This is an error message");

// Debug messages (may not show in all browsers by
default)
console.debug("Debug information");

// Testing assertions
let x = 5;
```

```
console.assert(x > 10, "x should be greater than 10"); //
Will show error

// Grouping related messages
console.group("User Information");
console.log("Name: John Doe");
console.log("Email: john@example.com");
console.log("Age: 28");
console.groupEnd();
```

Logging Variables and Data Types

Understanding how different data types appear in the console helps with debugging and development.

#javascript

```
// Primitive types
console.log("String:", "Hello World");
console.log("Number:", 42);
console.log("Boolean:", true);
console.log("Undefined:", undefined);
console.log("Null:", null);

// Objects and arrays
let person = {
    name: "Sarah",
    age: 25,
    city: "New York"
};
console.log("Person object:", person);
```

```javascript
let numbers = [1, 2, 3, 4, 5];
console.log("Numbers array:", numbers);

// Functions
function greetUser(name) {
    return `Hello, ${name}!`;
}
console.log("Function:", greetUser);
console.log("Function result:", greetUser("Tom"));
```

Advanced Console Techniques

Professional developers use sophisticated console techniques for efficient debugging and performance monitoring.

#javascript

```javascript
// Table format for arrays of objects
let users = [
    { name: "Alice", age: 28, city: "Boston" },
    { name: "Bob", age: 35, city: "Chicago" },
    { name: "Carol", age: 42, city: "Denver" }
];
console.table(users);

// Timing code execution
console.time("Loop execution");
for (let i = 0; i < 1000000; i++) {
    // Some operation
    Math.sqrt(i);
}
console.timeEnd("Loop execution");
```

```
// Counting occurrences
function processItem(item) {
    console.count("Items processed");
    // Process the item
}

processItem("item1");
processItem("item2");
processItem("item3");

// Clear the console
console.clear();

// Stack trace
function firstFunction() {
    secondFunction();
}

function secondFunction() {
    thirdFunction();
}

function thirdFunction() {
    console.trace("Execution path");
}

firstFunction();
```

String Formatting and Interpolation

Modern JavaScript provides powerful string formatting capabilities that make console output more informative and readable.

#javascript

```
// Template literals for string interpolation
let productName = "Laptop";
let price = 899.99;
let quantity = 2;

console.log(`Product: ${productName}`);
console.log(`Price: $${price}`);
console.log(`Total: $${price * quantity}`);

// Formatting with expressions
let user = { name: "John", age: 30 };
console.log(`User ${user.name} is ${user.age >= 18 ?
"adult" : "minor"}`);

// Multi-line strings
let receipt = `
Order Summary:
Product: ${productName}
Quantity: ${quantity}
Unit Price: $${price}
Total: $${(price * quantity).toFixed(2)}
`;
console.log(receipt);
```

Console Styling (Chrome/Firefox)

Some browsers support CSS styling in console output, making debug messages more visually distinctive.

#javascript

```
// Styled console messages (works in Chrome/Firefox)
console.log("%cSuccess!", "color: green; font-weight: bold; font-size: 16px;");
console.log("%cWarning!", "color: orange; font-weight: bold;");
console.log("%cError!", "color: red; font-weight: bold; background: yellow;");

// Multiple styles in one message
console.log(
    "%cAPI Call: %c/users/123 %cStatus: %c200 OK",
    "color: blue; font-weight: bold;",
    "color: black; font-family: monospace;",
    "color: blue; font-weight: bold;",
    "color: green; font-weight: bold;"
);
```

2.5 Common Mistakes to Avoid

Variable Declaration Mistakes

Proper variable declaration prevents scope issues and unexpected behavior that can plague JavaScript applications.

#javascript

```
// Mistake: Using variables without declaration
function calculateTotal() {
    price = 100;         // Creates global variable accidentally
    tax = price * 0.08; // Another accidental global
```

```
    return price + tax;
}

// Correct: Proper variable declaration
function calculateTotal() {
    let price = 100;        // Properly scoped variable
    let tax = price * 0.08; // Properly scoped variable
    return price + tax;
}

// Mistake: Redeclaring variables with var
var userName = "John";
var userName = "Jane";  // No error, but confusing

// Better: Use let/const appropriately
let userName = "John";
// let userName = "Jane";  // This would cause an error
(good!)

const MAX_USERS = 100;
// const MAX_USERS = 200;  // This would cause an error
(good!)
```

Semicolon-Related Errors

Missing semicolons can cause unexpected code behavior, especially with certain JavaScript constructs.

#javascript

```
// Mistake: Missing semicolon before IIFE
let result = function(x) { return x * 2; }(5)
```

```
(function() { console.log("This won't work as expected");
})()

// Correct: Proper semicolon placement
let result = function(x) { return x * 2; }(5);
(function() { console.log("This works correctly"); })();

// Mistake: Return statement with line break
function getData() {
    return
    {
        name: "John",
        age: 30
    };
}
console.log(getData()); // Returns undefined!

// Correct: Keep return value on same line or use
parentheses
function getData() {
    return {
        name: "John",
        age: 30
    };
}
```

Type Coercion Confusion

JavaScript's automatic type conversion can lead to unexpected results if not properly understood.

#javascript

```
// Mistake: Unexpected type coercion
console.log("5" + 3);      // "53" (string concatenation)
console.log("5" - 3);      // 2 (numeric subtraction)
console.log("5" * "2");    // 10 (both converted to
numbers)
console.log(true + 1);     // 2 (true becomes 1)

// Better: Explicit type conversion
let stringNumber = "5";
let actualNumber = 3;

console.log(Number(stringNumber) + actualNumber); // 8
console.log(parseInt(stringNumber) + actualNumber); // 8
console.log(stringNumber + String(actualNumber)); // "53"

// Mistake: Loose equality causing issues
console.log(0 == false);      // true
console.log("" == false);     // true
console.log(null == undefined); // true

// Better: Use strict equality
console.log(0 === false);      // false
console.log("" === false);     // false
console.log(null === undefined); // false
```

Scope and Hoisting Issues

Understanding how JavaScript handles variable and function hoisting prevents confusing behavior.

#javascript

```
// Mistake: Relying on hoisting behavior
console.log(myVar); // undefined (not an error, but confusing)
var myVar = "Hello";

console.log(myFunction()); // "This works" (function is hoisted)
function myFunction() {
    return "This works";
}

// Better: Declare variables before use
let myVariable = "Hello";
console.log(myVariable); // "Hello" (clear and predictable)

// Function expressions are not hoisted
// console.log(myFunc()); // Error: Cannot access 'myFunc' before initialization
let myFunc = function() {
    return "This is better";
};
console.log(myFunc()); // "This is better"
```

Array and Object Common Errors

Working with arrays and objects requires attention to reference behavior and proper syntax.

#javascript

```
// Mistake: Confusing array length with last index
```

```
let colors = ["red", "green", "blue"];
console.log(colors[colors.length]); // undefined (index 3
doesn't exist)

// Correct: Use length - 1 for last element
console.log(colors[colors.length - 1]); // "blue"

// Mistake: Modifying arrays while iterating
let numbers = [1, 2, 3, 4, 5];
for (let i = 0; i < numbers.length; i++) {
    if (numbers[i] % 2 === 0) {
        numbers.splice(i, 1); // This skips elements!
    }
}

// Better: Iterate backwards or use filter
let numbers = [1, 2, 3, 4, 5];
let oddNumbers = numbers.filter(num => num % 2 !== 0);

// Mistake: Object property access confusion
let user = {
    "first name": "John",
    age: 30
};
// console.log(user.first name); // Syntax error

// Correct: Use bracket notation for spaces in property
names
console.log(user["first name"]); // "John"
console.log(user.age); // 30 (dot notation works for
valid identifiers)
```

Function-Related Mistakes

Functions in JavaScript have specific behaviors that can cause issues if not properly understood.

#javascript

```javascript
// Mistake: Not understanding 'this' context
let person = {
    name: "Alice",
    greet: function() {
        return "Hello, " + this.name;
    }
};

let greetFunction = person.greet;
console.log(greetFunction()); // "Hello, undefined" (this
is not person)

// Better: Use bind or arrow functions
let boundGreet = person.greet.bind(person);
console.log(boundGreet()); // "Hello, Alice"

// Or use arrow functions (lexical this)
let person2 = {
    name: "Bob",
    greet: () => {
        return "Hello, " + this.name; // this refers to
global scope
    }
};
```

```
// Mistake: Not handling function parameters properly
function divide(a, b) {
    return a / b; // What if b is 0 or undefined?
}

// Better: Add parameter validation
function divide(a, b) {
    if (typeof a !== "number" || typeof b !== "number") {
        throw new Error("Both parameters must be
numbers");
    }
    if (b === 0) {
        throw new Error("Division by zero is not
allowed");
    }
    return a / b;
}
```

String and Number Operations

String and number operations in JavaScript require careful attention to avoid unexpected results.

#javascript

```
// Mistake: String concatenation vs addition confusion
let a = "10";
let b = "20";
console.log(a + b); // "1020" (string concatenation)

let x = 10;
let y = 20;
```

```
console.log(x + y); // 30 (numeric addition)

// Mixed types - unexpected results
console.log("10" + 5); // "105"
console.log(10 + "5"); // "105"

// Better: Be explicit about intentions
let num1 = parseInt("10");
let num2 = parseInt("20");
console.log(num1 + num2); // 30

let str1 = "10";
let str2 = "20";
console.log(str1 + str2); // "1020"

// Mistake: Not handling NaN properly
let result = parseInt("abc");
console.log(result); // NaN
console.log(result + 5); // NaN

// Better: Check for NaN
let userInput = "abc";
let parsed = parseInt(userInput);
if (isNaN(parsed)) {
    console.log("Invalid number input");
} else {
    console.log("Number:", parsed);
}
```

Essential Tips

- Master keyboard shortcuts for your code editor to quickly format code, navigate between files, and use multiple cursors for efficient editing.
- Always use a consistent coding style throughout your project, whether you choose 2-space or 4-space indentation, and maintain the same approach for naming conventions.
- Set up automatic code formatting tools like Prettier or ESLint in your development environment to catch syntax errors and maintain consistent formatting automatically.
- Practice reading error messages carefully - JavaScript error messages often contain the exact line number and description of syntax issues.
- Use browser developer tools extensively, not just for console.log() debugging, but also for setting breakpoints, inspecting variables, and stepping through code execution.

Actionable Strategies

- Configure your code editor with JavaScript-specific extensions that provide syntax highlighting, error detection, and intelligent code completion to catch mistakes as you type.
- Develop a habit of writing comments before writing code - outline what your function should do in plain English, then implement the logic underneath.
- Create a personal reference document with common JavaScript patterns you use frequently, including proper function syntax, object creation patterns, and array manipulation methods.
- Practice code review by reading other developers' JavaScript code on GitHub, paying attention to their formatting choices, naming conventions, and commenting strategies.
- Establish a debugging routine that starts with console.log() for simple issues, progresses to browser breakpoints for complex logic, and uses console.table() for data structure inspection.
- Build small projects that focus specifically on syntax mastery - create simple calculators, text manipulators, or data formatters that let you practice different aspects of JavaScript syntax.
- Join JavaScript communities and forums where you can ask questions about syntax confusion, share code for feedback, and learn from experienced developers' approaches to clean, readable code.

Chapter 3: Variables and Constants

Variables and constants form the foundation of data storage and manipulation in JavaScript. They serve as containers that hold values, allowing developers to store, retrieve, and modify information throughout program execution. Understanding how to properly declare, use, and manage variables is crucial for writing efficient and maintainable JavaScript code.

3.1 Declaring Variables with `var`, `let`, and `const`

JavaScript provides three primary keywords for declaring variables: `var`, `let`, and `const`. Each keyword has distinct characteristics, behaviors, and use cases that significantly impact how variables function within your code.

The `var` Keyword

The `var` keyword represents the original method for declaring variables in JavaScript. It has been part of the language since its inception and exhibits unique behaviors that distinguish it from modern alternatives.

#javascript

```javascript
var userName = "John Doe";
var age = 25;
var isActive = true;

console.log(userName); // Output: John Doe
console.log(age);      // Output: 25
console.log(isActive); // Output: true
```

Variables declared with `var` are function-scoped, meaning they are accessible throughout the entire function in which they are declared. If declared outside any function, they become globally scoped.

#javascript

```
function demonstrateVar() {
    if (true) {
        var message = "Hello from inside the block";
    }
    console.log(message); // Output: Hello from inside
the block
}

demonstrateVar();
```

Variable Hoisting with `var`

One of the most distinctive features of `var` is hoisting. JavaScript moves variable declarations to the top of their containing scope during compilation, though the assignment remains in its original position.

#javascript

```
console.log(hoistedVar); // Output: undefined (not an
error)
var hoistedVar = "I am hoisted";
console.log(hoistedVar); // Output: I am hoisted

// The above code is interpreted as:
// var hoistedVar;
// console.log(hoistedVar);
// hoistedVar = "I am hoisted";
// console.log(hoistedVar);
```

The `let` Keyword

The `let` keyword was introduced in ECMAScript 2015 (ES6) to address some of the issues associated with `var`. It provides block-scoped variable declarations, offering more predictable behavior.

#javascript

```
let productName = "Laptop";
let price = 999.99;
let inStock = true;

console.log(productName); // Output: Laptop
console.log(price);       // Output: 999.99
console.log(inStock);     // Output: true
```

Variables declared with `let` are confined to the block in which they are declared, providing better control over variable accessibility.

#javascript

```
function demonstrateLet() {
    if (true) {
        let blockScopedMessage = "Hello from the block";
        console.log(blockScopedMessage); // Output: Hello
from the block
    }
    // console.log(blockScopedMessage); // Error:
blockScopedMessage is not defined
}

demonstrateLet();
```

Temporal Dead Zone

Variables declared with `let` exist in a "temporal dead zone" from the start of the block until the declaration is reached. Accessing them before declaration results in a ReferenceError.

#javascript

```
console.log(beforeDeclaration); // ReferenceError: Cannot access 'beforeDeclaration' before initialization
let beforeDeclaration = "Now I exist";
console.log(beforeDeclaration); // Output: Now I exist
```

The `const` Keyword

The `const` keyword declares constants - variables that cannot be reassigned after their initial declaration. Like `let`, `const` is block-scoped and subject to the temporal dead zone.

#javascript

```
const API_URL = "https://api.example.com";
const MAX_RETRY_ATTEMPTS = 3;
const CONFIG = {
    timeout: 5000,
    retries: 3
};

console.log(API_URL);               // Output: https://api.example.com
console.log(MAX_RETRY_ATTEMPTS);    // Output: 3
console.log(CONFIG);                // Output: {timeout: 5000, retries: 3}
```

Reassignment Restrictions with `const`

Constants cannot be reassigned, but objects and arrays declared with `const` can still have their contents modified.

#javascript

```
const numbers = [1, 2, 3];
numbers.push(4); // This is allowed
console.log(numbers); // Output: [1, 2, 3, 4]

const user = { name: "Alice", age: 30 };
user.age = 31; // This is allowed
console.log(user); // Output: {name: "Alice", age: 31}

// numbers = [5, 6, 7]; // Error: Assignment to constant
variable
// user = { name: "Bob" }; // Error: Assignment to
constant variable
```

3.2 Understanding Scope in JavaScript

Scope determines where variables can be accessed within your code. JavaScript implements several types of scope that govern variable visibility and accessibility.

Global Scope

Variables declared outside any function or block have global scope. They are accessible from anywhere in the program.

#javascript

```
var globalVar = "I am global";
let globalLet = "I am also global";
const GLOBAL_CONST = "I am a global constant";
```

```
function accessGlobalVariables() {
    console.log(globalVar);      // Output: I am global
    console.log(globalLet);      // Output: I am also
global
    console.log(GLOBAL_CONST);  // Output: I am a global
constant
}

accessGlobalVariables();
```

Function Scope

Variables declared within a function are only accessible within that function. This applies to variables declared with `var`, `let`, and `const`.

#javascript

```
function calculateTotal(price, taxRate) {
    var subtotal = price;
    let tax = price * taxRate;
    const total = subtotal + tax;

    console.log(`Subtotal: ${subtotal}`);
    console.log(`Tax: ${tax}`);
    console.log(`Total: ${total}`);

    return total;
}

calculateTotal(100, 0.08);
```

```
// console.log(subtotal); // Error: subtotal is not
defined
// console.log(tax);       // Error: tax is not defined
// console.log(total);     // Error: total is not defined
```

Block Scope

Block scope applies to variables declared with `let` and `const` within curly braces `{}`. Variables declared with `var` do not respect block scope.

#javascript

```
function demonstrateBlockScope() {
    if (true) {
        var varVariable = "I ignore block scope";
        let letVariable = "I respect block scope";
        const constVariable = "I also respect block
scope";
    }

    console.log(varVariable);   // Output: I ignore block
scope
    // console.log(letVariable);   // Error: letVariable
is not defined
    // console.log(constVariable); // Error:
constVariable is not defined
}

demonstrateBlockScope();
```

Lexical Scope and Closures

JavaScript uses lexical scoping, meaning inner functions have access to variables in their outer scope. This enables the creation of closures.

#javascript

```
function outerFunction(x) {
    const outerVariable = x;

    function innerFunction(y) {
        const innerVariable = y;
        console.log(`Outer: ${outerVariable}, Inner:
${innerVariable}`);
        return outerVariable + innerVariable;
    }

    return innerFunction;
}

const addFive = outerFunction(5);
console.log(addFive(3)); // Output: Outer: 5, Inner: 3,
then 8
```

Scope Chain

When JavaScript looks for a variable, it searches through the scope chain, starting from the current scope and moving outward until it finds the variable or reaches the global scope.

#javascript

```
const globalMessage = "Global";

function level1() {
    const level1Message = "Level 1";
```

```
    function level2() {
        const level2Message = "Level 2";

        function level3() {
            console.log(globalMessage);  // Found in
global scope
            console.log(level1Message);  // Found in
level1 scope
            console.log(level2Message);  // Found in
level2 scope

            const level3Message = "Level 3";
            console.log(level3Message);  // Found in
current scope
        }

        level3();
    }

    level2();
}

level1();
```

3.3 Naming Conventions and Best Practices

Proper naming conventions improve code readability, maintainability, and collaboration among developers. JavaScript follows specific conventions that have become industry standards.

Camel Case Convention

JavaScript uses camelCase for variable and function names. The first letter is lowercase, and each subsequent word begins with an uppercase letter.

#javascript

```
let firstName = "John";
let lastName = "Doe";
let emailAddress = "john.doe@email.com";
let phoneNumber = "123-456-7890";
let dateOfBirth = new Date("1990-01-01");

function calculateAge(birthDate) {
    const currentDate = new Date();
    const ageInMilliseconds = currentDate - birthDate;
    const ageInYears = Math.floor(ageInMilliseconds /
(365.25 * 24 * 60 * 60 * 1000));
    return ageInYears;
}
```

Constant Naming

Constants, especially those representing configuration values or fixed data, are typically written in SCREAMING_SNAKE_CASE.

#javascript

```
const MAX_LOGIN_ATTEMPTS = 3;
const API_BASE_URL = "https://api.example.com";
const DEFAULT_TIMEOUT = 5000;
const ERROR_MESSAGES = {
    INVALID_EMAIL: "Please enter a valid email address",
```

```
    PASSWORD_TOO_SHORT: "Password must be at least 8
characters long",
    NETWORK_ERROR: "Network connection failed"
};
```

Descriptive and Meaningful Names

Variable names should clearly describe their purpose or the data they contain. Avoid abbreviations and single-letter variables except for loop counters.

#javascript

```javascript
// Poor naming
let x = 25;
let u = "John";
let d = new Date();

// Good naming
let userAge = 25;
let userName = "John";
let currentDate = new Date();

// Descriptive function names
function validateEmailAddress(email) {
    const emailRegex = /^[^\s@]+@[^\s@]+\.[^\s@]+$/;
    return emailRegex.test(email);
}

function calculateShippingCost(weight, distance,
shippingMethod) {
    const baseRate = 5.00;
    const weightMultiplier = 0.50;
```

```
    const distanceMultiplier = 0.10;

    let cost = baseRate + (weight * weightMultiplier) +
(distance * distanceMultiplier);

    if (shippingMethod === "express") {
        cost *= 1.5;
    }

    return cost;
}
```

Boolean Variable Naming

Boolean variables should use prefixes like `is`, `has`, `can`, or `should` to make their purpose clear.

#javascript

```
let isLoggedIn = false;
let hasPermission = true;
let canEdit = false;
let shouldValidate = true;
let isLoading = false;
let hasError = false;

function checkUserPermissions(user) {
    const isAdmin = user.role === "admin";
    const isOwner = user.id === resource.ownerId;
    const hasActiveSubscription =
user.subscription.status === "active";
```

```
    return isAdmin || isOwner || hasActiveSubscription;
}
```

Avoiding Reserved Words

JavaScript has reserved words that cannot be used as variable names. Understanding these restrictions prevents naming conflicts.

#javascript

```
// Invalid variable names (reserved words)
// let class = "JavaScript";      // Error
// let function = "myFunction";  // Error
// let var = "variable";         // Error

// Valid alternative names
let className = "JavaScriptClass";
let functionName = "myFunction";
let variableName = "variable";
```

3.4 Reassigning Values and Mutability

Understanding how variables can be modified after declaration is crucial for managing program state and preventing unintended changes.

Reassigning Variables Declared with `let`

Variables declared with `let` can be reassigned to new values, including values of different types.

#javascript

```
let counter = 0;
console.log(counter); // Output: 0

counter = 10;
console.log(counter); // Output: 10

counter = "ten";
console.log(counter); // Output: ten

counter = true;
console.log(counter); // Output: true

counter = { value: 42 };
console.log(counter); // Output: {value: 42}
```

Reassigning Variables Declared with `var`

Variables declared with `var` behave similarly to `let` regarding reassignment, but with different scoping rules.

#javascript

```
var message = "Hello";
console.log(message); // Output: Hello

message = "Goodbye";
console.log(message); // Output: Goodbye

var message = "Hello Again"; // Redeclaration is allowed
with var
console.log(message); // Output: Hello Again
```

Immutability with `const`

Variables declared with `const` cannot be reassigned, but the contents of objects and arrays can still be modified.

#javascript

```
const user = {
    name: "Alice",
    age: 30,
    email: "alice@email.com"
};

// Modifying object properties is allowed
user.age = 31;
user.email = "alice.new@email.com";
console.log(user); // Output: {name: "Alice", age: 31,
email: "alice.new@email.com"}

// Adding new properties is allowed
user.phone = "123-456-7890";
console.log(user); // Output: {name: "Alice", age: 31,
email: "alice.new@email.com", phone: "123-456-7890"}

// Reassigning the entire object is not allowed
// user = { name: "Bob" }; // Error: Assignment to
constant variable
```

Deep Immutability

To achieve true immutability for objects and arrays, use methods like `Object.freeze()` or consider using immutable data structures.

#javascript

```
const frozenUser = Object.freeze({
    name: "Bob",
    age: 25,
    email: "bob@email.com"
});

// Attempting to modify properties fails silently in non-strict mode
frozenUser.age = 26;
console.log(frozenUser.age); // Output: 25 (unchanged)

// In strict mode, this would throw an error
"use strict";
// frozenUser.age = 26; // TypeError: Cannot assign to read-only property
```

Mutating Arrays

Arrays declared with `const` can have their contents modified but cannot be reassigned.

#javascript

```
const fruits = ["apple", "banana", "orange"];

// Modifying array contents is allowed
fruits.push("grape");
fruits[0] = "pear";
console.log(fruits); // Output: ["pear", "banana", "orange", "grape"]
```

```
// Array methods that modify the original array
fruits.pop();
fruits.unshift("strawberry");
console.log(fruits); // Output: ["strawberry", "pear",
"banana", "orange"]

// Reassigning the entire array is not allowed
// fruits = ["new", "array"]; // Error: Assignment to
constant variable
```

3.5 Choosing Between `let` and `const`

The decision between `let` and `const` depends on whether you need to reassign the variable after its initial declaration. This choice impacts code clarity, performance, and helps prevent accidental modifications.

When to Use `const`

Use `const` when the variable value will not be reassigned. This applies to primitive values that remain constant and reference values where the reference itself won't change.

`#javascript`

```javascript
// Configuration values
const API_ENDPOINT = "https://api.example.com/v1";
const MAX_RETRY_ATTEMPTS = 3;
const TIMEOUT_DURATION = 5000;

// Mathematical constants
const PI = 3.14159;
const GRAVITY = 9.81;
```

```javascript
// Objects and arrays that won't be reassigned
const userPreferences = {
    theme: "dark",
    language: "en",
    notifications: true
};

const shoppingCart = [];

// Function expressions
const calculateDiscount = function(price, percentage) {
    return price * (percentage / 100);
};

// Arrow functions
const formatCurrency = (amount) => {
    return new Intl.NumberFormat('en-US', {
        style: 'currency',
        currency: 'USD'
    }).format(amount);
};
```

When to Use `let`

Use `let` when the variable value needs to be reassigned during program execution. This includes loop counters, accumulator variables, and any value that changes over time.

#javascript

```javascript
// Loop counters
```

```
for (let i = 0; i < 10; i++) {
    console.log(`Iteration ${i}`);
}

// Accumulator variables
let totalPrice = 0;
const items = [10, 20, 30, 40];

for (let item of items) {
    totalPrice += item;
}

console.log(`Total: ${totalPrice}`); // Output: Total:
100

// Conditional assignments
let userRole;
if (user.permissions.includes("admin")) {
    userRole = "administrator";
} else if (user.permissions.includes("edit")) {
    userRole = "editor";
} else {
    userRole = "viewer";
}

// Variables that change during processing
let currentStep = 1;
let isProcessing = true;
let errorMessage = null;

function processData(data) {
```

```
    currentStep = 1;
    isProcessing = true;

    try {
        // Step 1: Validate data
        if (!data || data.length === 0) {
            throw new Error("No data provided");
        }
        currentStep = 2;

        // Step 2: Process data
        let processedData = data.map(item =>
item.toUpperCase());
        currentStep = 3;

        // Step 3: Save results
        console.log("Data processed successfully");
        isProcessing = false;
        return processedData;

    } catch (error) {
        errorMessage = error.message;
        isProcessing = false;
        throw error;
    }
}
```

Performance Considerations

While the performance difference is minimal in most cases, `const` can provide slight optimizations because the JavaScript engine knows the binding won't change.

#javascript

```javascript
// Preferred approach for better performance and clarity
const users = [
    { name: "Alice", age: 30 },
    { name: "Bob", age: 25 },
    { name: "Charlie", age: 35 }
];

const processUsers = (userList) => {
    const processedUsers = userList.map(user => {
        const fullName = `${user.name} (${user.age} years
old)`;
        return {
            ...user,
            fullName,
            isAdult: user.age >= 18
        };
    });

    return processedUsers;
};

// Use let only when reassignment is necessary
let currentIndex = 0;
let selectedUser = users[currentIndex];

function selectNextUser() {
    currentIndex = (currentIndex + 1) % users.length;
```

```
    selectedUser = users[currentIndex];
    return selectedUser;
}
```

Default to `const` Rule

A good practice is to default to using `const` and only use `let` when you know the variable needs to be reassigned. This approach makes your code more predictable and helps prevent accidental modifications.

#javascript

```
// Good practice: Start with const
const calculateOrderTotal = (items, taxRate = 0.08) => {
    const subtotal = items.reduce((sum, item) => sum +
item.price, 0);
    const tax = subtotal * taxRate;
    const total = subtotal + tax;

    return {
        subtotal,
        tax,
        total
    };
};

// Use let only when reassignment is needed
const findLargestNumber = (numbers) => {
    let largest = numbers[0];

    for (let i = 1; i < numbers.length; i++) {
        if (numbers[i] > largest) {
```

```
            largest = numbers[i];
        }
    }

    return largest;
};
```

Essential Tips

- Always initialize variables when declaring them to avoid undefined values and make your intentions clear.
- Use meaningful names that describe the variable's purpose rather than its type or implementation details.
- Keep variable scope as narrow as possible to reduce complexity and potential conflicts.
- Group related variable declarations together to improve code organization and readability.
- Consider using destructuring assignment to extract values from objects and arrays more elegantly.

Actionable Strategies

- Establish a consistent naming convention across your entire project and enforce it through code reviews or linting tools.
- Create a style guide that specifies when to use `var`, `let`, and `const` based on your project's requirements and team preferences.
- Implement ESLint rules that enforce `const` usage when variables are never reassigned and prevent the use of `var` in modern codebases.
- Use TypeScript or JSDoc comments to document variable types and purposes, especially for complex objects and functions.
- Refactor legacy code that uses `var` to use `let` and `const` systematically, testing thoroughly to ensure scope changes don't break functionality.
- Create utility functions for common variable operations like deep cloning objects to maintain immutability when needed.

- Develop a habit of reviewing variable declarations during code reviews to ensure they follow best practices and maintain consistency.

Chapter 4: Data Types and Type Conversion

JavaScript's type system forms the foundation of how data is stored, manipulated, and processed in your applications. Understanding data types and type conversion mechanisms is crucial for writing robust, predictable code and avoiding common pitfalls that plague many JavaScript developers.

4.1 Primitive Data Types: Strings, Numbers, Booleans

JavaScript recognizes several primitive data types that represent the most basic forms of data. These primitives are immutable, meaning their values cannot be changed directly - instead, operations on primitives create new values.

String Data Type

Strings represent textual data in JavaScript and can be created using single quotes, double quotes, or backticks (template literals). Each approach offers different capabilities and use cases.

#javascript

```
// Single quotes
let singleQuoted = 'Hello World';

// Double quotes
let doubleQuoted = "Hello World";

// Template literals (ES6+)
let templateLiteral = `Hello World`;

// Multiline strings with template literals
let multiline = `This is a
multiline string
```

```
using template literals`;
```

Template literals provide powerful string interpolation capabilities, allowing you to embed expressions directly within strings:

#javascript

```
let name = "Alice";
let age = 30;
let greeting = `Hello, my name is ${name} and I am ${age}
years old.`;
console.log(greeting); // "Hello, my name is Alice and I
am 30 years old."

// Complex expressions in template literals
let price = 19.99;
let tax = 0.08;
let total = `Total cost: $${(price * (1 +
tax)).toFixed(2)}`;
console.log(total); // "Total cost: $21.59"
```

String Methods and Properties

Strings come with numerous built-in methods for manipulation and analysis:

#javascript

```
let text = "JavaScript Programming";

// Length property
console.log(text.length); // 21

// Case conversion
```

```
console.log(text.toLowerCase()); // "javascript
programming"
console.log(text.toUpperCase()); // "JAVASCRIPT
PROGRAMMING"

// Substring extraction
console.log(text.slice(0, 10)); // "JavaScript"
console.log(text.substring(11)); // "Programming"

// Character access
console.log(text[0]); // "J"
console.log(text.charAt(4)); // "S"

// Search operations
console.log(text.indexOf("Script")); // 4
console.log(text.includes("Program")); // true

// String replacement
console.log(text.replace("JavaScript", "Python")); //
"Python Programming"
```

Escape Characters

Special characters within strings require escape sequences:

#javascript

```
let escaped = "She said, \"Hello World!\"";
let newlineExample = "First line\nSecond line";
let tabExample = "Column1\tColumn2";
let backslashExample = "Path: C:\\Users\\Documents";

console.log(escaped); // She said, "Hello World!"
```

```
console.log(newlineExample);
// First line
// Second line
```

Number Data Type

JavaScript uses a single number type to represent both integers and floating-point numbers, following the IEEE 754 double-precision floating-point standard.

#javascript

```
// Integer representation
let integer = 42;
let negativeInteger = -17;

// Floating-point representation
let decimal = 3.14159;
let scientific = 2.5e6; // 2,500,000
let smallNumber = 1.23e-4; // 0.000123

// Special numeric values
let infinity = Infinity;
let negativeInfinity = -Infinity;
let notANumber = NaN;
```

Numeric Operations and Methods

JavaScript provides extensive support for mathematical operations:

#javascript

```
let a = 10;
```

```
let b = 3;

// Basic arithmetic
console.log(a + b); // 13
console.log(a - b); // 7
console.log(a * b); // 30
console.log(a / b); // 3.3333333333333335
console.log(a % b); // 1 (modulo/remainder)
console.log(a ** b); // 1000 (exponentiation)

// Math object methods
console.log(Math.round(3.7)); // 4
console.log(Math.floor(3.7)); // 3
console.log(Math.ceil(3.2)); // 4
console.log(Math.max(5, 10, 3)); // 10
console.log(Math.min(5, 10, 3)); // 3
console.log(Math.random()); // Random number 0-1

// Number methods
let num = 123.456789;
console.log(num.toFixed(2)); // "123.46"
console.log(num.toPrecision(5)); // "123.46"
console.log(Number.isInteger(123)); // true
console.log(Number.isInteger(123.45)); // false
```

Floating-Point Precision Issues

Understanding JavaScript's floating-point arithmetic limitations prevents common calculation errors:

#javascript

```
// Precision issues
console.log(0.1 + 0.2); // 0.30000000000000004 (not 0.3!)
console.log(0.1 + 0.2 === 0.3); // false

// Solutions for precision
function addPrecise(a, b, precision = 10) {
    return parseFloat((a + b).toFixed(precision));
}

console.log(addPrecise(0.1, 0.2, 1)); // 0.3

// Using Number.EPSILON for comparisons
function isEqual(a, b) {
    return Math.abs(a - b) < Number.EPSILON;
}

console.log(isEqual(0.1 + 0.2, 0.3)); // true
```

Boolean Data Type

Booleans represent logical values and form the basis of conditional logic in JavaScript applications.

#javascript

```
// Direct boolean values
let isActive = true;
let isComplete = false;

// Boolean results from comparisons
let isGreater = 10 > 5; // true
```

```
let isEqual = "hello" === "world"; // false
let isLessOrEqual = 3 <= 3; // true

// Logical operations
let a = true;
let b = false;

console.log(a && b); // false (AND)
console.log(a || b); // true (OR)
console.log(!a); // false (NOT)
console.log(!!a); // true (double negation - converts to
boolean)
```

Truthy and Falsy Values

JavaScript's boolean evaluation extends beyond true/false values:

#javascript

```
// Falsy values (evaluate to false)
console.log(Boolean(false)); // false
console.log(Boolean(0)); // false
console.log(Boolean(-0)); // false
console.log(Boolean(0n)); // false (BigInt zero)
console.log(Boolean("")); // false (empty string)
console.log(Boolean(null)); // false
console.log(Boolean(undefined)); // false
console.log(Boolean(NaN)); // false

// Truthy values (everything else)
console.log(Boolean(true)); // true
console.log(Boolean(1)); // true
```

```
console.log(Boolean(-1)); // true
console.log(Boolean("hello")); // true
console.log(Boolean(" ")); // true (space is not empty)
console.log(Boolean([])); // true (empty array)
console.log(Boolean({})); // true (empty object)
```

Short-Circuit Evaluation

Understanding how logical operators handle evaluation optimization:

#javascript

```
// AND short-circuit
let result1 = false && console.log("This won't execute");
let result2 = true && "This will be returned";

// OR short-circuit
let result3 = true || console.log("This won't execute");
let result4 = false || "This will be returned";

// Practical applications
let user = { name: "John" };
let displayName = user.name || "Guest"; // "John"

let emptyUser = {};
let defaultName = emptyUser.name || "Anonymous"; //
"Anonymous"
```

4.2 Complex Types: Objects, Arrays, Functions

Complex data types in JavaScript allow you to store and organize multiple values and create sophisticated data structures and behaviors.

Objects

Objects represent collections of key-value pairs and serve as the foundation for complex data modeling in JavaScript.

Object Creation and Access

#javascript

```javascript
// Object literal notation
let person = {
    name: "Sarah",
    age: 28,
    city: "New York",
    isEmployed: true
};

// Accessing properties
console.log(person.name); // "Sarah" (dot notation)
console.log(person["age"]); // 28 (bracket notation)

// Dynamic property access
let property = "city";
console.log(person[property]); // "New York"

// Adding new properties
person.email = "sarah@example.com";
person["phone"] = "555-1234";

// Modifying existing properties
person.age = 29;
person["city"] = "Boston";
```

Advanced Object Features

javascript

```
// Nested objects
let company = {
    name: "Tech Corp",
    address: {
        street: "123 Main St",
        city: "San Francisco",
        zipCode: "94105"
    },
    employees: {
        count: 150,
        departments: ["Engineering", "Sales",
"Marketing"]
    }
};

// Accessing nested properties
console.log(company.address.city); // "San Francisco"
console.log(company.employees.departments[0]); //
"Engineering"

// Object methods
let calculator = {
    value: 0,
    add: function(num) {
        this.value += num;
        return this;
    },
    multiply: function(num) {
        this.value *= num;
```

```
        return this;
    },
    getResult: function() {
        return this.value;
    }
};

// Method chaining
let result = calculator.add(5).multiply(3).getResult();
// 15
```

Object Destructuring

ES6 introduced destructuring assignment for cleaner object property extraction:

#javascript

```
let student = {
    name: "Mike",
    grade: "A",
    subjects: ["Math", "Science", "History"],
    contact: {
        email: "mike@school.edu",
        phone: "555-0123"
    }
};

// Basic destructuring
let { name, grade } = student;
console.log(name); // "Mike"
console.log(grade); // "A"
```

```
// Renaming variables
let { name: studentName, grade: studentGrade } = student;

// Default values
let { name: fullName, age = 18 } = student;

// Nested destructuring
let { contact: { email, phone } } = student;
console.log(email); // "mike@school.edu"
```

Arrays

Arrays are ordered collections of elements that can hold multiple values of any type.

Array Creation and Basic Operations

#javascript

```
// Array creation methods
let numbers = [1, 2, 3, 4, 5];
let mixed = ["hello", 42, true, null, { name: "Object" }];
let empty = [];
let constructed = new Array(5); // Creates array with 5 empty slots

// Accessing elements
console.log(numbers[0]); // 1 (first element)
console.log(numbers[numbers.length - 1]); // 5 (last element)

// Modifying arrays
numbers[2] = 10; // [1, 2, 10, 4, 5]
```

```
numbers.push(6); // Add to end: [1, 2, 10, 4, 5, 6]
numbers.unshift(0); // Add to beginning: [0, 1, 2, 10, 4,
5, 6]
let lastElement = numbers.pop(); // Remove from end:
returns 6
let firstElement = numbers.shift(); // Remove from
beginning: returns 0
```

Array Methods for Data Manipulation
#javascript

```
let fruits = ["apple", "banana", "orange", "grape"];

// Searching methods
console.log(fruits.indexOf("banana")); // 1
console.log(fruits.includes("orange")); // true
console.log(fruits.find(fruit => fruit.length > 5)); //
"banana"

// Transformation methods
let upperFruits = fruits.map(fruit =>
fruit.toUpperCase());
// ["APPLE", "BANANA", "ORANGE", "GRAPE"]

let longFruits = fruits.filter(fruit => fruit.length >
5);
// ["banana", "orange"]

let totalLength = fruits.reduce((sum, fruit) => sum +
fruit.length, 0);
// 20

// Iteration methods
```

```
fruits.forEach((fruit, index) => {
    console.log(`${index}: ${fruit}`);
});

// Array joining and slicing
console.log(fruits.join(", ")); // "apple, banana,
orange, grape"
console.log(fruits.slice(1, 3)); // ["banana", "orange"]
```

Multidimensional Arrays
#javascript

```
// 2D array (matrix)
let matrix = [
    [1, 2, 3],
    [4, 5, 6],
    [7, 8, 9]
];

// Accessing 2D array elements
console.log(matrix[1][2]); // 6

// Iterating through 2D arrays
for (let i = 0; i < matrix.length; i++) {
    for (let j = 0; j < matrix[i].length; j++) {
        console.log(`matrix[${i}][${j}] =
${matrix[i][j]}`);
    }
}

// Using nested forEach
```

```
matrix.forEach((row, rowIndex) => {
    row.forEach((cell, colIndex) => {
        console.log(`Row ${rowIndex}, Col ${colIndex}:
${cell}`);
    });
});
```

Functions

Functions are reusable blocks of code that can accept parameters and return values, making them first-class objects in JavaScript.

Function Declaration and Expression

#javascript

```
// Function declaration
function greet(name) {
    return `Hello, ${name}!`;
}

// Function expression
let sayGoodbye = function(name) {
    return `Goodbye, ${name}!`;
};

// Arrow function (ES6)
let welcome = (name) => `Welcome, ${name}!`;

// Arrow function with multiple parameters
let add = (a, b) => a + b;

// Arrow function with block body
```

```
let processData = (data) => {
    let processed = data.map(item => item * 2);
    return processed.filter(item => item > 10);
};
```

Function Parameters and Arguments
#javascript

```
// Default parameters
function createUser(name, age = 18, role = "user") {
    return {
        name: name,
        age: age,
        role: role
    };
}

console.log(createUser("John")); // { name: "John", age:
18, role: "user" }
console.log(createUser("Jane", 25, "admin")); // { name:
"Jane", age: 25, role: "admin" }

// Rest parameters
function sum(...numbers) {
    return numbers.reduce((total, num) => total + num,
0);
}

console.log(sum(1, 2, 3, 4, 5)); // 15

// Destructuring parameters
function displayUser({ name, age, email }) {
```

```
    console.log(`Name: ${name}, Age: ${age}, Email:
${email}`);
}

let user = { name: "Bob", age: 30, email:
"bob@example.com" };
displayUser(user);
```

Higher-Order Functions

Functions that operate on other functions, either by taking them as arguments or returning them:

#javascript

```
// Function that takes another function as parameter
function executeOperation(a, b, operation) {
    return operation(a, b);
}

let multiply = (x, y) => x * y;
let divide = (x, y) => x / y;

console.log(executeOperation(10, 2, multiply)); // 20
console.log(executeOperation(10, 2, divide)); // 5

// Function that returns another function
function createMultiplier(factor) {
    return function(number) {
        return number * factor;
    };
}
```

```
let double = createMultiplier(2);
let triple = createMultiplier(3);

console.log(double(5)); // 10
console.log(triple(4)); // 12
```

4.3 Type Checking with `typeof`

The `typeof` operator provides runtime type information, though it has some quirks that developers must understand.

Basic typeof Usage

#javascript

```
// Primitive types
console.log(typeof "hello"); // "string"
console.log(typeof 42); // "number"
console.log(typeof true); // "boolean"
console.log(typeof undefined); // "undefined"
console.log(typeof Symbol("id")); // "symbol"
console.log(typeof 123n); // "bigint"

// Function type
console.log(typeof function() {}); // "function"

// Object types (all return "object")
console.log(typeof {}); // "object"
console.log(typeof []); // "object"
console.log(typeof null); // "object" (historical quirk)
```

```
console.log(typeof new Date()); // "object"
console.log(typeof /regex/); // "object"
```

typeof Limitations and Workarounds

The `typeof` operator has several limitations that require additional checking strategies:

#javascript

```
// Distinguishing between different object types
function getDetailedType(value) {
    if (value === null) return "null";
    if (Array.isArray(value)) return "array";
    if (value instanceof Date) return "date";
    if (value instanceof RegExp) return "regexp";
    return typeof value;
}

console.log(getDetailedType(null)); // "null"
console.log(getDetailedType([])); // "array"
console.log(getDetailedType(new Date())); // "date"
console.log(getDetailedType(/pattern/)); // "regexp"

// More comprehensive type checking
function comprehensiveTypeCheck(value) {
    // Handle null specifically
    if (value === null) return "null";

    // Handle primitive types
    let type = typeof value;
    if (type !== "object") return type;
```

```
    // Handle object subtypes
    if (Array.isArray(value)) return "array";
    if (value instanceof Date) return "date";
    if (value instanceof RegExp) return "regexp";
    if (value instanceof Error) return "error";

    // Check for plain objects
    if (value.constructor === Object) return
"plainObject";

    return "object";
}
```

Practical Type Checking Patterns

#javascript

```
// Safe property access
function safeGetProperty(obj, property) {
    if (typeof obj !== "object" || obj === null) {
        return undefined;
    }
    return obj[property];
}

// Function validation
function validateFunction(fn, functionName) {
    if (typeof fn !== "function") {
        throw new Error(`${functionName} must be a
function`);
```

```
    }
}

// Multiple type checking
function processInput(input) {
    switch (typeof input) {
        case "string":
            return input.trim().toLowerCase();
        case "number":
            return input.toFixed(2);
        case "boolean":
            return input ? "yes" : "no";
        case "object":
            if (input === null) return "null value";
            if (Array.isArray(input)) return `array with
${input.length} items`;
            return "object type";
        default:
            return "unknown type";
    }
}
```

4.4 Type Conversion: Implicit vs Explicit

JavaScript performs automatic type conversion (coercion) in many situations, but explicit conversion provides better control and predictability.

Implicit Type Conversion (Coercion)

JavaScript automatically converts types in various contexts, which can lead to unexpected results:

String Coercion
#javascript

```
// Addition with strings (concatenation)
console.log("5" + 3); // "53"
console.log(5 + "3"); // "53"
console.log("Hello" + " " + "World"); // "Hello World"

// Template literals always coerce to strings
let age = 25;
console.log(`I am ${age} years old`); // "I am 25 years
old"

// String coercion in other contexts
console.log("Value: " + true); // "Value: true"
console.log("Items: " + [1, 2, 3]); // "Items: 1,2,3"
console.log("Object: " + {}); // "Object: [object
Object]"
```

Numeric Coercion
#javascript

```
// Arithmetic operations (except +) coerce to numbers
console.log("10" - 5); // 5
console.log("10" * "2"); // 20
console.log("20" / "4"); // 5
console.log("15" % "4"); // 3

// Unary plus operator
console.log(+"42"); // 42
console.log(+true); // 1
console.log(+false); // 0
```

```
console.log(+""); // 0
console.log(+"hello"); // NaN

// Comparison operations
console.log("10" > 5); // true
console.log("20" < "3"); // true (lexicographic
comparison!)
console.log("20" < 3); // false (numeric comparison)
```

Boolean Coercion
#javascript

```
// Logical contexts
if ("hello") console.log("Truthy string"); // Executes
if (0) console.log("Won't execute"); // Doesn't execute
if ([]) console.log("Empty array is truthy"); // Executes

// Logical operators
console.log("" || "default"); // "default"
console.log("value" || "default"); // "value"
console.log(null && "won't reach"); // null
console.log("test" && "reached"); // "reached"
```

Explicit Type Conversion

Explicit conversion provides predictable results and clearer code intent:

String Conversion
#javascript

```
// String() constructor
console.log(String(123)); // "123"
```

```
console.log(String(true)); // "true"
console.log(String(null)); // "null"
console.log(String(undefined)); // "undefined"

// toString() method
let num = 42;
console.log(num.toString()); // "42"
console.log(num.toString(2)); // "101010" (binary)
console.log(num.toString(16)); // "2a" (hexadecimal)

// JSON.stringify for complex objects
let obj = { name: "John", age: 30 };
console.log(JSON.stringify(obj)); //
'{"name":"John","age":30}'
```

Number Conversion
#javascript

```
// Number() constructor
console.log(Number("123")); // 123
console.log(Number("123.45")); // 123.45
console.log(Number("")); // 0
console.log(Number(" ")); // 0
console.log(Number("hello")); // NaN
console.log(Number(true)); // 1
console.log(Number(false)); // 0

// parseInt() and parseFloat()
console.log(parseInt("123")); // 123
console.log(parseInt("123.45")); // 123
console.log(parseInt("123px")); // 123
```

```
console.log(parseFloat("123.45")); // 123.45
console.log(parseFloat("123.45px")); // 123.45

// With radix parameter
console.log(parseInt("1010", 2)); // 10 (binary to decimal)
console.log(parseInt("FF", 16)); // 255 (hexadecimal to decimal)
```

Boolean Conversion
#javascript

```
// Boolean() constructor
console.log(Boolean(1)); // true
console.log(Boolean(0)); // false
console.log(Boolean("")); // false
console.log(Boolean("hello")); // true
console.log(Boolean([])); // true
console.log(Boolean({})); // true

// Double negation (!! operator)
console.log(!!"hello"); // true
console.log(!!0); // false
console.log(!![]); // true
```

Common Coercion Pitfalls

Understanding these scenarios helps avoid bugs:

#javascript

```
// Array to string conversion issues
```

```
console.log([1, 2, 3] + [4, 5, 6]); // "1,2,34,5,6"
console.log([] + []); // ""
console.log([] + {}); // "[object Object]"
console.log({} + []); // "[object Object]"

// Equality comparison surprises
console.log(0 == false); // true
console.log("" == false); // true
console.log("0" == false); // true
console.log(null == undefined); // true
console.log(null == 0); // false
console.log(undefined == 0); // false

// Use strict equality to avoid coercion
console.log(0 === false); // false
console.log("" === false); // false
console.log(null === undefined); // false
```

4.5 Parsing Numbers and Booleans from Strings

Converting string representations to numeric and boolean values requires understanding various parsing methods and their behaviors.

Number Parsing Methods

parseInt() Function

The `parseInt()` function parses a string and returns an integer:

#javascript

```
// Basic integer parsing
console.log(parseInt("123")); // 123
console.log(parseInt("123.45")); // 123 (stops at
decimal)
console.log(parseInt("  456  ")); // 456 (ignores
whitespace)

// Parsing with non-numeric characters
console.log(parseInt("123px")); // 123
console.log(parseInt("width: 300px")); // NaN (doesn't
start with number)
console.log(parseInt("$50")); // NaN

// Using radix parameter
console.log(parseInt("1010", 2)); // 10 (binary)
console.log(parseInt("77", 8)); // 63 (octal)
console.log(parseInt("FF", 16)); // 255 (hexadecimal)
console.log(parseInt("123", 10)); // 123 (decimal -
always specify!)

// Edge cases
console.log(parseInt("")); // NaN
console.log(parseInt("  ")); // NaN
console.log(parseInt("0x10")); // 16 (hex prefix
recognized)
```

parseFloat() Function

The `parseFloat()` function parses a string and returns a floating-point number:

#javascript

```
// Basic float parsing
console.log(parseFloat("123.45")); // 123.45
console.log(parseFloat("123")); // 123
console.log(parseFloat("  456.78  ")); // 456.78

// Scientific notation
console.log(parseFloat("1.23e-4")); // 0.000123
console.log(parseFloat("5.67E+2")); // 567

// Parsing with mixed content
console.log(parseFloat("123.45px")); // 123.45
console.log(parseFloat("price: $19.99")); // NaN
console.log(parseFloat("3.14159 is pi")); // 3.14159

// Multiple decimal points
console.log(parseFloat("123.45.67")); // 123.45 (stops at second decimal)
```

Number() Constructor vs Parsing Functions

Understanding the differences between conversion approaches:

#javascript

```
let testStrings = ["123", "123.45", "123px", "", "   ", "0x10"];

testStrings.forEach(str => {
    console.log(`"${str}":`);
    console.log(`  Number(): ${Number(str)}`);
    console.log(`  parseInt(): ${parseInt(str, 10)}`);
    console.log(`  parseFloat(): ${parseFloat(str)}`);
```

```
    console.log("---");
});

// Output analysis:
// Number() is strict - returns NaN for any invalid content
// parseInt()/parseFloat() are lenient - parse valid prefixes
```

Advanced Number Parsing Techniques

Safe Number Parsing with Validation
#javascript

```
function safeParseInt(str, radix = 10) {
    // Validate input
    if (typeof str !== "string") return NaN;

    // Trim whitespace
    str = str.trim();

    // Check if string is empty
    if (str === "") return NaN;

    // Parse the number
    let result = parseInt(str, radix);

    // Verify the entire string was valid
    if (isNaN(result)) return NaN;

    // Check if there were trailing non-numeric characters
```

```
    let reconstructed = result.toString(radix);
    if (radix === 10 && !str.startsWith(reconstructed)) {
        console.warn(`Warning: "${str}" contains non-
numeric characters`);
    }

    return result;
}

console.log(safeParseInt("123")); // 123
console.log(safeParseInt("123px")); // 123 (with warning)
console.log(safeParseInt("abc")); // NaN
```

Currency and Formatted Number Parsing
#javascript

```
function parseCurrency(currencyString) {
    // Remove currency symbols and formatting
    let cleaned = currencyString
        .replace(/[$,]/g, "") // Remove $ and commas
        .trim();

    let result = parseFloat(cleaned);
    return isNaN(result) ? 0 : result;
}

console.log(parseCurrency("$1,234.56")); // 1234.56
console.log(parseCurrency("$12,345.67")); // 12345.67
console.log(parseCurrency("Invalid")); // 0

// International number parsing
```

```
function parseInternationalNumber(numString, locale =
"en-US") {
    try {
        // Remove locale-specific formatting
        if (locale === "de-DE") {
            // German: 1.234,56
            numString = numString.replace(/\./g,
"").replace(",", ".");
        } else if (locale === "fr-FR") {
            // French: 1 234,56
            numString = numString.replace(/\s/g,
"").replace(",", ".");
        }

        return parseFloat(numString);
    } catch (error) {
        return NaN;
    }
}
```

Boolean Parsing from Strings

JavaScript doesn't have a native parseBoolean function, but several approaches handle string-to-boolean conversion:

String-Based Boolean Parsing
#javascript

```
function parseBoolean(value) {
    // Handle non-string inputs
    if (typeof value === "boolean") return value;
    if (typeof value !== "string") return Boolean(value);
```

```
    // Convert to Lowercase for case-insensitive
comparison
    let normalized = value.toLowerCase().trim();

    // Define true values
    let trueValues = ["true", "yes", "1", "on",
"enabled"];
    let falseValues = ["false", "no", "0", "off",
"disabled"];

    if (trueValues.includes(normalized)) return true;
    if (falseValues.includes(normalized)) return false;

    // Default behavior for ambiguous values
    return Boolean(value);
}

// Test cases
console.log(parseBoolean("true")); // true
console.log(parseBoolean("True")); // true
console.log(parseBoolean("yes")); // true
console.log(parseBoolean("1")); // true
console.log(parseBoolean("false")); // false
console.log(parseBoolean("no")); // false
console.log(parseBoolean("0")); // false
console.log(parseBoolean("maybe")); // true (non-empty
string)
```

Numeric Boolean Parsing

#javascript

```
function parseNumericBoolean(value) {
```

```
    let num = Number(value);
    if (isNaN(num)) return null; // Invalid input
    return num !== 0;
}

console.log(parseNumericBoolean("1")); // true
console.log(parseNumericBoolean("0")); // false
console.log(parseNumericBoolean("42")); // true
console.log(parseNumericBoolean("-1")); // true
console.log(parseNumericBoolean("0.0")); // false
console.log(parseNumericBoolean("abc")); // null

#### JSON-Safe Boolean Parsing
```

#```javascript

```
function parseJSONBoolean(value) {
    try {
        // Handle already parsed booleans
        if (typeof value === "boolean") return value;

        // Parse JSON-valid boolean strings
        let parsed = JSON.parse(value.toLowerCase());

        // Ensure result is actually boolean
        return typeof parsed === "boolean" ? parsed :
null;
    } catch (error) {
        return null; // Invalid JSON boolean
    }
```

```
}

console.log(parseJSONBoolean("true")); // true
console.log(parseJSONBoolean("false")); // false
console.log(parseJSONBoolean("True")); // true
console.log(parseJSONBoolean("1")); // null (not JSON
boolean)
console.log(parseJSONBoolean("yes")); // null (not JSON
boolean)
```

Form Data and User Input Parsing

Real-world applications often need to parse user input from forms and APIs:

#javascript

```
// Comprehensive form data parser
class FormDataParser {
    static parseField(value, expectedType) {
        if (value === null || value === undefined) return
null;

        // Convert to string for processing
        let stringValue = String(value).trim();
        if (stringValue === "") return null;

        switch (expectedType.toLowerCase()) {
            case "number":
                return this.parseNumber(stringValue);
            case "integer":
                return this.parseInteger(stringValue);
            case "boolean":
```

```
                return this.parseBoolean(stringValue);
            case "string":
                return stringValue;
            default:
                return stringValue;
        }
    }

    static parseNumber(value) {
        // Handle negative numbers
        let cleaned = value.replace(/[^\d.-]/g, "");
        let result = parseFloat(cleaned);
        return isNaN(result) ? null : result;
    }

    static parseInteger(value) {
        let result = this.parseNumber(value);
        return result !== null ? Math.floor(result) :
null;
    }

    static parseBoolean(value) {
        let normalized = value.toLowerCase();
        if (["true", "yes", "1",
"on"].includes(normalized)) return true;
        if (["false", "no", "0",
"off"].includes(normalized)) return false;
        return null;
    }
}
```

```
// Usage example
let formData = {
    age: "25",
    price: "$19.99",
    isActive: "true",
    count: "42px"
};

Object.keys(formData).forEach(key => {
    let original = formData[key];
    let asNumber = FormDataParser.parseField(original,
"number");
    let asBoolean = FormDataParser.parseField(original,
"boolean");

    console.log(`${key}: "${original}" -> number:
${asNumber}, boolean: ${asBoolean}`);
});
```

Error Handling in Type Conversion

Robust applications must handle conversion failures gracefully:

#javascript

```
// Safe conversion with fallbacks
function safeConvert(value, targetType, fallback = null)
{
    try {
        switch (targetType) {
            case "number":
                let num = Number(value);
```

```
            return isNaN(num) ? fallback : num;

        case "integer":
            let int = parseInt(value, 10);
            return isNaN(int) ? fallback : int;

        case "float":
            let float = parseFloat(value);
            return isNaN(float) ? fallback : float;

        case "boolean":
            if (typeof value === "boolean") return
value;
            if (typeof value === "string") {
                let lower =
value.toLowerCase().trim();
                if (["true", "yes",
"1"].includes(lower)) return true;
                if (["false", "no",
"0"].includes(lower)) return false;
            }
            return fallback;

        case "string":
            return value !== null && value !==
undefined ? String(value) : fallback;

        default:
            return fallback;
    }
} catch (error) {
```

```
        console.warn(`Conversion error:
${error.message}`);
        return fallback;
    }
}

// Testing safe conversion
console.log(safeConvert("123", "number", 0)); // 123
console.log(safeConvert("abc", "number", 0)); // 0
console.log(safeConvert("true", "boolean", false)); //
true
console.log(safeConvert("maybe", "boolean", false)); //
false
```

Performance Considerations

Different parsing methods have varying performance characteristics:

#javascript

```
// Performance comparison function
function compareParsingPerformance() {
    let testData = Array.from({length: 10000}, (_, i) =>
`${i}.${i}`);

    console.time("Number() conversion");
    testData.forEach(str => Number(str));
    console.timeEnd("Number() conversion");

    console.time("parseFloat() conversion");
    testData.forEach(str => parseFloat(str));
    console.timeEnd("parseFloat() conversion");
```

```
    console.time("Unary + conversion");
    testData.forEach(str => +str);
    console.timeEnd("Unary + conversion");
}

// Generally: unary + ≈ Number() > parseFloat() for pure numeric strings
// parseFloat() is more forgiving but slower for clean numeric data
```

Best Practices for Type Conversion

Understanding when and how to apply different conversion strategies:

#javascript

```
// Context-aware parsing strategy
class TypeConverter {
    // For API responses - strict parsing
    static parseAPIResponse(data, schema) {
        let result = {};

        for (let [key, expectedType] of Object.entries(schema)) {
            if (!(key in data)) {
                result[key] = null;
                continue;
            }

            let value = data[key];
```

```
            switch (expectedType) {
                case "number":
                    result[key] = typeof value ===
"number" ? value : Number(value);
                    if (isNaN(result[key])) {
                        throw new Error(`Invalid number
for field ${key}: ${value}`);
                    }
                    break;

                case "boolean":
                    result[key] = Boolean(value);
                    break;

                case "string":
                    result[key] = String(value);
                    break;

                default:
                    result[key] = value;
            }
        }

        return result;
    }

    // For user input - lenient parsing with validation
    static parseUserInput(input, expectedType, options =
{}) {
        let {
            allowEmpty = false,
```

```
            min = null,
            max = null,
            defaultValue = null
        } = options;

        // Handle empty input
        if (!input || (typeof input === "string" &&
input.trim() === "")) {
            return allowEmpty ? defaultValue : null;
        }

        let result;

        switch (expectedType) {
            case "number":
            case "integer":
                // Remove common non-numeric characters
                let cleaned =
String(input).replace(/[,$%]/g, "");
                result = expectedType === "integer" ?
parseInt(cleaned, 10) : parseFloat(cleaned);

                if (isNaN(result)) return defaultValue;

                // Apply range validation
                if (min !== null && result < min) return
defaultValue;
                if (max !== null && result > max) return
defaultValue;

                return result;
```

```
            case "boolean":
                return this.parseBoolean(input);

            default:
                return String(input);
        }
    }

    static parseBoolean(value) {
        if (typeof value === "boolean") return value;

        let stringValue =
String(value).toLowerCase().trim();
        let truthyValues = ["true", "yes", "1", "on",
"enabled", "active"];
        let falsyValues = ["false", "no", "0", "off",
"disabled", "inactive"];

        if (truthyValues.includes(stringValue)) return
true;
        if (falsyValues.includes(stringValue)) return
false;

        // For ambiguous cases, use JavaScript's
truthiness
        return Boolean(value);
    }
}

// Usage examples
let apiData = { age: "25", active: "1", name: "John" };
```

```
let schema = { age: "number", active: "boolean", name: "string" };

try {
    let parsed = TypeConverter.parseAPIResponse(apiData, schema);
    console.log(parsed); // { age: 25, active: true, name: "John" }
} catch (error) {
    console.error("API parsing failed:", error.message);
}

// User input parsing
console.log(TypeConverter.parseUserInput("$25.50", "number")); // 25.5
console.log(TypeConverter.parseUserInput("yes", "boolean")); // true
console.log(TypeConverter.parseUserInput("", "number", { allowEmpty: true, defaultValue: 0 })); // 0
```

Key Takeaways

- Understanding JavaScript's type system and conversion mechanisms provides the foundation for writing robust applications. Primitive types offer predictable behavior when handled correctly, while complex types enable sophisticated data modeling. The distinction between implicit and explicit conversion determines code reliability and maintainability.
- Type checking with `typeof` requires awareness of its limitations, particularly with object subtypes and null values. Combining `typeof` with additional checks creates comprehensive type validation systems.
- String parsing for numbers and booleans demands understanding the differences between strict conversion methods like `Number()` and lenient parsing functions like `parseInt()` and `parseFloat()`. Context-appropriate parsing strategies improve both user experience and data integrity.

- The choice between implicit and explicit conversion affects code readability and debugging difficulty. Explicit conversion makes intentions clear and reduces unexpected behavior, while understanding implicit conversion helps identify potential issues in existing code.

Essential Tips

- Always specify the radix parameter when using `parseInt()` to avoid unexpected octal interpretation of numbers with leading zeros.
- Use `Number.isNaN()` instead of `isNaN()` for reliable NaN checking, as the global `isNaN()` function performs type coercion that can produce misleading results.
- Implement comprehensive type checking functions that go beyond `typeof` to distinguish between arrays, null values, and different object types for more robust code.
- Consider using strict equality (===) instead of loose equality (==) to avoid unintended type coercion in comparisons.
- Create parsing utilities that handle edge cases and provide meaningful fallback values rather than relying on default JavaScript conversion behavior.

Actionable Strategies

- Build a custom type validation library that combines `typeof` checks with instanceof operations and Array.isArray() to create comprehensive type detection for your specific use cases.
- Establish consistent patterns for handling user input by creating specialized parsing functions that validate ranges, formats, and types appropriate to your application domain.
- Implement error boundaries around type conversion operations using try-catch blocks and provide user-friendly error messages when conversion fails.
- Create unit tests for all type conversion scenarios in your application, including edge cases like empty strings, null values, and malformed input to ensure consistent behavior.
- Use TypeScript or JSDoc annotations to document expected types for function parameters and return values, making type expectations explicit for other developers.

- Develop a configuration-driven approach to form validation that maps field names to expected types and validation rules, reducing repetitive parsing code.
- Cache the results of expensive type conversion operations when processing large datasets, and consider using typed arrays for numeric data that requires consistent type handling.

Chapter 5: Operators in JavaScript

Operators form the backbone of JavaScript programming, enabling you to perform calculations, make comparisons, assign values, and create complex logical expressions. Understanding operators thoroughly is crucial for writing effective JavaScript code, as they appear in virtually every program you'll create.

5.1 Arithmetic Operators

Arithmetic operators allow you to perform mathematical calculations on numeric values. JavaScript provides a comprehensive set of arithmetic operators that handle both basic and advanced mathematical operations.

Basic Arithmetic Operations

The fundamental arithmetic operators include addition (+), subtraction (-), multiplication (*), division (/), and modulus (%). Each operator serves a specific mathematical purpose and behaves predictably with numeric values.

#javascript

```
let a = 15;
let b = 4;

// Addition
let sum = a + b; // 19
console.log("Sum:", sum);

// Subtraction
let difference = a - b; // 11
console.log("Difference:", difference);
```

```
// Multiplication
let product = a * b; // 60
console.log("Product:", product);

// Division
let quotient = a / b; // 3.75
console.log("Quotient:", quotient);

// Modulus (remainder)
let remainder = a % b; // 3
console.log("Remainder:", remainder);
```

Understanding the Modulus Operator

The modulus operator (%) returns the remainder after division, making it particularly useful for determining if numbers are even or odd, creating cycling patterns, or wrapping values within specific ranges.

#javascript

```
// Check if a number is even or odd
function isEven(number) {
    return number % 2 === 0;
}

console.log(isEven(8)); // true
console.log(isEven(7)); // false

// Create a cycling pattern (0, 1, 2, 0, 1, 2, ...)
for (let i = 0; i < 10; i++) {
    console.log(i % 3);
}
```

```
// Wrap array indices
let colors = ['red', 'green', 'blue'];
let index = 5;
let wrappedIndex = index % colors.length; // 2
console.log(colors[wrappedIndex]); // 'blue'
```

Exponentiation Operator

JavaScript includes the exponentiation operator (**) for raising numbers to powers, eliminating the need for Math.pow() in many cases.

#javascript

```
let base = 2;
let exponent = 3;

// Using exponentiation operator
let result1 = base ** exponent; // 8

// Equivalent using Math.pow()
let result2 = Math.pow(base, exponent); // 8

// Complex calculations
let compound = 1000 * (1 + 0.05) ** 10; // Compound
interest calculation
console.log("Compound result:", compound);

// Square roots using fractional exponents
let squareRoot = 16 ** 0.5; // 4
console.log("Square root:", squareRoot);
```

Unary Operators

Unary operators work on single operands and include increment (++), decrement (--), unary plus (+), and unary minus (-).

#javascript

```
let count = 5;


// Pre-increment: increment first, then use value
let preIncrement = ++count; // count becomes 6,
preIncrement is 6
console.log("Pre-increment:", preIncrement, "Count:",
count);


count = 5; // Reset


// Post-increment: use value first, then increment
let postIncrement = count++; // postIncrement is 5, then
count becomes 6
console.log("Post-increment:", postIncrement, "Count:",
count);


// Pre-decrement and post-decrement work similarly
let x = 10;
console.log(--x); // 9 (x is decremented first)
console.log(x--); // 9 (x is used first, then decremented
to 8)
console.log(x);   // 8


// Unary plus and minus
let str = "42";
let num = +str; // Converts string to number: 42
```

```
let negative = -num; // -42
```

Type Coercion in Arithmetic Operations

JavaScript automatically converts data types during arithmetic operations, which can lead to unexpected results if not understood properly.

#javascript

```javascript
// Number and string addition
console.log(5 + "3"); // "53" (concatenation)
console.log("5" + 3); // "53" (concatenation)

// Other operations convert strings to numbers
console.log("10" - 3); // 7
console.log("10" * 3); // 30
console.log("10" / 2); // 5

// Boolean to number conversion
console.log(true + 1);  // 2 (true becomes 1)
console.log(false * 5); // 0 (false becomes 0)

// Null and undefined behavior
console.log(null + 5);      // 5 (null becomes 0)
console.log(undefined + 5); // NaN (undefined becomes
NaN)
```

5.2 Comparison Operators

Comparison operators evaluate relationships between values and return boolean results (true or false). These operators are essential for conditional statements, loops, and data validation.

Equality and Inequality Operators

JavaScript provides both loose equality (==) and strict equality (===) operators, each with different type coercion behaviors.

#javascript

```
let num = 5;
let str = "5";
let bool = true;

// Loose equality (==) performs type coercion
console.log(num == str);   // true (string "5" converted to number 5)
console.log(1 == bool);    // true (boolean true converted to number 1)
console.log(0 == false);   // true (boolean false converted to number 0)
console.log(null == undefined); // true (special case)

// Strict equality (===) requires same type and value
console.log(num === str);  // false (different types)
console.log(1 === bool);   // false (different types)
console.log(5 === 5);      // true (same type and value)

// Inequality operators
console.log(num != str);   // false (loose inequality)
console.log(num !== str);  // true (strict inequality)
```

Relational Operators

Relational operators compare the relative order or magnitude of values, primarily used with numbers and strings.

#javascript

```
let x = 10;
let y = 20;
let z = "30";

// Numeric comparisons
console.log(x < y);   // true
console.log(x > y);   // false
console.log(x <= 10); // true
console.log(y >= 20); // true

// String comparisons (lexicographic order)
console.log("apple" < "banana"); // true
console.log("Apple" < "apple");  // true (uppercase letters come first)
console.log("10" < "9");         // true (string comparison, not numeric)

// Mixed type comparisons
console.log(y < z);   // true (20 < 30, string "30" converted to number)
console.log("20" < "3"); // true (string comparison, not numeric)

// Date comparisons
let date1 = new Date("2023-01-01");
let date2 = new Date("2023-12-31");
console.log(date1 < date2); // true
```

Special Cases and Edge Behaviors

Understanding how comparison operators handle special values prevents common programming errors.

#javascript

```javascript
// NaN comparisons
console.log(NaN === NaN); // false (NaN is never equal to itself)
console.log(NaN == NaN);  // false
console.log(isNaN(NaN));  // true (use isNaN() to check for NaN)

// Infinity comparisons
console.log(Infinity > 1000000); // true
console.log(-Infinity < -1000000); // true
console.log(Infinity === Infinity); // true

// Array and object comparisons
let arr1 = [1, 2, 3];
let arr2 = [1, 2, 3];
let arr3 = arr1;

console.log(arr1 == arr2);  // false (different objects)
console.log(arr1 === arr2); // false (different objects)
console.log(arr1 === arr3); // true (same reference)

// Type coercion in comparisons
console.log([] == false);   // true (empty array converts to 0, false converts to 0)
console.log("" == false);   // true (empty string converts to 0)
```

```
console.log(" " == false);  // false (space is not empty string)
```

5.3 Logical Operators (&&, ||, !)

Logical operators combine or modify boolean expressions, enabling complex conditional logic and control flow in your programs.

The Logical AND Operator (&&)

The AND operator returns true only when both operands are truthy. It employs short-circuit evaluation, meaning if the first operand is falsy, the second operand is not evaluated.

#javascript

```
// Basic boolean logic
console.log(true && true);   // true
console.log(true && false);  // false
console.log(false && true);  // false

// Short-circuit evaluation
let count = 0;
false && count++; // count++ is not executed
console.log(count); // 0

true && count++; // count++ is executed
console.log(count); // 1

// Practical applications
let user = {
    name: "John",
```

```
    age: 25,
    isActive: true
};

// Check multiple conditions
if (user.age >= 18 && user.isActive) {
    console.log("User can access premium features");
}

// Safe property access
user.profile && user.profile.avatar &&
console.log(user.profile.avatar);

// Conditional assignment
let defaultSettings = { theme: "light" };
let userSettings = user.settings || defaultSettings;
let finalTheme = userSettings && userSettings.theme &&
userSettings.theme;
```

The Logical OR Operator (||)

The OR operator returns true when at least one operand is truthy. Like AND, it uses short-circuit evaluation, stopping at the first truthy value.

#javascript

```
// Basic boolean logic
console.log(true || false);   // true
console.log(false || true);   // true
console.log(false || false);  // false

// Default value assignment
```

```
function greetUser(name) {
    name = name || "Guest"; // If name is falsy, use
"Guest"
    console.log("Hello, " + name);
}

greetUser("Alice"); // "Hello, Alice"
greetUser("");      // "Hello, Guest"
greetUser();        // "Hello, Guest"

// Multiple fallback values
let config = {
    apiUrl: process.env.API_URL ||
localStorage.getItem('apiUrl') ||
'https://api.default.com'
};

// Conditional execution
let hasPermission = user.isAdmin || user.isModerator ||
user.hasSpecialAccess;
hasPermission && performSensitiveOperation();
```

The Logical NOT Operator (!)

The NOT operator inverts the truthiness of its operand, converting truthy values to false and falsy values to true.

#javascript

```
// Basic negation
console.log(!true);   // false
console.log(!false);  // true
```

```
// Double negation for boolean conversion
console.log(!!"hello");    // true (non-empty string is truthy)
console.log(!!0);          // false (0 is falsy)
console.log(!![]);         // true (empty array is truthy)
console.log(!!null);       // false (null is falsy)

// Practical applications
let isLoggedOut = !user.isLoggedIn;
let isEmpty = !array.length;
let isInvalid = !isValid(userInput);

// Conditional logic with NOT
if (!user.hasSubscription) {
    showSubscriptionOffer();
}

// Toggle boolean values
let isVisible = true;
isVisible = !isVisible; // Now false

// Complex conditions
let canEdit = user.isOwner && !document.isLocked && !user.isRestricted;
```

Combining Logical Operators

Complex logical expressions combine multiple operators using parentheses to control evaluation order.

#javascript

```
let user = {
    age: 25,
    isActive: true,
    role: "editor",
    hasSubscription: false
};

// Complex permission check
let canAccessFeature = (user.age >= 18 && user.isActive)
&&
                       (user.role === "admin" ||
user.hasSubscription);

// Multiple condition groups
let shouldShowContent = (user.isLoggedIn &&
user.isActive) ||
                        (user.isGuest &&
content.isPublic);

// Nested logical operations
let canPerformAction = user.isActive &&
                       (user.role === "admin" ||
                        (user.role === "editor" &&
document.isEditable)) &&
                       !user.isBlocked;


// Short-circuit patterns for error handling
function processUser(userData) {
    userData &&
    userData.profile &&
    userData.profile.email &&
    sendWelcomeEmail(userData.profile.email);
```

```
}
```

Truthy and Falsy Values

Understanding JavaScript's concept of truthy and falsy values is crucial for effective use of logical operators.

#javascript

```
// Falsy values in JavaScript
console.log(!!false);     // false
console.log(!!0);         // false
console.log(!!-0);        // false
console.log(!!"");        // false
console.log(!!null);      // false
console.log(!!undefined); // false
console.log(!!NaN);       // false

// Everything else is truthy
console.log(!!"hello");   // true
console.log(!!1);         // true
console.log(!!-1);        // true
console.log(!![]);        // true (empty array is
truthy!)
console.log(!!{});        // true (empty object is
truthy!)
console.log(!!" ");       // true (space character is
truthy)


// Practical implications
let items = [];
if (items) { // This will always be true, even for empty
arrays!
```

```
    console.log("This runs even for empty arrays");
}

// Correct way to check for empty arrays
if (items.length) {
    console.log("Array has items");
}
```

5.4 Assignment Operators (+=, -=, etc.)

Assignment operators provide concise ways to update variable values by combining assignment with arithmetic or other operations.

Basic Assignment and Compound Assignment

The basic assignment operator (=) assigns a value to a variable, while compound assignment operators combine assignment with operations.

#javascript

```
let score = 100;
let multiplier = 2;
let bonus = 50;

// Basic assignment
score = 150;

// Addition assignment
score += bonus; // Equivalent to: score = score + bonus
console.log(score); // 200
```

```
// Subtraction assignment
score -= 25; // Equivalent to: score = score - 25
console.log(score); // 175

// Multiplication assignment
score *= multiplier; // Equivalent to: score = score *
multiplier
console.log(score); // 350

// Division assignment
score /= 2; // Equivalent to: score = score / 2
console.log(score); // 175

// Modulus assignment
score %= 100; // Equivalent to: score = score % 100
console.log(score); // 75

// Exponentiation assignment
score **= 2; // Equivalent to: score = score ** 2
console.log(score); // 5625
```

String Concatenation Assignment

The addition assignment operator works with strings for concatenation, making it easy to build strings incrementally.

#javascript

```
let message = "Hello";
let userName = "Alice";
let punctuation = "!";
```

```
// String concatenation assignment
message += " "; // "Hello "
message += userName; // "Hello Alice"
message += punctuation; // "Hello Alice!"

console.log(message); // "Hello Alice!"

// Building HTML strings
let html = "<div>";
html += "<h1>Welcome</h1>";
html += "<p>Thank you for visiting</p>";
html += "</div>";

// Building formatted output
let report = "Sales Report\n";
report += "============\n";
report += "Total Sales: $" + totalSales + "\n";
report += "Orders: " + orderCount + "\n";
```

Advanced Assignment Patterns

Assignment operators can be used in sophisticated patterns for data manipulation and algorithm implementation.

#javascript

```
// Array manipulation
let numbers = [1, 2, 3, 4, 5];
let sum = 0;

// Calculate sum using compound assignment
for (let i = 0; i < numbers.length; i++) {
```

```
    sum += numbers[i];
}

// Object property updates
let player = {
    health: 100,
    mana: 50,
    experience: 0
};

// Update player stats
player.health -= 20; // Take damage
player.mana += 10;   // Restore mana
player.experience *= 1.5; // Experience bonus

// Counter patterns
let attempts = 0;
let maxAttempts = 3;

while (attempts < maxAttempts) {
    attempts += 1;
    if (tryOperation()) {
        break;
    }
}

// Accumulator patterns
let inventory = {};
let items = ["sword", "shield", "potion", "sword",
"potion"];
```

```
// Count items
for (let item of items) {
    inventory[item] = (inventory[item] || 0) + 1;
}
```

Bitwise Assignment Operators

JavaScript includes bitwise assignment operators for low-level bit manipulation operations.

#javascript

```
let flags = 0b1010; // Binary: 1010 (decimal 10)

// Bitwise AND assignment
flags &= 0b1100; // flags = flags & 0b1100
console.log(flags.toString(2)); // "1000"

// Bitwise OR assignment
flags |= 0b0011; // flags = flags | 0b0011
console.log(flags.toString(2)); // "1011"

// Bitwise XOR assignment
flags ^= 0b0101; // flags = flags ^ 0b0101
console.log(flags.toString(2)); // "1110"

// Left shift assignment
let value = 5; // Binary: 101
value <<= 2; // Shift left by 2 positions
console.log(value); // 20 (Binary: 10100)

// Right shift assignment
```

```
value >>= 1; // Shift right by 1 position
console.log(value); // 10 (Binary: 1010)
```

Logical Assignment Operators (ES2021)

Modern JavaScript includes logical assignment operators that combine logical operations with assignment.

#javascript

```
let config = {
    theme: null,
    language: "en",
    debug: false
};

// Logical OR assignment (||=)
config.theme ||= "default"; // Only assigns if theme is falsy
console.log(config.theme); // "default"

config.language ||= "fr"; // Won't assign because language is truthy
console.log(config.language); // "en"

// Logical AND assignment (&&=)
let settings = {
    notifications: true,
    sound: true
};
```

```
settings.notifications &&= hasPermission(); // Only
assigns if notifications is truthy
settings.sound &&= settings.notifications; // Chain
conditions

// Nullish coalescing assignment (??=)
let userPrefs = {
    theme: null,
    fontSize: undefined,
    language: "es"
};

userPrefs.theme ??= "light"; // Assigns only if null or
undefined
userPrefs.fontSize ??= 16;   // Assigns only if null or
undefined
userPrefs.language ??= "en"; // Won't assign because
language is not null/undefined

console.log(userPrefs); // { theme: "light", fontSize:
16, language: "es" }
```

5.5 Ternary Operators and Practical Uses

The ternary operator provides a concise way to write conditional expressions, offering an alternative to if-else statements for simple conditional logic.

Basic Ternary Syntax and Usage

The ternary operator follows the pattern: `condition ? valueIfTrue : valueIfFalse`, evaluating the condition and returning one of two values based on the result.

#javascript

```
let age = 20;
let status = age >= 18 ? "adult" : "minor";
console.log(status); // "adult"

// Equivalent if-else statement
let status2;
if (age >= 18) {
    status2 = "adult";
} else {
    status2 = "minor";
}

// Function parameter defaults
function greet(name) {
    let displayName = name ? name : "Guest";
    // More concise: let displayName = name || "Guest";
    return "Hello, " + displayName;
}

// Immediate value assignment
let temperature = 75;
let weatherAdvice = temperature > 70 ? "Wear light
clothes" : "Dress warmly";

// Boolean flag setting
let hasData = dataArray.length > 0 ? true : false;
// More concise: let hasData = dataArray.length > 0;
```

Nested Ternary Operators

Multiple conditions can be handled using nested ternary operators, though readability should be considered carefully.

#javascript

```
let score = 85;

// Nested ternary for grade assignment
let grade = score >= 90 ? "A" :
           score >= 80 ? "B" :
           score >= 70 ? "C" :
           score >= 60 ? "D" : "F";

console.log(grade); // "B"

// Complex condition handling
let user = { age: 25, isPremium: true, isActive: true };

let accessLevel = user.age >= 18 ?
                    (user.isPremium ?
                        (user.isActive ? "premium-active"
: "premium-inactive") :
                        "standard") :
                    "restricted";

// Weather condition example
let temperature = 32;
let humidity = 80;

let comfort = temperature > 80 ?
                (humidity > 70 ? "hot and humid" : "hot
and dry") :
              temperature < 32 ?
```

```
                 (humidity > 50 ? "cold and damp" : "cold
and dry") :
                 "comfortable";
```

Ternary Operators in Function Returns

Ternary operators excel in function return statements, providing clean, readable conditional returns.

#javascript

```
// Simple validation function
function isValidEmail(email) {
    return email && email.includes("@") ? true : false;
    // Even better: return email && email.includes("@");
}

// Mathematical utility functions
function absolute(number) {
    return number >= 0 ? number : -number;
}

function max(a, b) {
    return a > b ? a : b;
}

function clamp(value, min, max) {
    return value < min ? min : (value > max ? max :
value);
}

// String formatting functions
```

```
function pluralize(count, singular, plural) {
    return count === 1 ? singular : (plural || singular +
"s");
}

console.log(pluralize(1, "item")); // "item"
console.log(pluralize(3, "item")); // "items"
console.log(pluralize(0, "child", "children")); //
"children"

// Status determination
function getOrderStatus(order) {
    return order.shipped ?
           (order.delivered ? "Delivered" : "In Transit")
:
           (order.processed ? "Processing" : "Pending");
}
```

Ternary Operators with Objects and Arrays

Ternary operators work effectively with object properties and array operations, enabling dynamic data structure manipulation.

#javascript

```
// Dynamic object property assignment
let user = {
    name: "John",
    age: 17
};

let userProfile = {
```

```
    name: user.name,
    status: user.age >= 18 ? "adult" : "minor",
    permissions: user.age >= 18 ? ["read", "write",
"delete"] : ["read"],
    theme: user.preferences ? user.preferences.theme :
"default"
};

// Conditional array filtering
let numbers = [1, 2, 3, 4, 5, 6, 7, 8, 9, 10];
let evenNumbers = numbers.filter(n => n % 2 === 0 ? true
: false);
// More concise: let evenNumbers = numbers.filter(n => n
% 2 === 0);

// Dynamic CSS class assignment
function getButtonClass(type, disabled) {
    return `btn ${type === "primary" ? "btn-primary" :
"btn-secondary"} ${disabled ? "disabled" : ""}`;
}

// Conditional API endpoint selection
let apiEndpoint = isDevelopment ?
                  "http://localhost:3000/api" :
                  "https://api.production.com";

// Dynamic content rendering
let content = hasData ?
              data.map(item =>
`<li>${item.name}</li>`).join("") :
              "<li>No items available</li>";
```

Performance Considerations and Best Practices

Understanding when and how to use ternary operators effectively improves both code performance and readability.

#javascript

```javascript
// Good: Simple, clear conditions
let message = isLoggedIn ? "Welcome back!" : "Please log in";

// Avoid: Overly complex nested ternaries
// This is hard to read and maintain
let result = condition1 ?
             (condition2 ?
              (condition3 ? value1 : value2) :
              (condition4 ? value3 : value4)) :
             (condition5 ? value5 : value6);

// Better: Use if-else or switch for complex logic
let result;
if (condition1 && condition2 && condition3) {
    result = value1;
} else if (condition1 && condition2) {
    result = value2;
} else if (condition1 && condition4) {
    result = value3;
} else {
    result = getDefaultValue();
}

// Performance: Ternary vs if-else
```

```
// Both have similar performance, choose based on
readability

// Ternary operator short-circuits evaluation
let value = expensiveCheck() ? expensiveOperation() :
cheapDefault();
// expensiveOperation() only runs if expensiveCheck()
returns true

// Avoid side effects in ternary conditions
// Bad: condition with side effects
let result = (counter++, counter > 5) ? "high" : "low";

// Good: separate side effects from conditions
counter++;
let result = counter > 5 ? "high" : "low";
```

Real-World Application Examples

Practical examples demonstrate how ternary operators solve common programming challenges elegantly.

#javascript

```
// Form validation
function validateForm(formData) {
    return {
        nameValid: formData.name ? formData.name.length >
0 : false,
        emailValid: formData.email ?
/\S+@\S+\.\S+/.test(formData.email) : false,
        ageValid: formData.age ? formData.age >= 13 :
false,
```

```
        passwordStrong: formData.password ?
formData.password.length >= 8 : false
    };
}

// Shopping cart calculations
function calculateDiscount(cart) {
    let total = cart.total;
    let discount = total > 100 ?
                   (total > 200 ? 0.15 : 0.10) :
                   (cart.items.length > 5 ? 0.05 : 0);
    return total * discount;
}

// User interface state management
function getUIState(user, data) {
    return {
        showSpinner: data.loading ? true : false,
        showError: data.error ? true : false,
        showContent: !data.loading && !data.error &&
data.items ? true : false,
        showEmptyState: !data.loading && !data.error &&
!data.items ? true : false,
        userActions: user.isAdmin ?
                     ["create", "read", "update",
"delete"] :
                     ["read"]
    };
}

// Date and time formatting
function formatTimeAgo(timestamp) {
```

```
    let now = Date.now();
    let diff = now - timestamp;
    let minutes = Math.floor(diff / 60000);

    return minutes < 1 ? "just now" :
           minutes < 60 ? `${minutes} minutes ago` :
           minutes < 1440 ? `${Math.floor(minutes / 60)}
hours ago` :
           `${Math.floor(minutes / 1440)} days ago`;
}
```

Essential Tips

- **Always use strict equality (===) instead of loose equality (==) to avoid unexpected type coercion issues** - This prevents bugs caused by JavaScript's automatic type conversion and makes your code more predictable and maintainable.
- **Understand operator precedence to write clear expressions without excessive parentheses** - Knowing that multiplication happens before addition, and logical AND before logical OR, helps you write more readable code and avoid calculation errors.
- **Use compound assignment operators (+=, -=, =) to make your code more concise and expressive* - These operators not only reduce typing but also clearly communicate your intent to modify existing values rather than reassign them.
- **Leverage short-circuit evaluation in logical operators for performance optimization and safe property access** - The && and || operators stop evaluating once the result is determined, which can prevent errors and improve performance in conditional checks.
- **Keep ternary operators simple and readable, using if-else statements for complex conditional logic** - While ternary operators are powerful for simple conditions, nested or complex ternary expressions can make code difficult to understand and maintain.

Actionable Strategies

- **Create a personal reference sheet of operator precedence rules and keep it handy while coding** - Write down the order of operations for arithmetic, comparison, and logical operators, and refer to it until the precedence becomes second nature.
- **Practice writing validation functions using comparison and logical operators to build proficiency** - Create functions that validate user input, check data ranges, and verify object properties to strengthen your understanding of how operators work together.
- **Implement a consistent style guide for when to use ternary operators versus if-else statements in your projects** - Establish rules like "use ternary for simple value assignment, use if-else for complex logic or multiple statements" to maintain code consistency.
- **Use console.log() to experiment with type coercion behavior and build an intuitive understanding** - Test different combinations of data types with various operators to see how JavaScript handles automatic type conversion.
- **Refactor existing if-else chains into appropriate operator expressions where it improves readability** - Look for opportunities to simplify conditional logic using logical operators or ternary expressions without sacrificing code clarity.
- **Master the modulus operator for creating cycling patterns, determining odd/even numbers, and implementing wraparound logic** - Practice using % for tasks like array index wrapping, creating alternating patterns, and validating divisibility rules.
- **Develop debugging skills by understanding how operator precedence affects expression evaluation** - When encountering unexpected results in calculations or conditions, systematically check if operator precedence is causing the issue and use parentheses to clarify your intentions.

Chapter 6: Strings in Depth

Strings represent one of the most fundamental data types in JavaScript, serving as the building blocks for text manipulation, user interface development, and data processing. This chapter provides comprehensive coverage of string operations, from basic declaration to advanced manipulation techniques that professional developers use daily.

6.1 Declaring and Concatenating Strings

String Declaration Methods

JavaScript offers multiple approaches to declare strings, each with distinct characteristics and use cases. Understanding these methods forms the foundation for effective string manipulation.

Single Quote Declaration

Single quotes provide the most straightforward method for string declaration:

#javascript

```
let message = 'Hello, World!';
let productName = 'JavaScript Programming Guide';
let userInput = 'Enter your password';
```

Single quotes work exceptionally well for strings containing double quotes:

#javascript

```
let htmlAttribute = 'class="container main-content"';
let quotedText = 'She said "JavaScript is amazing!"';
```

Double Quote Declaration

Double quotes offer identical functionality to single quotes but prove useful when your string contains apostrophes:

#javascript

```
let contractionExample = "Don't worry about JavaScript complexity";
let possessiveForm = "John's coding skills improved significantly";
let complexSentence = "The developer's toolkit includes various frameworks";
```

Backtick Declaration (Template Literals)

Backticks enable template literals, providing powerful string interpolation capabilities:

#javascript

```
let templateString = `This is a template literal`;
let dynamicContent = `Current timestamp: ${new Date()}`;
```

String Concatenation Techniques

Traditional Concatenation with Plus Operator

The plus operator (+) remains the most widely recognized concatenation method:

#javascript

```
let firstName = 'John';
let lastName = 'Doe';
let fullName = firstName + ' ' + lastName;
```

```
console.log(fullName); // Output: John Doe

let greeting = 'Hello, ' + fullName + '! Welcome to
JavaScript programming.';
console.log(greeting); // Output: Hello, John Doe!
Welcome to JavaScript programming.
```

Complex Concatenation Examples

Building dynamic strings often requires multiple concatenation operations:

#javascript

```
let productPrice = 29.99;
let currency = 'USD';
let taxRate = 0.08;
let totalPrice = productPrice * (1 + taxRate);

let priceDisplay = 'Product Price: ' + currency + ' ' +
productPrice +
                   ' (Tax: ' + (taxRate * 100) + '%)' +
                   ' Total: ' + currency + ' ' +
totalPrice.toFixed(2);
console.log(priceDisplay);
// Output: Product Price: USD 29.99 (Tax: 8%) Total: USD
32.39
```

Assignment Concatenation

The plus-equals operator (+=) provides a shorthand for appending strings:

#javascript

```
let buildString = 'JavaScript';
```

```
buildString += ' is';
buildString += ' a powerful';
buildString += ' programming language';
console.log(buildString); // Output: JavaScript is a
powerful programming language
```

Performance Considerations

For large-scale string concatenation, consider performance implications:

#javascript

```
// Less efficient for multiple concatenations
let result = '';
for (let i = 0; i < 1000; i++) {
    result += 'Item ' + i + ' ';
}

// More efficient using array join
let items = [];
for (let i = 0; i < 1000; i++) {
    items.push('Item ' + i);
}
let efficientResult = items.join(' ');
```

6.2 String Methods

Length Property

The length property returns the number of characters in a string, including spaces and special characters:

#javascript

```
let sampleText = 'JavaScript Programming';
console.log(sampleText.length); // Output: 21

let emptyString = '';
console.log(emptyString.length); // Output: 0

let stringWithSpaces = '   Leading and trailing spaces
';
console.log(stringWithSpaces.length); // Output: 35
```

Practical Length Applications
#javascript

```
function validatePassword(password) {
    if (password.length < 8) {
        return 'Password must be at least 8 characters
long';
    } else if (password.length > 50) {
        return 'Password cannot exceed 50 characters';
    }
    return 'Password length is acceptable';
}

console.log(validatePassword('abc')); // Output: Password
must be at least 8 characters long
console.log(validatePassword('securePassword123')); //
Output: Password length is acceptable
```

Case Conversion Methods

toUpperCase() Method

Converts all characters to uppercase:

#javascript

```
let originalText = 'JavaScript Programming';
let upperCaseText = originalText.toUpperCase();
console.log(upperCaseText); // Output: JAVASCRIPT
PROGRAMMING

// Practical application for case-insensitive comparison
let userInput = 'JAVASCRIPT';
let expectedValue = 'javascript';
if (userInput.toUpperCase() ===
expectedValue.toUpperCase()) {
    console.log('Match found!');
}
```

toLowerCase() Method

Converts all characters to lowercase:

#javascript

```
let mixedCaseText = 'JavaScript PROGRAMMING Guide';
let lowerCaseText = mixedCaseText.toLowerCase();
console.log(lowerCaseText); // Output: javascript
programming guide

// Email validation example
function normalizeEmail(email) {
    return email.toLowerCase().trim();
}
```

```
let emailInput = '  USER@EXAMPLE.COM  ';
let normalizedEmail = normalizeEmail(emailInput);
console.log(normalizedEmail); // Output: user@example.com
```

String Extraction Methods

slice() Method

Extracts a section of a string and returns a new string:

#javascript

```
let fullText = 'JavaScript Programming Language';
let extractedText = fullText.slice(0, 10);
console.log(extractedText); // Output: JavaScript

// Negative indices
let lastPart = fullText.slice(-8);
console.log(lastPart); // Output: Language

// Range extraction
let middlePart = fullText.slice(11, 22);
console.log(middlePart); // Output: Programming
```

substring() Method

Similar to slice but handles negative values differently:

#javascript

```
let text = 'JavaScript Programming';
let substring1 = text.substring(0, 10);
```

```
console.log(substring1); // Output: JavaScript

let substring2 = text.substring(11);
console.log(substring2); // Output: Programming

// Negative values treated as 0
let substring3 = text.substring(-5, 10);
console.log(substring3); // Output: JavaScript
```

substr() Method (Deprecated)

Though deprecated, understanding substr() helps with legacy code:

#javascript

```
let text = 'JavaScript Programming';
let substr1 = text.substr(0, 10); // Start at 0, take 10 characters
console.log(substr1); // Output: JavaScript

let substr2 = text.substr(11, 11); // Start at 11, take 11 characters
console.log(substr2); // Output: Programming
```

String Trimming Methods

trim() Method

Removes whitespace from both ends of a string:

#javascript

```
let messyString = '   JavaScript Programming   ';
let cleanString = messyString.trim();
```

```
console.log(cleanString); // Output: JavaScript Programming
console.log(cleanString.length); // Output: 21

// Form input validation
function validateInput(input) {
    let trimmedInput = input.trim();
    if (trimmedInput.length === 0) {
        return 'Input cannot be empty';
    }
    return trimmedInput;
}
```

trimStart() and trimEnd() Methods

Removes whitespace from the beginning or end specifically:

#javascript

```
let textWithSpaces = '   JavaScript Programming   ';
let trimmedStart = textWithSpaces.trimStart();
let trimmedEnd = textWithSpaces.trimEnd();

console.log(`"${trimmedStart}"`); // Output: "JavaScript Programming   "
console.log(`"${trimmedEnd}"`); // Output: "   JavaScript Programming"
```

String Replacement Methods

replace() Method

Replaces the first occurrence of a substring:

#javascript

```
let originalText = 'JavaScript is great. JavaScript is powerful.';
let replacedText = originalText.replace('JavaScript', 'Python');
console.log(replacedText); // Output: Python is great. JavaScript is powerful.

// Using regular expressions for global replacement
let globalReplace = originalText.replace(/JavaScript/g, 'Python');
console.log(globalReplace); // Output: Python is great. Python is powerful.
```

replaceAll() Method

Replaces all occurrences of a substring:

#javascript

```
let text = 'JavaScript is great. JavaScript is powerful. JavaScript is versatile.';
let replacedAll = text.replaceAll('JavaScript', 'TypeScript');
console.log(replacedAll); // Output: TypeScript is great. TypeScript is powerful. TypeScript is versatile.
```

String Splitting Methods

split() Method

Converts a string into an array of substrings:

#javascript

```
let csvData = 'John,Doe,30,Engineer';
let dataArray = csvData.split(',');
console.log(dataArray); // Output: ['John', 'Doe', '30', 'Engineer']

let sentence = 'JavaScript is a programming language';
let words = sentence.split(' ');
console.log(words); // Output: ['JavaScript', 'is', 'a', 'programming', 'language']

// Limiting split results
let limitedSplit = sentence.split(' ', 3);
console.log(limitedSplit); // Output: ['JavaScript', 'is', 'a']
```

6.3 Template Literals and Interpolation

Basic Template Literal Syntax

Template literals revolutionize string creation by enabling embedded expressions and multiline strings:

#javascript

```
let name = 'John';
let age = 30;
let profession = 'Developer';

let introduction = `Hello, my name is ${name}. I am ${age} years old and work as a ${profession}.`;
console.log(introduction);
// Output: Hello, my name is John. I am 30 years old and work as a Developer.
```

```
```

Expression Interpolation

Template literals support complex expressions within placeholders:

#javascript

```
let price = 29.99;
let quantity = 3;
let taxRate = 0.08;

let receipt = `
Order Summary:
Quantity: ${quantity}
Unit Price: $${price}
Subtotal: $${(price * quantity).toFixed(2)}
Tax (${(taxRate * 100)}%): $${(price * quantity *
taxRate).toFixed(2)}
Total: $${(price * quantity * (1 + taxRate)).toFixed(2)}
`;
console.log(receipt);
```

Function Calls in Template Literals

Template literals can execute functions within interpolation:

#javascript

```
function getCurrentDate() {
    return new Date().toLocaleDateString();
}
```

```
function getRandomNumber() {
    return Math.floor(Math.random() * 100);
}

let dynamicMessage = `
Today's date: ${getCurrentDate()}
Random number: ${getRandomNumber()}
Calculation result: ${Math.sqrt(144)}
`;
console.log(dynamicMessage);
```

Conditional Logic in Template Literals

Implement conditional logic directly within template literals:

#javascript

```
let user = {
    name: 'Alice',
    isLoggedIn: true,
    isPremium: false,
    messageCount: 5
};

let statusMessage = `
Welcome, ${user.name}!
Status: ${user.isLoggedIn ? 'Online' : 'Offline'}
Account Type: ${user.isPremium ? 'Premium Member' :
'Standard Member'}
Messages: ${user.messageCount > 0 ? `${user.messageCount}
new messages` : 'No new messages'}
`;
```

```
console.log(statusMessage);
```

Multiline String Capabilities

Template literals naturally handle multiline strings without escape characters:

#javascript

```
let htmlTemplate = `
<!DOCTYPE html>
<html lang="en">
<head>
    <meta charset="UTF-8">
    <meta name="viewport" content="width=device-width,
initial-scale=1.0">
    <title>JavaScript Application</title>
</head>
<body>
    <h1>Welcome to JavaScript</h1>
    <p>This is a multiline HTML template.</p>
</body>
</html>
`;
console.log(htmlTemplate);
```

Tagged Template Literals

Advanced template literal functionality using tag functions:

#javascript

```
function highlight(strings, ...values) {
```

```
    let result = '';
    strings.forEach((string, i) => {
        result += string;
        if (i < values.length) {
            result += `<mark>${values[i]}</mark>`;
        }
    });
    return result;
}

let searchTerm = 'JavaScript';
let content = 'Programming';
let highlightedText = highlight`Learning ${searchTerm}
for ${content} development`;
console.log(highlightedText);
// Output: Learning <mark>JavaScript</mark> for
<mark>Programming</mark> development
```

6.4 Searching within Strings

indexOf() Method

Returns the index of the first occurrence of a substring:

#javascript

```
let text = 'JavaScript Programming Language';
let position = text.indexOf('Script');
console.log(position); // Output: 4

let notFound = text.indexOf('Python');
console.log(notFound); // Output: -1
```

```
// Case-sensitive search
let caseSensitive = text.indexOf('script');
console.log(caseSensitive); // Output: -1
```

Advanced indexOf() Usage

#javascript

```
let email = 'user@example.com';
let atPosition = email.indexOf('@');
let dotPosition = email.indexOf('.', atPosition);

if (atPosition > 0 && dotPosition > atPosition) {
    console.log('Valid email format');
    console.log(`Username: ${email.substring(0,
atPosition)}`);
    console.log(`Domain: ${email.substring(atPosition +
1, dotPosition)}`);
    console.log(`Extension: ${email.substring(dotPosition
+ 1)}`);
}
```

lastIndexOf() Method

Finds the last occurrence of a substring:

#javascript

```
let text = 'JavaScript Programming with JavaScript
frameworks';
let firstOccurrence = text.indexOf('JavaScript');
let lastOccurrence = text.lastIndexOf('JavaScript');
```

```
console.log(`First occurrence: ${firstOccurrence}`); // Output: 0
console.log(`Last occurrence: ${lastOccurrence}`); // Output: 28
```

includes() Method

Returns a boolean indicating whether a substring exists:

#javascript

```
let userAgent = 'Mozilla/5.0 (Windows NT 10.0; Win64; x64) AppleWebKit/537.36';
let isMobile = userAgent.includes('Mobile');
let isChrome = userAgent.includes('Chrome');
let isFirefox = userAgent.includes('Firefox');

console.log(`Mobile device: ${isMobile}`); // Output: false
console.log(`Chrome browser: ${isChrome}`); // Output: true
console.log(`Firefox browser: ${isFirefox}`); // Output: false
```

Practical includes() Applications

#javascript

```
function validateFileType(filename) {
    let allowedTypes = ['.jpg', '.jpeg', '.png', '.gif', '.pdf', '.doc', '.docx'];
    let isValid = allowedTypes.some(type => filename.toLowerCase().includes(type));
    return isValid;
}
```

```
console.log(validateFileType('document.pdf')); // Output:
true
console.log(validateFileType('image.exe')); // Output:
false
```

startsWith() and endsWith() Methods

Check if a string begins or ends with specific characters:

#javascript

```
let filename = 'javascript-tutorial.pdf';
let isJavaScriptFile = filename.startsWith('javascript');
let isPdfFile = filename.endsWith('.pdf');

console.log(`JavaScript file: ${isJavaScriptFile}`); //
Output: true
console.log(`PDF file: ${isPdfFile}`); // Output: true

// URL validation example
function isSecureUrl(url) {
    return url.startsWith('https://');
}

function isImageFile(filename) {
    return filename.endsWith('.jpg') ||
           filename.endsWith('.jpeg') ||
           filename.endsWith('.png') ||
           filename.endsWith('.gif');
}
```

search() Method

Uses regular expressions for pattern matching:

#javascript

```
let text = 'JavaScript Programming 2024';
let numberPattern = text.search(/\d+/);
console.log(numberPattern); // Output: 23

let emailText = 'Contact us at support@example.com for
assistance';
let emailPattern = emailText.search(/[a-zA-Z0-9._%+-
]+@[a-zA-Z0-9.-]+\.[a-zA-Z]{2,}/);
console.log(emailPattern); // Output: 14
```

match() Method

Returns an array of matches or null:

#javascript

```
let text = 'JavaScript Programming Language 2024';
let words = text.match(/\b\w+\b/g);
console.log(words); // Output: ['JavaScript',
'Programming', 'Language', '2024']

let phoneNumber = 'Call us at (555) 123-4567 or (555)
987-6543';
let phoneNumbers = phoneNumber.match(/\(\d{3}\)\s\d{3}-
\d{4}/g);
console.log(phoneNumbers); // Output: ['(555) 123-4567',
'(555) 987-6543']
```

6.5 Escaping Characters and Multiline Strings

Escape Sequences in JavaScript

JavaScript uses backslash () as the escape character for special characters:

#javascript

```
let quotedString = "She said, \"JavaScript is amazing!\"";
console.log(quotedString); // Output: She said, "JavaScript is amazing!"


let apostropheString = 'Don\'t worry about JavaScript complexity';
console.log(apostropheString); // Output: Don't worry about JavaScript complexity


let pathString = 'C:\\Users\\Documents\\javascript-project';
console.log(pathString); // Output: C:\Users\Documents\javascript-project
```

Common Escape Sequences

Newline and Tab Characters

#javascript

```
let formattedText = 'Line 1\nLine 2\nLine 3';
console.log(formattedText);
// Output:
// Line 1
// Line 2
// Line 3
```

```
let tabbedText = 'Column 1\tColumn 2\tColumn 3';
console.log(tabbedText); // Output: Column 1    Column 2
Column 3
```

Special Character Escaping
#javascript

```
let specialChars = 'Backslash: \\ Newline: \\n Tab: \\t
Quote: \\" Apostrophe: \\\'';
console.log(specialChars);
// Output: Backslash: \ Newline: \n Tab: \t Quote: "
Apostrophe: \'


let unicodeExample = 'Unicode heart: \u2764 Unicode star:
\u2605';
console.log(unicodeExample); // Output: Unicode heart: ❤
Unicode star: ★
```

Multiline String Techniques

Using Escape Sequences
#javascript

```
let multilineString = 'This is line one\n' +
                      'This is line two\n' +
                      'This is line three';
console.log(multilineString);
```

Using Template Literals
#javascript

```
let templateMultiline = `
```

```
    This is line one
    This is line two
    This is line three
`;
console.log(templateMultiline);
```

Preserving Indentation

#javascript

```
let codeExample = `
function greetUser(name) {
    if (name) {
        console.log(\`Hello, \${name}!\`);
    } else {
        console.log('Hello, Guest!');
    }
}
`;
console.log(codeExample);
```

Raw String Literals

Using String.raw for literal backslash interpretation:

#javascript

```
let rawString = String.raw`C:\Users\Documents\javascript-
project\file.txt`;
console.log(rawString); // Output:
C:\Users\Documents\javascript-project\file.txt


let regexPattern = String.raw`\d{3}-\d{2}-\d{4}`;
```

```
console.log(regexPattern); // Output: \d{3}-\d{2}-\d{4}
```

Practical Escaping Examples

JSON String Handling

#javascript

```
let jsonString = '{"name": "John", "message": "He said, \\"Hello, World!\\""}';
let parsedJson = JSON.parse(jsonString);
console.log(parsedJson.message); // Output: He said, "Hello, World!"
```

HTML Content Generation

#javascript

```
let htmlContent = `
<div class="container">
    <h1>Welcome to JavaScript</h1>
    <p>This is a paragraph with "quoted text" and 'apostrophes'.</p>
    <code>let message = "Hello, World!";</code>
</div>
`;
document.body.innerHTML = htmlContent;
```

File Path Handling

#javascript

```
function createFilePath(directory, filename) {
    // Handle different operating systems
```

```
    let separator = process.platform === 'win32' ? '\\' :
'/';
    return `${directory}${separator}${filename}`;
}

let windowsPath = createFilePath('C:\\Users\\Documents',
'file.txt');
let unixPath = createFilePath('/home/user/documents',
'file.txt');
```

Advanced String Manipulation

Combining Multiple Techniques

#javascript

```
function formatUserProfile(user) {
    let profile = `
        User Profile:
        Name: ${user.name}
        Email: ${user.email}
        Status: ${user.isActive ? 'Active' : 'Inactive'}
        Last Login: ${user.lastLogin || 'Never'}
        Preferences: ${JSON.stringify(user.preferences,
null, 2)}
    `;
    return profile.trim();
}

let user = {
    name: 'John Doe',
    email: 'john@example.com',
    isActive: true,
```

```
    lastLogin: '2024-01-15',
    preferences: {
        theme: 'dark',
        notifications: true
    }
};

console.log(formatUserProfile(user));
```

Text Processing Pipeline

#javascript

```
function processText(input) {
    return input
        .trim()                          // Remove
whitespace
        .toLowerCase()                   // Convert to
lowercase
        .replace(/[^\w\s]/g, '')        // Remove
punctuation
        .replace(/\s+/g, ' ')           // Normalize
spaces
        .split(' ')                     // Split into
words
        .filter(word => word.length > 2) // Filter short
words
        .join(' ');                     // Rejoin
}

let rawText = '   JavaScript   Programming!!!  Is
AMAZING...   ';
let cleanText = processText(rawText);
```

```
console.log(cleanText); // Output: javascript programming
amazing
```

Essential Tips

- Use template literals for complex string composition instead of concatenation chains, as they improve readability and maintainability while reducing syntax errors.
- Always validate string inputs before processing them, checking for null, undefined, or empty values to prevent runtime errors in your applications.
- Leverage built-in string methods like trim(), toLowerCase(), and includes() for common operations rather than writing custom functions, as they are optimized and well-tested.
- Consider performance implications when working with large strings or performing many string operations, using techniques like array joining for multiple concatenations.
- Master regular expressions for advanced string searching and manipulation, as they provide powerful pattern matching capabilities beyond basic string methods.

Actionable Strategies

- Create utility functions for common string operations like email validation, phone number formatting, and text sanitization to maintain consistency across your applications.
- Implement comprehensive input validation that combines multiple string methods to check length, format, and content requirements simultaneously.
- Use template literals with embedded functions to create dynamic content generators that can adapt to different data structures and formatting requirements.
- Establish naming conventions for string variables that clearly indicate their purpose and content type, making your code more maintainable and self-documenting.
- Build reusable string formatting functions that handle edge cases like null values, empty strings, and special characters to avoid repetitive error handling.

- Optimize string processing workflows by chaining methods efficiently and avoiding unnecessary intermediate variable assignments that consume memory.

Develop debugging techniques specifically for string manipulation, including console logging with delimiters to visualize whitespace and special characters clearly.

Chapter 7: Numbers and Math

Numbers form the foundation of computational logic in JavaScript. Understanding how to manipulate numerical data effectively determines your ability to build robust applications that handle calculations, data processing, and mathematical operations with precision and reliability.

7.1 Basic Number Operations

Understanding JavaScript Number Types

JavaScript uses a single number type to represent all numeric values, whether integers or floating-point numbers. This unified approach simplifies development but requires understanding of precision limitations and type coercion behaviors.

#javascript

```
// All numbers in JavaScript are stored as 64-bit
floating point
let integer = 42;
let decimal = 3.14159;
let scientific = 2.5e6; // 2,500,000
let negative = -17.5;

console.log(typeof integer); // "number"
console.log(typeof decimal); // "number"
```

Arithmetic Operators in Detail

JavaScript provides standard arithmetic operators that follow mathematical precedence rules. Understanding operator precedence prevents calculation errors and ensures predictable results.

#javascript

```
// Basic arithmetic operations
let addition = 15 + 25;          // 40
let subtraction = 100 - 35;      // 65
let multiplication = 8 * 7;      // 56
let division = 84 / 12;          // 7
let modulus = 17 % 5;            // 2 (remainder)
let exponentiation = 2 ** 8;     // 256

// Complex expressions with precedence
let result = 10 + 5 * 3;         // 25 (not 45)
let grouped = (10 + 5) * 3;      // 45

// Increment and decrement operators
let counter = 5;
counter++;     // Post-increment: returns 5, then
increments to 6
++counter;     // Pre-increment: increments to 7, then
returns 7
counter--;     // Post-decrement: returns 7, then
decrements to 6
--counter;     // Pre-decrement: decrements to 5, then
returns 5
```

Assignment Operators for Efficient Calculations

Assignment operators combine arithmetic operations with variable assignment, providing concise syntax for common mathematical operations.

#javascript

```
let value = 20;
```

```
value += 10;     // value = value + 10; Result: 30
value -= 5;      // value = value - 5;  Result: 25
value *= 2;      // value = value * 2;  Result: 50
value /= 4;      // value = value / 4;  Result: 12.5
value %= 7;      // value = value % 7;  Result: 5.5
value **= 2;     // value = value ** 2; Result: 30.25
```

Handling Number Precision and Floating Point Arithmetic

JavaScript's floating-point arithmetic can produce unexpected results due to binary representation limitations. Understanding these quirks prevents calculation errors in financial and scientific applications.

#javascript

```
// Floating point precision issues
console.log(0.1 + 0.2);          // 0.30000000000000004
(not 0.3)
console.log(0.1 + 0.2 === 0.3); // false

// Solutions for precision issues
function addPrecise(a, b, decimals = 10) {
    return parseFloat((a + b).toFixed(decimals));
}

console.log(addPrecise(0.1, 0.2, 1)); // 0.3

// Using epsilon for comparison
function isEqual(a, b, epsilon = Number.EPSILON) {
    return Math.abs(a - b) < epsilon;
}
```

```
console.log(isEqual(0.1 + 0.2, 0.3)); // true
```

Number Conversion and Type Coercion

JavaScript automatically converts between numbers and strings in many contexts. Understanding explicit and implicit conversion helps prevent unexpected behavior.

#javascript

```javascript
// Explicit conversion
let stringNumber = "123";
let converted = Number(stringNumber);      // 123
let parsed = parseInt("123.45");           // 123
let floatParsed = parseFloat("123.45");    // 123.45

// Implicit conversion (type coercion)
let result1 = "5" * 2;       // 10 (string converted to number)
let result2 = "5" + 2;       // "52" (number converted to string)
let result3 = "5" - 2;       // 3 (string converted to number)

// Unary plus operator for conversion
let quickConvert = +"42";    // 42 (number)
```

7.2 Math Object and Useful Functions

Introduction to the Math Object

The Math object provides a comprehensive collection of mathematical constants and functions. Unlike other objects, Math is not a constructor and all properties and methods are static.

#javascript

```
// Math object properties (constants)
console.log(Math.PI);     // 3.141592653589793
console.log(Math.E);      // 2.718281828459045
console.log(Math.LN2);    // 0.6931471805599453
console.log(Math.SQRT2); // 1.4142135623730951
```

Essential Math Methods for Everyday Programming

Math.floor() - Rounding Down

The `Math.floor()` function returns the largest integer less than or equal to a given number, effectively rounding down to the nearest integer.

#javascript

```
console.log(Math.floor(4.7));     // 4
console.log(Math.floor(4.2));     // 4
console.log(Math.floor(-4.7));    // -5 (rounds toward
negative infinity)
console.log(Math.floor(-4.2));    // -5

// Practical applications
function getPageNumber(itemIndex, itemsPerPage) {
    return Math.floor(itemIndex / itemsPerPage) + 1;
}

console.log(getPageNumber(15, 10)); // 2 (item 15 is on
page 2)
```

Math.ceil() - Rounding Up

The `Math.ceil()` function returns the smallest integer greater than or equal to a given number, effectively rounding up to the nearest integer.

#javascript

```
console.log(Math.ceil(4.1));      // 5
console.log(Math.ceil(4.9));      // 5
console.log(Math.ceil(-4.1));     // -4 (rounds toward positive infinity)
console.log(Math.ceil(-4.9));     // -4

// Calculate required pages for pagination
function calculateTotalPages(totalItems, itemsPerPage) {
    return Math.ceil(totalItems / itemsPerPage);
}

console.log(calculateTotalPages(95, 10)); // 10 pages needed
```

Math.round() - Standard Rounding

The `Math.round()` function returns the nearest integer, using standard rounding rules (0.5 rounds up).

#javascript

```
console.log(Math.round(4.4));     // 4
console.log(Math.round(4.5));     // 5
console.log(Math.round(4.6));     // 5
console.log(Math.round(-4.5));    // -4
console.log(Math.round(-4.6));    // -5
```

Math.random() - Generating Random Numbers

The `Math.random()` function returns a pseudo-random number between 0 (inclusive) and 1 (exclusive). This forms the basis for generating random numbers in various ranges.

#javascript

```
// Basic random number (0 to 1)
console.log(Math.random()); // 0.7834592847362847

// Random integer between min and max (inclusive)
function randomInt(min, max) {
    return Math.floor(Math.random() * (max - min + 1)) +
min;
}

console.log(randomInt(1, 6));    // Simulates dice roll
(1-6)
console.log(randomInt(10, 20)); // Random number between
10-20

// Random decimal in range
function randomFloat(min, max) {
    return Math.random() * (max - min) + min;
}

console.log(randomFloat(1.5, 5.5)); // Random decimal
between 1.5-5.5
```

Advanced Math Functions

Power and Root Operations
#javascript

```
// Power operations
console.log(Math.pow(2, 8));        // 256 (2^8)
console.log(Math.pow(9, 0.5));      // 3 (square root of 9)
console.log(Math.sqrt(16));         // 4 (square root)
console.log(Math.cbrt(27));         // 3 (cube root)

// Exponentiation operator (ES2016)
console.log(2 ** 8);                // 256 (equivalent to
Math.pow(2, 8))
```

Absolute Values and Sign Operations
#javascript

```
console.log(Math.abs(-15));         // 15
console.log(Math.abs(15));          // 15
console.log(Math.sign(-15));        // -1
console.log(Math.sign(15));         // 1
console.log(Math.sign(0));          // 0
```

Maximum and Minimum Values
#javascript

```
console.log(Math.max(10, 5, 15, 3));          // 15
console.log(Math.min(10, 5, 15, 3));          // 3

// Using with arrays
let numbers = [10, 5, 15, 3, 8];
console.log(Math.max(...numbers));            // 15 (spread
operator)
```

```
console.log(Math.min.apply(null, numbers)); // 3 (apply
method)
```

7.3 Rounding and Formatting Numbers

Precision Control with toFixed()

The `toFixed()` method formats a number using fixed-point notation, specifying the number of decimal places to display.

#javascript

```
let price = 19.99567;
console.log(price.toFixed(2));    // "19.99" (string)
console.log(price.toFixed(0));    // "20" (string)
console.log(price.toFixed(4));    // "19.9957" (string)

// Converting back to number
let formatted = parseFloat(price.toFixed(2)); // 19.99
(number)

// Financial calculations
function calculateTotal(subtotal, taxRate) {
    let total = subtotal * (1 + taxRate);
    return parseFloat(total.toFixed(2));
}

console.log(calculateTotal(99.99, 0.08)); // 107.99
```

Exponential Notation with toExponential()

The `toExponential()` method returns a string representing the number in exponential notation.

#javascript

```
let largeNumber = 1234567;
console.log(largeNumber.toExponential());    //
"1.234567e+6"
console.log(largeNumber.toExponential(2));   // "1.23e+6"

let smallNumber = 0.000123;
console.log(smallNumber.toExponential());    // "1.23e-4"
console.log(smallNumber.toExponential(3));   // "1.230e-
4"
```

Precision with toPrecision()

The `toPrecision()` method returns a string representing the number to a specified precision.

#javascript

```
let number = 123.456;
console.log(number.toPrecision());     // "123.456"
console.log(number.toPrecision(4));    // "123.5"
console.log(number.toPrecision(2));    // "1.2e+2"
console.log(number.toPrecision(6));    // "123.456"
```

Custom Rounding Functions

JavaScript's built-in rounding functions may not always meet specific requirements. Creating custom rounding functions provides greater control over rounding behavior.

#javascript

```
// Round to specific decimal places
function roundToDecimal(number, decimals) {
    const factor = Math.pow(10, decimals);
    return Math.round(number * factor) / factor;
}

console.log(roundToDecimal(3.14159, 2)); // 3.14
console.log(roundToDecimal(3.14159, 4)); // 3.1416

// Banker's rounding (round half to even)
function bankersRound(number, decimals) {
    const factor = Math.pow(10, decimals);
    const shifted = number * factor;
    const rounded = Math.round(shifted);

    if (Math.abs(shifted - rounded) === 0.5) {
        return (rounded % 2 === 0 ? rounded : rounded -
Math.sign(rounded)) / factor;
    }
    return rounded / factor;
}

// Always round up for positive, down for negative
function roundAwayFromZero(number) {
    return number >= 0 ? Math.ceil(number) :
Math.floor(number);
}
```

Number Formatting for Display

Creating user-friendly number displays requires formatting functions that handle various locales and number types.

#javascript

```
// Add thousand separators
function addThousandSeparators(number) {
    return
number.toString().replace(/\B(?=(\d{3})+(?!\d))/g, ",");
}

console.log(addThousandSeparators(1234567)); //
"1,234,567"

// Format currency
function formatCurrency(amount, currency = "$") {
    return currency +
addThousandSeparators(amount.toFixed(2));
}

console.log(formatCurrency(1234.567)); // "$1,234.57"

// Format percentage
function formatPercentage(decimal, decimals = 1) {
    return (decimal * 100).toFixed(decimals) + "%";
}

console.log(formatPercentage(0.1567, 2)); // "15.67%"
```

7.4 Working with Decimal and Integers

Integer Detection and Validation

Distinguishing between integers and floating-point numbers enables appropriate handling of different numeric types in applications.

#javascript

```
// Check if number is integer
console.log(Number.isInteger(42));         // true
console.log(Number.isInteger(42.0));       // true
console.log(Number.isInteger(42.1));       // false

// Custom integer check function
function isWholeNumber(value) {
    return Number.isInteger(value) && value >= 0;
}

console.log(isWholeNumber(5));      // true
console.log(isWholeNumber(-5));     // false
console.log(isWholeNumber(5.5));  // false
```

Safe Integer Limits

JavaScript has limitations on integer precision due to its floating-point representation. Understanding these limits prevents calculation errors with large integers.

#javascript

```
console.log(Number.MAX_SAFE_INTEGER);     //
9007199254740991
console.log(Number.MIN_SAFE_INTEGER);     // -
9007199254740991

// Check if integer is safe
```

```
console.log(Number.isSafeInteger(9007199254740991));  //
true
console.log(Number.isSafeInteger(9007199254740992));  //
false

// Safe integer operations
function safeAdd(a, b) {
    const result = a + b;
    if (Number.isSafeInteger(result)) {
        return result;
    }
    throw new Error("Result exceeds safe integer range");
}
```

Working with BigInt for Large Integers

For integers beyond the safe integer range, JavaScript provides the BigInt type for arbitrary precision integer arithmetic.

#javascript

```
// Creating BigInt values
let bigInt1 = 9007199254740992n;        // 'n' suffix
let bigInt2 = BigInt("9007199254740993");
let bigInt3 = BigInt(9007199254740994);

// BigInt operations
console.log(bigInt1 + bigInt2);         //
18014398509481985n
console.log(bigInt1 * 2n);              //
18014398509481984n

// Cannot mix BigInt with regular numbers
```

```
// console.log(bigInt1 + 5);                // TypeError
console.log(bigInt1 + 5n);                  //
9007199254740997n

// Converting between BigInt and Number
console.log(Number(bigInt1));               //
9007199254740992 (if safe)
console.log(BigInt(42));                    // 42n
```

Decimal Precision Management

Managing decimal precision prevents accumulation of floating-point errors in calculations involving monetary values or scientific data.

#javascript

```
// Decimal arithmetic with precision control
class DecimalNumber {
    constructor(value, precision = 2) {
        this.precision = precision;
        this.factor = Math.pow(10, precision);
        this.value = Math.round(value * this.factor);
    }

    add(other) {
        const result = (this.value + other.value) /
this.factor;
        return new DecimalNumber(result, this.precision);
    }

    subtract(other) {
        const result = (this.value - other.value) /
this.factor;
```

```
        return new DecimalNumber(result, this.precision);
    }

    multiply(other) {
        const result = (this.value * other.value) /
(this.factor * this.factor);
        return new DecimalNumber(result, this.precision);
    }

    toString() {
        return (this.value /
this.factor).toFixed(this.precision);
    }
}

// Usage example
let price1 = new DecimalNumber(19.99, 2);
let price2 = new DecimalNumber(5.01, 2);
let total = price1.add(price2);
console.log(total.toString()); // "25.00"
```

Integer Division and Modulo Operations

Understanding integer division and modulo operations enables efficient algorithms for various programming scenarios.

#javascript

```
// Integer division simulation
function integerDivision(dividend, divisor) {
    return Math.floor(dividend / divisor);
}
```

```
console.log(integerDivision(17, 5));  // 3

// Modulo applications
function isEven(number) {
    return number % 2 === 0;
}

function isOdd(number) {
    return number % 2 !== 0;
}

// Circular array indexing
function getCircularIndex(index, arrayLength) {
    return index % arrayLength;
}

console.log(getCircularIndex(15, 10)); // 5 (wraps
around)

// Check if number is divisible
function isDivisibleBy(number, divisor) {
    return number % divisor === 0;
}

console.log(isDivisibleBy(15, 3)); // true
console.log(isDivisibleBy(15, 4)); // false
```

7.5 Dealing with NaN and Infinity

Understanding NaN (Not a Number)

NaN represents computational errors or undefined mathematical operations. Proper NaN handling prevents application crashes and unexpected behavior.

#javascript

```
// Operations that produce NaN
console.log(0 / 0);                // NaN
console.log(Math.sqrt(-1));        // NaN
console.log(parseInt("hello"));    // NaN
console.log("hello" * 2);          // NaN

// NaN properties
console.log(typeof NaN);           // "number"
console.log(NaN === NaN);          // false (NaN is not
equal to itself)
console.log(NaN == NaN);           // false

// Checking for NaN
console.log(Number.isNaN(NaN));           // true
console.log(Number.isNaN("hello"));       // false
console.log(isNaN("hello"));              // true (coerces
to number first)
console.log(isNaN("123"));                // false
```

Safe NaN Detection Functions

Creating robust NaN detection functions ensures accurate identification of invalid numeric values.

#javascript

```
// Strict NaN check
```

```javascript
function isActuallyNaN(value) {
    return Number.isNaN(value);
}

// Check if value becomes NaN when converted to number
function becomesNaN(value) {
    return isNaN(value);
}

// Safe number validation
function isValidNumber(value) {
    return typeof value === 'number' &&
!Number.isNaN(value) && isFinite(value);
}

console.log(isValidNumber(42));        // true
console.log(isValidNumber(NaN));       // false
console.log(isValidNumber(Infinity));  // false
console.log(isValidNumber("42"));      // false
```

Working with Infinity

JavaScript represents positive and negative infinity, which can result from mathematical operations or explicit assignment.

#javascript

```javascript
// Operations that produce Infinity
console.log(1 / 0);                // Infinity
console.log(-1 / 0);               // -Infinity
console.log(Math.pow(10, 1000)); // Infinity
```

```
// Infinity properties
console.log(typeof Infinity);          // "number"
console.log(Infinity > 1000000);       // true
console.log(-Infinity < -1000000);     // true

// Checking for Infinity
console.log(Number.isFinite(42));          // true
console.log(Number.isFinite(Infinity));    // false
console.log(Number.isFinite(-Infinity));   // false
console.log(Number.isFinite(NaN));         // false

// Global isFinite vs Number.isFinite
console.log(isFinite("42"));               // true
(coerces to number)
console.log(Number.isFinite("42"));        // false (no
coercion)
```

Error Prevention and Validation Strategies

Implementing comprehensive validation prevents NaN and Infinity from propagating through calculations.

#javascript

```
// Safe division function
function safeDivide(numerator, denominator) {
    if (denominator === 0) {
        throw new Error("Division by zero");
    }

    const result = numerator / denominator;
```

```
    if (!Number.isFinite(result)) {
        throw new Error("Result is not a finite number");
    }

    return result;
}

// Safe mathematical operations
function safeMath(operation, ...args) {
    try {
        const result = operation(...args);

        if (Number.isNaN(result)) {
            throw new Error("Operation resulted in NaN");
        }

        if (!Number.isFinite(result)) {
            throw new Error("Operation resulted in
Infinity");
        }

        return result;
    } catch (error) {
        console.error("Mathematical operation failed:",
error.message);
        return null;
    }
}

// Usage examples
console.log(safeMath(Math.sqrt, 16));   // 4
```

```
console.log(safeMath(Math.sqrt, -16));  // null (logs
error)
console.log(safeMath((a, b) => a / b, 10, 2)); // 5
```

Input Validation and Sanitization

Validating user input and external data prevents NaN and Infinity from entering calculations.

#javascript

```
// Comprehensive number validation
function validateNumber(input, options = {}) {
    const {
        allowNaN = false,
        allowInfinity = false,
        min = -Infinity,
        max = Infinity,
        mustBeInteger = false
    } = options;

    // Convert to number if string
    const num = typeof input === 'string' ?
parseFloat(input) : input;

    // Check if it's a number
    if (typeof num !== 'number') {
        return { valid: false, error: "Not a number" };
    }

    // Check for NaN
    if (Number.isNaN(num) && !allowNaN) {
```

```
        return { valid: false, error: "Value is NaN" };
    }

    // Check for Infinity
    if (!Number.isFinite(num) && !allowInfinity) {
        return { valid: false, error: "Value is infinite"
};
    }

    // Check range
    if (num < min || num > max) {
        return { valid: false, error: `Value out of range
[${min}, ${max}]` };
    }

    // Check if integer required
    if (mustBeInteger && !Number.isInteger(num)) {
        return { valid: false, error: "Value must be an
integer" };
    }

    return { valid: true, value: num };
}

// Usage examples
console.log(validateNumber("42"));           // { valid:
true, value: 42 }
console.log(validateNumber("hello"));        // { valid:
false, error: "Value is NaN" }
console.log(validateNumber(150, { min: 0, max: 100 }));
// { valid: false, error: "Value out of range [0, 100]" }
```

Fallback Strategies for Invalid Numbers

Implementing fallback strategies maintains application functionality when encountering invalid numeric values.

#javascript

```javascript
// Default value fallback
function getNumberWithDefault(value, defaultValue = 0) {
    const num = Number(value);
    return Number.isFinite(num) ? num : defaultValue;
}

console.log(getNumberWithDefault("42"));     // 42
console.log(getNumberWithDefault("hello"));  // 0
console.log(getNumberWithDefault("hello", -1)); // -1

// Clamping values to valid range
function clampNumber(value, min, max) {
    const num = Number(value);

    if (Number.isNaN(num)) {
        return min;
    }

    if (num === Infinity) {
        return max;
    }

    if (num === -Infinity) {
        return min;
    }
```

```
    return Math.min(Math.max(num, min), max);
}

console.log(clampNumber(150, 0, 100));   // 100
console.log(clampNumber(-50, 0, 100));   // 0
console.log(clampNumber("hello", 0, 100)); // 0
```

Essential Tips

- Always use `Number.isNaN()` instead of the global `isNaN()` function to avoid type coercion issues when checking for NaN values.
- Store monetary values as integers (cents) rather than decimals to avoid floating-point precision errors in financial calculations.
- Use `Math.random()` with proper scaling and flooring to generate random integers within specific ranges, ensuring uniform distribution.
- Implement input validation functions that check for both NaN and Infinity before performing mathematical operations on user-provided data.
- Apply the `Number.isInteger()` method to verify whole numbers rather than using modulo operations or string parsing techniques.

Actionable Strategies

- Create utility functions for common mathematical operations like percentage calculations, tax computations, and unit conversions to maintain consistency across your applications.
- Implement comprehensive error handling in mathematical functions that gracefully handle edge cases like division by zero, negative square roots, and overflow conditions.
- Build custom rounding functions that match your specific business requirements, such as banker's rounding for financial applications or ceiling functions for resource allocation.
- Design number formatting functions that handle different locales and currencies, making your applications internationally compatible from the start.

- Establish consistent precision standards throughout your application by creating decimal classes or using libraries that handle arbitrary precision arithmetic.
- Develop validation pipelines that sanitize and verify numeric input from forms, APIs, and user interactions before processing them in calculations.
- Create debugging utilities that log mathematical operations and their results, helping identify precision issues and calculation errors during development and testing phases.

Chapter 8: Arrays

Arrays represent one of the most fundamental and powerful data structures in JavaScript. They serve as ordered collections that can store multiple values under a single variable name, making them essential for managing lists of related data. Understanding arrays and their methods forms the backbone of effective JavaScript programming.

8.1 Creating and Accessing Arrays

Array Declaration Syntax

JavaScript provides multiple ways to create arrays, each with its own use cases and advantages. The most common approach uses square bracket notation, which offers clarity and simplicity.

#javascript

```
// Array literal notation (most common)
let fruits = ['apple', 'banana', 'orange'];
let numbers = [1, 2, 3, 4, 5];
let mixed = ['hello', 42, true, null];

// Array constructor
let emptyArray = new Array();
let sizedArray = new Array(5); // Creates array with 5
empty slots
let constructorArray = new Array('red', 'green', 'blue');

// Creating arrays with Array.of()
let specificArray = Array.of(1, 2, 3, 4);
let singleElement = Array.of(5); // Creates [5], not
array with 5 slots
```

Dynamic Array Creation

Arrays in JavaScript are dynamic, meaning they can grow and shrink during runtime. This flexibility allows for powerful data manipulation without worrying about predefined sizes.

#javascript

```
// Starting with empty array and building it
let dynamicArray = [];
dynamicArray[0] = 'first';
dynamicArray[1] = 'second';
dynamicArray[5] = 'sixth'; // Creates sparse array with
undefined elements

console.log(dynamicArray); // ['first', 'second',
undefined, undefined, undefined, 'sixth']
console.log(dynamicArray.length); // 6
```

Array Index Access

Array elements are accessed using zero-based indexing, where the first element has index 0, the second has index 1, and so forth.

#javascript

```
let colors = ['red', 'green', 'blue', 'yellow'];

// Accessing elements
console.log(colors[0]); // 'red'
console.log(colors[2]); // 'blue'
console.log(colors[10]); // undefined (out of bounds)
```

```
// Negative indexing (using array length)
console.log(colors[colors.length - 1]); // 'yellow' (last element)
console.log(colors[colors.length - 2]); // 'blue' (second to last)
```

Array Properties and Characteristics

The length property provides crucial information about array size and enables various array operations.

#javascript

```
let students = ['Alice', 'Bob', 'Charlie'];

console.log(students.length); // 3

// Modifying length property
students.length = 5; // Extends array with undefined elements
console.log(students); // ['Alice', 'Bob', 'Charlie', undefined, undefined]

students.length = 2; // Truncates array
console.log(students); // ['Alice', 'Bob']
```

Multi-dimensional Arrays

JavaScript supports arrays within arrays, creating multi-dimensional structures perfect for representing complex data like matrices or tables.

#javascript

```
// Two-dimensional array (matrix)
```

```
let matrix = [
    [1, 2, 3],
    [4, 5, 6],
    [7, 8, 9]
];

// Accessing elements in 2D array
console.log(matrix[0][0]); // 1
console.log(matrix[1][2]); // 6
console.log(matrix[2][1]); // 8

// Practical example: student grades
let grades = [
    ['Math', 85, 92, 78],
    ['Science', 91, 88, 95],
    ['English', 87, 84, 90]
];

console.log(grades[0][0]); // 'Math'
console.log(grades[1][3]); // 95
```

8.2 Array Methods: push, pop, shift, unshift

The push() Method

The push() method adds one or more elements to the end of an array and returns the new length. This method modifies the original array directly.

#javascript

```
let fruits = ['apple', 'banana'];
```

```
// Adding single element
let newLength = fruits.push('orange');
console.log(fruits); // ['apple', 'banana', 'orange']
console.log(newLength); // 3

// Adding multiple elements
fruits.push('grape', 'kiwi', 'mango');
console.log(fruits); // ['apple', 'banana', 'orange',
'grape', 'kiwi', 'mango']

// Practical example: building a shopping cart
let cart = [];
cart.push({item: 'laptop', price: 999});
cart.push({item: 'mouse', price: 25});
cart.push({item: 'keyboard', price: 75});
console.log(cart.length); // 3
```

The pop() Method

The pop() method removes and returns the last element from an array. If the array is empty, it returns undefined.

#javascript

```
let numbers = [1, 2, 3, 4, 5];

// Removing last element
let lastElement = numbers.pop();
console.log(lastElement); // 5
console.log(numbers); // [1, 2, 3, 4]

// Removing from empty array
```

```
let empty = [];
console.log(empty.pop()); // undefined

// Practical example: undo functionality
let history = ['action1', 'action2', 'action3'];
let lastAction = history.pop(); // Remove and get last
action
console.log(`Undoing: ${lastAction}`); // Undoing:
action3
```

The shift() Method

The shift() method removes and returns the first element from an array, shifting all remaining elements down by one position.

#javascript

```
let queue = ['first', 'second', 'third'];

// Removing first element
let firstElement = queue.shift();
console.log(firstElement); // 'first'
console.log(queue); // ['second', 'third']

// Processing queue items
let tasks = ['task1', 'task2', 'task3'];
while (tasks.length > 0) {
    let currentTask = tasks.shift();
    console.log(`Processing: ${currentTask}`);
}
// Output:
// Processing: task1
```

```
// Processing: task2
// Processing: task3
```

The unshift() Method

The unshift() method adds one or more elements to the beginning of an array and returns the new length.

#javascript

```
let animals = ['cat', 'dog'];

// Adding single element at beginning
let newLength = animals.unshift('bird');
console.log(animals); // ['bird', 'cat', 'dog']
console.log(newLength); // 3

// Adding multiple elements
animals.unshift('fish', 'hamster');
console.log(animals); // ['fish', 'hamster', 'bird',
'cat', 'dog']

// Practical example: priority queue
let priorityQueue = ['normal task'];
priorityQueue.unshift('urgent task'); // Add urgent task
at front
priorityQueue.unshift('critical task'); // Add critical
task at front
console.log(priorityQueue); // ['critical task', 'urgent
task', 'normal task']
```

Method Chaining and Combined Operations

These methods can be combined to create powerful array manipulations:

#javascript

```
let data = [1, 2, 3];

// Chaining operations
data.push(4).push is undefined, but we can do sequential
operations
data.push(4);
data.push(5);
let removed = data.shift(); // Remove first element
data.unshift(0); // Add at beginning

console.log(data); // [0, 2, 3, 4, 5]
console.log(removed); // 1

// Stack implementation using push/pop
class Stack {
    constructor() {
        this.items = [];
    }

    push(element) {
        this.items.push(element);
    }

    pop() {
        return this.items.pop();
    }

    peek() {
```

```
        return this.items[this.items.length - 1];
    }

    isEmpty() {
        return this.items.length === 0;
    }
}

let stack = new Stack();
stack.push(10);
stack.push(20);
console.log(stack.pop()); // 20
```

8.3 Iterating Over Arrays (for, forEach)

Traditional for Loop

The traditional for loop provides complete control over array iteration, allowing access to both index and value.

#javascript

```
let colors = ['red', 'green', 'blue', 'yellow'];

// Basic for loop
for (let i = 0; i < colors.length; i++) {
    console.log(`Index ${i}: ${colors[i]}`);
}

// Reverse iteration
for (let i = colors.length - 1; i >= 0; i--) {
    console.log(`Reverse Index ${i}: ${colors[i]}`);
```

```
}

// Skip every other element
for (let i = 0; i < colors.length; i += 2) {
    console.log(`Even index ${i}: ${colors[i]}`);
}
```

for...of Loop

The for...of loop provides a cleaner syntax when you only need the values, not the indices.

#javascript

```
let fruits = ['apple', 'banana', 'orange'];

// Iterating over values
for (let fruit of fruits) {
    console.log(fruit);
}

// Getting both index and value with entries()
for (let [index, fruit] of fruits.entries()) {
    console.log(`${index}: ${fruit}`);
}

// Practical example: calculating total
let prices = [19.99, 29.99, 39.99, 49.99];
let total = 0;

for (let price of prices) {
    total += price;
```

```
}
console.log(`Total: $${total.toFixed(2)}`); // Total:
$139.96
```

for...in Loop

The for...in loop iterates over enumerable properties, including array indices.

#javascript

```
let animals = ['cat', 'dog', 'bird'];

// Using for...in (gets indices as strings)
for (let index in animals) {
    console.log(`Index ${index}: ${animals[index]}`);
}

// Be careful with for...in and arrays with additional
properties
let specialArray = ['a', 'b', 'c'];
specialArray.customProperty = 'custom';

for (let index in specialArray) {
    console.log(`${index}: ${specialArray[index]}`);
}
// Output includes: customProperty: custom
```

The forEach() Method

The forEach() method executes a provided function for each array element, offering a functional programming approach.

#javascript

```
let numbers = [1, 2, 3, 4, 5];

// Basic forEach usage
numbers.forEach(function(number) {
    console.log(number * 2);
});

// Arrow function syntax
numbers.forEach(number => console.log(number * 2));

// Access to index and array
numbers.forEach((number, index, array) => {
    console.log(`Element ${number} at index ${index} of
array [${array}]`);
});

// Practical example: processing user data
let users = [
    { name: 'Alice', age: 25 },
    { name: 'Bob', age: 30 },
    { name: 'Charlie', age: 35 }
];

users.forEach((user, index) => {
    console.log(`User ${index + 1}: ${user.name} is
${user.age} years old`);
});
```

Performance Considerations and Best Practices

Different iteration methods have varying performance characteristics:

#javascript

```
let largeArray = new Array(1000000).fill(0).map((_, i) =>
i);

// Performance test function
function performanceTest(name, callback) {
    let start = performance.now();
    callback();
    let end = performance.now();
    console.log(`${name}: ${end - start} milliseconds`);
}

// Testing different iteration methods
performanceTest('Traditional for loop', () => {
    let sum = 0;
    for (let i = 0; i < largeArray.length; i++) {
        sum += largeArray[i];
    }
});

performanceTest('for...of loop', () => {
    let sum = 0;
    for (let num of largeArray) {
        sum += num;
    }
});

performanceTest('forEach method', () => {
    let sum = 0;
    largeArray.forEach(num => sum += num);
```

```
});
```

Breaking and Continuing in Loops

Control flow differs between traditional loops and forEach:

#javascript

```
let numbers = [1, 2, 3, 4, 5, 6, 7, 8, 9, 10];

// Traditional for loop with break and continue
for (let i = 0; i < numbers.length; i++) {
    if (numbers[i] % 2 === 0) continue; // Skip even
numbers
    if (numbers[i] > 7) break; // Stop at numbers greater
than 7
    console.log(numbers[i]);
}
// Output: 1, 3, 5, 7

// forEach cannot use break/continue - use return instead
numbers.forEach(number => {
    if (number % 2 === 0) return; // Similar to continue
    if (number > 7) return; // Cannot break early
    console.log(number);
});
// Output: 1, 3, 5, 7, 9 (cannot break early)

// Alternative: use some() or every() for early
termination
numbers.some(number => {
    if (number % 2 === 0) return false; // Continue
```

```
    if (number > 7) return true; // Break
    console.log(number);
    return false;
});
```

8.4 Sorting and Reversing Arrays

The reverse() Method

The reverse() method reverses the order of elements in an array in place, modifying the original array.

#javascript

```
let numbers = [1, 2, 3, 4, 5];

// Reversing the array
numbers.reverse();
console.log(numbers); // [5, 4, 3, 2, 1]

// Reversing strings
let letters = ['a', 'b', 'c', 'd'];
letters.reverse();
console.log(letters); // ['d', 'c', 'b', 'a']

// Creating a reversed copy without modifying original
let original = [1, 2, 3, 4, 5];
let reversed = [...original].reverse(); // Spread
operator creates copy
console.log(original); // [1, 2, 3, 4, 5]
console.log(reversed); // [5, 4, 3, 2, 1]
```

Basic sort() Method

The sort() method sorts array elements in place and returns the sorted array. By default, it converts elements to strings and sorts alphabetically.

#javascript

```
let fruits = ['banana', 'apple', 'orange', 'grape'];

// Default alphabetical sort
fruits.sort();
console.log(fruits); // ['apple', 'banana', 'grape',
'orange']

// Sorting numbers (watch out for default behavior)
let numbers = [10, 5, 40, 25, 1000, 1];
numbers.sort();
console.log(numbers); // [1, 10, 1000, 25, 40, 5] -
sorted as strings!

// Case-sensitive sorting
let words = ['apple', 'Apple', 'APPLE', 'banana'];
words.sort();
console.log(words); // ['APPLE', 'Apple', 'apple',
'banana']
```

Custom Sorting with Compare Functions

To sort numbers correctly or implement custom sorting logic, provide a compare function:

#javascript

```
let numbers = [10, 5, 40, 25, 1000, 1];

// Ascending numerical sort
numbers.sort((a, b) => a - b);
console.log(numbers); // [1, 5, 10, 25, 40, 1000]

// Descending numerical sort
numbers.sort((a, b) => b - a);
console.log(numbers); // [1000, 40, 25, 10, 5, 1]

// Case-insensitive string sorting
let words = ['apple', 'Apple', 'APPLE', 'banana'];
words.sort((a, b) =>
a.toLowerCase().localeCompare(b.toLowerCase()));
console.log(words); // ['apple', 'Apple', 'APPLE',
'banana']
```

Sorting Objects

Sorting arrays of objects requires custom compare functions based on object properties:

#javascript

```
let students = [
    { name: 'Alice', grade: 85, age: 20 },
    { name: 'Bob', grade: 92, age: 19 },
    { name: 'Charlie', grade: 78, age: 21 },
    { name: 'David', grade: 92, age: 18 }
];

// Sort by grade (ascending)
```

```
students.sort((a, b) => a.grade - b.grade);
console.log(students);

// Sort by name (alphabetical)
students.sort((a, b) => a.name.localeCompare(b.name));
console.log(students);

// Sort by multiple criteria (grade descending, then age ascending)
students.sort((a, b) => {
    if (a.grade !== b.grade) {
        return b.grade - a.grade; // Grade descending
    }
    return a.age - b.age; // Age ascending for same grade
});
console.log(students);
```

Advanced Sorting Techniques

#javascript

```
// Sorting by string length
let words = ['cat', 'elephant', 'dog', 'butterfly', 'ant'];
words.sort((a, b) => a.length - b.length);
console.log(words); // ['cat', 'dog', 'ant', 'elephant', 'butterfly']

// Random shuffle (Fisher-Yates algorithm)
function shuffle(array) {
    let shuffled = [...array];
```

```
    for (let i = shuffled.length - 1; i > 0; i--) {
        let j = Math.floor(Math.random() * (i + 1));
        [shuffled[i], shuffled[j]] = [shuffled[j],
shuffled[i]];
    }
    return shuffled;
}

let deck = ['A', 'K', 'Q', 'J', '10', '9', '8', '7'];
let shuffledDeck = shuffle(deck);
console.log(shuffledDeck);

// Stable sorting with original indices
let items = [
    { name: 'apple', category: 'fruit' },
    { name: 'carrot', category: 'vegetable' },
    { name: 'banana', category: 'fruit' },
    { name: 'broccoli', category: 'vegetable' }
];

// Add original indices
items.forEach((item, index) => item.originalIndex =
index);

// Sort by category, maintaining original order for same
category
items.sort((a, b) => {
    if (a.category !== b.category) {
        return a.category.localeCompare(b.category);
    }
    return a.originalIndex - b.originalIndex;
```

```
});
console.log(items);
```

8.5 Searching Arrays (indexOf, includes)

The indexOf() Method

The indexOf() method returns the first index at which a given element can be found, or -1 if not present.

#javascript

```
let fruits = ['apple', 'banana', 'orange', 'banana', 'grape'];

// Basic usage
console.log(fruits.indexOf('banana')); // 1 (first occurrence)
console.log(fruits.indexOf('grape')); // 4
console.log(fruits.indexOf('kiwi')); // -1 (not found)

// Starting search from specific index
console.log(fruits.indexOf('banana', 2)); // 3 (starts search from index 2)

// Practical example: checking if element exists
function hasElement(array, element) {
    return array.indexOf(element) !== -1;
}

console.log(hasElement(fruits, 'apple')); // true
console.log(hasElement(fruits, 'kiwi')); // false
```

The lastIndexOf() Method

The lastIndexOf() method returns the last index at which a given element can be found:

#javascript

```
let letters = ['a', 'b', 'c', 'b', 'd', 'b'];

console.log(letters.indexOf('b')); // 1 (first occurrence)
console.log(letters.lastIndexOf('b')); // 5 (last occurrence)

// Search backwards from specific position
console.log(letters.lastIndexOf('b', 4)); // 3 (last occurrence before index 4)

// Finding all occurrences
function findAllIndices(array, element) {
    let indices = [];
    let index = array.indexOf(element);

    while (index !== -1) {
        indices.push(index);
        index = array.indexOf(element, index + 1);
    }

    return indices;
}

console.log(findAllIndices(letters, 'b')); // [1, 3, 5]
```

The includes() Method

The includes() method determines whether an array contains a certain element, returning true or false:

#javascript

```
let numbers = [1, 2, 3, 4, 5];

// Basic usage
console.log(numbers.includes(3)); // true
console.log(numbers.includes(6)); // false

// Starting search from specific index
console.log(numbers.includes(3, 3)); // false (starts
from index 3)

// Case sensitivity with strings
let names = ['Alice', 'Bob', 'Charlie'];
console.log(names.includes('alice')); // false (case
sensitive)
console.log(names.includes('Alice')); // true

// Working with NaN
let values = [1, 2, NaN, 4];
console.log(values.includes(NaN)); // true
console.log(values.indexOf(NaN)); // -1 (indexOf can't
find NaN)
```

Advanced Search Methods

Beyond basic searching, JavaScript provides powerful methods for complex search operations:

#javascript

```
// Using find() for object searches
let users = [
    { id: 1, name: 'Alice', active: true },
    { id: 2, name: 'Bob', active: false },
    { id: 3, name: 'Charlie', active: true }
];

// Find first user matching condition
let activeUser = users.find(user => user.active);
console.log(activeUser); // { id: 1, name: 'Alice',
active: true }

// Find index of first user matching condition
let activeUserIndex = users.findIndex(user =>
user.active);
console.log(activeUserIndex); // 0

// Check if any user is active
let hasActiveUser = users.some(user => user.active);
console.log(hasActiveUser); // true

// Check if all users are active
let allUsersActive = users.every(user => user.active);
console.log(allUsersActive); // false

// Filter all active users
let activeUsers = users.filter(user => user.active);
console.log(activeUsers); // Array with Alice and Charlie
```

Search Performance Optimization

For large arrays or frequent searches, consider these optimization strategies:

#javascript

```javascript
// Binary search for sorted arrays (much faster than linear search)
function binarySearch(sortedArray, target) {
    let left = 0;
    let right = sortedArray.length - 1;

    while (left <= right) {
        let mid = Math.floor((left + right) / 2);

        if (sortedArray[mid] === target) {
            return mid;
        } else if (sortedArray[mid] < target) {
            left = mid + 1;
        } else {
            right = mid - 1;
        }
    }

    return -1; // Not found
}

let sortedNumbers = [1, 3, 5, 7, 9, 11, 13, 15];
console.log(binarySearch(sortedNumbers, 7)); // 3
console.log(binarySearch(sortedNumbers, 6)); // -1
```

```
// Using Set for O(1) lookups
let largeArray = Array.from({length: 10000}, (_, i) =>
i);
let searchSet = new Set(largeArray);

// Much faster for multiple searches
console.log(searchSet.has(5000)); // true, O(1) operation
console.log(largeArray.includes(5000)); // true, but O(n)
operation

// Creating search index for objects
function createSearchIndex(array, key) {
    let index = new Map();
    array.forEach((item, idx) => {
        if (!index.has(item[key])) {
            index.set(item[key], []);
        }
        index.get(item[key]).push({item, index: idx});
    });
    return index;
}

let products = [
    { id: 1, name: 'Laptop', category: 'Electronics' },
    { id: 2, name: 'Book', category: 'Education' },
    { id: 3, name: 'Phone', category: 'Electronics' }
];

let categoryIndex = createSearchIndex(products,
'category');
console.log(categoryIndex.get('Electronics')); // All
electronics products
```

Practical Search Applications

#javascript

```
// Implementing autocomplete functionality
function autocomplete(array, query) {
    return array.filter(item =>

item.toLowerCase().startsWith(query.toLowerCase())
    );
}

let cities = ['New York', 'Los Angeles', 'Chicago',
'Houston', 'Phoenix'];
console.log(autocomplete(cities, 'new')); // ['New York']
console.log(autocomplete(cities, 'l')); // ['Los
Angeles']

// Finding duplicates
function findDuplicates(array) {
    let seen = new Set();
    let duplicates = new Set();

    for (let item of array) {
        if (seen.has(item)) {
            duplicates.add(item);
        } else {
            seen.add(item);
        }
    }
```

```
    return Array.from(duplicates);
}

let numbers = [1, 2, 3, 2, 4, 3, 5];
console.log(findDuplicates(numbers)); // [2, 3]

// Searching with multiple conditions
function searchProducts(products, criteria) {
    return products.filter(product => {
        return Object.keys(criteria).every(key => {
            if (typeof criteria[key] === 'string') {
                return
product[key].toLowerCase().includes(criteria[key].toLower
Case());
            }
            return product[key] === criteria[key];
        });
    });
}

let inventory = [
    { name: 'Gaming Laptop', price: 1200, category:
'Electronics', inStock: true },
    { name: 'Office Chair', price: 300, category:
'Furniture', inStock: false },
    { name: 'Wireless Mouse', price: 50, category:
'Electronics', inStock: true }
];

let searchResults = searchProducts(inventory, {
    category: 'Electronics',
```

```
    inStock: true
});
console.log(searchResults); // Gaming Laptop and Wireless
Mouse
```

Essential Tips

- Use array literals `[]` instead of the Array constructor for cleaner, more predictable code creation.
- Always check if an element exists before accessing it to avoid runtime errors, especially when dealing with dynamic arrays.
- Consider using `const` for arrays when you don't plan to reassign the entire array, as it prevents accidental reassignment while still allowing array modification.
- Cache array length in loops when dealing with large datasets to improve performance, as accessing the length property repeatedly can be costly.
- Use destructuring assignment to extract multiple array elements efficiently in a single statement.

Actionable Strategies

- Implement proper error handling when searching arrays by checking return values from methods like `indexOf()` before using them as indices.
- Choose the most appropriate iteration method based on your needs: use traditional for loops when you need index control, forEach for simple operations, and for...of for value-only iteration.
- Leverage method chaining with array methods like `filter()`, `map()`, and `reduce()` to create more readable and functional code patterns.
- Create reusable utility functions for common array operations such as finding duplicates, removing elements, or custom sorting logic.
- Use spread operator syntax for creating array copies and combining arrays instead of manual iteration or concatenation methods.
- Implement proper type checking and validation when working with arrays that might contain mixed data types or when accepting arrays as function parameters.

- Practice using modern array methods like `find()`, `some()`, `every()`, and `includes()` to write more expressive and maintainable code compared to traditional loop-based approaches.

Chapter 9: Objects and JSON

Objects represent one of the most fundamental and powerful data structures in JavaScript. They serve as the foundation for organizing and manipulating complex data, allowing developers to create sophisticated applications that mirror real-world entities and relationships. Understanding objects and JSON (JavaScript Object Notation) opens the door to advanced programming concepts and modern web development practices.

9.1 Creating and Accessing Objects

Object Fundamentals

Objects in JavaScript are collections of key-value pairs, where keys (also called properties) are strings or symbols, and values can be any data type including functions, arrays, or other objects. This flexibility makes objects incredibly versatile for representing complex data structures.

Object Creation Methods

Object Literal Syntax

The most common and straightforward method for creating objects uses the object literal syntax with curly braces:

#javascript

```
const person = {
    firstName: "Sarah",
    lastName: "Johnson",
    age: 28,
    city: "New York"
};
```

```
const product = {
    id: 1001,
    name: "Wireless Headphones",
    price: 199.99,
    inStock: true,
    colors: ["black", "white", "blue"]
};
```

Constructor Function Approach

Constructor functions provide a template for creating multiple objects with similar structures:

#javascript

```
function Car(make, model, year, color) {
    this.make = make;
    this.model = model;
    this.year = year;
    this.color = color;
    this.isRunning = false;
}

const myCar = new Car("Toyota", "Camry", 2023, "silver");
const friendsCar = new Car("Honda", "Civic", 2022,
"red");

console.log(myCar.make); // "Toyota"
console.log(friendsCar.model); // "Civic"
```

Object.create() Method

This method creates a new object with a specified prototype:

#javascript

```
const vehiclePrototype = {
    start: function() {
        this.isRunning = true;
        console.log(`${this.make} ${this.model} is now
running`);
    },
    stop: function() {
        this.isRunning = false;
        console.log(`${this.make} ${this.model} has
stopped`);
    }
};

const motorcycle = Object.create(vehiclePrototype);
motorcycle.make = "Harley-Davidson";
motorcycle.model = "Street 750";
motorcycle.type = "cruiser";

motorcycle.start(); // "Harley-Davidson Street 750 is now
running"
```

Property Access Methods

Dot Notation

Dot notation provides the most readable way to access object properties when the property name is known at write time:

#javascript

```
const student = {
    name: "Alex Chen",
```

```
    grade: "A",
    subjects: ["Math", "Science", "History"],
    gpa: 3.8
};

console.log(student.name); // "Alex Chen"
console.log(student.gpa); // 3.8
console.log(student.subjects[0]); // "Math"
```

Bracket Notation

Bracket notation offers more flexibility, especially when property names contain spaces, special characters, or are stored in variables:

#javascript

```
const restaurant = {
    "restaurant name": "The Golden Spoon",
    "opening hours": "9:00 AM - 10:00 PM",
    cuisine: "Italian",
    rating: 4.5
};

console.log(restaurant["restaurant name"]); // "The
Golden Spoon"
console.log(restaurant["opening hours"]); // "9:00 AM -
10:00 PM"

// Dynamic property access
const propertyName = "rating";
console.log(restaurant[propertyName]); // 4.5

// Using variables for property names
```

```javascript
const userInput = "cuisine";
console.log(restaurant[userInput]); // "Italian"
```

Property Modification

Objects in JavaScript are mutable, meaning their properties can be changed after creation:

#javascript

```javascript
const employee = {
    name: "Maria Rodriguez",
    position: "Software Developer",
    salary: 75000,
    department: "Engineering"
};

// Modifying existing properties
employee.salary = 80000;
employee.position = "Senior Software Developer";

// Adding new properties
employee.startDate = "2023-01-15";
employee.skills = ["JavaScript", "Python", "React"];

console.log(employee);
/* Output:
{
    name: "Maria Rodriguez",
    position: "Senior Software Developer",
    salary: 80000,
    department: "Engineering",
```

```
    startDate: "2023-01-15",
    skills: ["JavaScript", "Python", "React"]
}
*/
```

Property Deletion

The `delete` operator removes properties from objects:

#javascript

```
const book = {
    title: "The Great Gatsby",
    author: "F. Scott Fitzgerald",
    pages: 180,
    isbn: "978-0-7432-7356-5",
    tempProperty: "will be deleted"
};

delete book.tempProperty;
delete book.isbn;

console.log(book);
/* Output:
{
    title: "The Great Gatsby",
    author: "F. Scott Fitzgerald",
    pages: 180
}
*/
```

9.2 Object Properties and Methods

Understanding Methods

Methods are functions that belong to objects, enabling objects to perform actions and manipulate their own data. They provide encapsulation and organization by keeping related functionality together.

Defining Methods

Method Definition in Object Literals

#javascript

```
const calculator = {
    result: 0,
    add: function(num) {
        this.result += num;
        return this;
    },
    subtract: function(num) {
        this.result -= num;
        return this;
    },
    multiply: function(num) {
        this.result *= num;
        return this;
    },
    divide: function(num) {
        if (num !== 0) {
            this.result /= num;
        } else {
            console.log("Cannot divide by zero");
```

```
        }
        return this;
    },
    clear: function() {
        this.result = 0;
        return this;
    },
    getValue: function() {
        return this.result;
    }
};

// Method chaining
calculator.add(10).multiply(2).subtract(5).divide(3);
console.log(calculator.getValue()); // 5
```

ES6 Method Shorthand

Modern JavaScript provides a shorter syntax for defining methods:

#javascript

```
const shoppingCart = {
    items: [],
    total: 0,

    addItem(name, price, quantity = 1) {
        const item = {
            name: name,
            price: price,
            quantity: quantity,
            subtotal: price * quantity
```

```
        };
        this.items.push(item);
        this.updateTotal();
    },

    removeItem(name) {
        this.items = this.items.filter(item => item.name
!== name);
        this.updateTotal();
    },

    updateTotal() {
        this.total = this.items.reduce((sum, item) => sum
+ item.subtotal, 0);
    },

    getItemCount() {
        return this.items.reduce((count, item) => count +
item.quantity, 0);
    },

    displayCart() {
        console.log("Shopping Cart:");
        this.items.forEach(item => {
            console.log(`${item.name} - $${item.price} x
${item.quantity} = $${item.subtotal}`);
        });
        console.log(`Total: $${this.total.toFixed(2)}`);
        console.log(`Items: ${this.getItemCount()}`);
    }
};
```

```
shoppingCart.addItem("Laptop", 999.99, 1);
shoppingCart.addItem("Mouse", 29.99, 2);
shoppingCart.addItem("Keyboard", 89.99, 1);
shoppingCart.displayCart();
```

The this Keyword

The `this` keyword refers to the object that owns the method currently being executed:

#javascript

```
const bankAccount = {
    accountNumber: "12345-67890",
    balance: 1000.00,
    accountHolder: "John Smith",

    deposit(amount) {
        if (amount > 0) {
            this.balance += amount;
            console.log(`Deposited $${amount}. New
balance: $${this.balance}`);
        } else {
            console.log("Deposit amount must be
positive");
        }
    },

    withdraw(amount) {
        if (amount > 0 && amount <= this.balance) {
            this.balance -= amount;
```

```
            console.log(`Withdrew $${amount}. New
balance: $${this.balance}`);
        } else if (amount > this.balance) {
            console.log("Insufficient funds");
        } else {
            console.log("Withdrawal amount must be
positive");
        }
    },

    getBalance() {
        return this.balance;
    },

    getAccountInfo() {
        return {
            number: this.accountNumber,
            holder: this.accountHolder,
            balance: this.balance
        };
    }
};

bankAccount.deposit(250);
bankAccount.withdraw(100);
console.log(bankAccount.getAccountInfo());
```

Property Descriptors and Attributes

JavaScript provides fine-grained control over object properties through property descriptors:

#javascript

```
const secureObject = {};

Object.defineProperty(secureObject, 'readOnlyProperty', {
    value: "Cannot be changed",
    writable: false,
    enumerable: true,
    configurable: false
});

Object.defineProperty(secureObject, 'hiddenProperty', {
    value: "Not visible in loops",
    writable: true,
    enumerable: false,
    configurable: true
});

// Attempting to modify read-only property
secureObject.readOnlyProperty = "New value"; // Won't work
console.log(secureObject.readOnlyProperty); // "Cannot be changed"

// Hidden property won't appear in for...in loops
for (let key in secureObject) {
    console.log(key); // Only shows "readOnlyProperty"
}
```

Getters and Setters

Getters and setters provide controlled access to object properties:

#javascript

```
const temperature = {
    _celsius: 0,

    get celsius() {
        return this._celsius;
    },

    set celsius(value) {
        if (typeof value === 'number') {
            this._celsius = value;
        } else {
            console.log("Temperature must be a number");
        }
    },

    get fahrenheit() {
        return (this._celsius * 9/5) + 32;
    },

    set fahrenheit(value) {
        if (typeof value === 'number') {
            this._celsius = (value - 32) * 5/9;
        } else {
            console.log("Temperature must be a number");
        }
    },

    get kelvin() {
        return this._celsius + 273.15;
```

```
    },

    set kelvin(value) {
        if (typeof value === 'number' && value >= 0) {
            this._celsius = value - 273.15;
        } else {
            console.log("Kelvin must be a positive 
number");
        }
    }
};

temperature.celsius = 25;
console.log(`${temperature.celsius}°C = 
${temperature.fahrenheit}°F = ${temperature.kelvin}K`);

temperature.fahrenheit = 68;
console.log(`${temperature.celsius}°C = 
${temperature.fahrenheit}°F = ${temperature.kelvin}K`);
```

9.3 Nesting Objects and Arrays

Complex Data Structures

Real-world applications often require sophisticated data organization through nested objects and arrays, creating hierarchical structures that represent complex relationships and data models.

Nested Objects

Objects can contain other objects as properties, creating deep data structures:

#javascript

```
const company = {
    name: "TechCorp Solutions",
    founded: 2018,
    headquarters: {
        address: {
            street: "123 Innovation Drive",
            city: "San Francisco",
            state: "California",
            zipCode: "94105",
            country: "USA"
        },
        coordinates: {
            latitude: 37.7749,
            longitude: -122.4194
        }
    },
    departments: {
        engineering: {
            name: "Engineering",
            head: "Alice Johnson",
            employees: 45,
            budget: 2500000,
            projects: ["Project Alpha", "Project Beta",
"Project Gamma"]
        },
        marketing: {
            name: "Marketing",
            head: "Bob Williams",
            employees: 12,
```

```
            budget: 800000,
            campaigns: ["Summer Launch", "Holiday
Promotion"]
        },
        sales: {
            name: "Sales",
            head: "Carol Davis",
            employees: 20,
            budget: 1200000,
            regions: ["North America", "Europe", "Asia-
Pacific"]
        }
    },
    financial: {
        revenue: {
            2021: 15000000,
            2022: 18500000,
            2023: 22000000
        },
        expenses: {
            2021: 12000000,
            2022: 14500000,
            2023: 17000000
        }
    }
};

// Accessing nested properties
console.log(company.headquarters.address.city); // "San
Francisco"
console.log(company.departments.engineering.employees);
// 45
```

```
console.log(company.financial.revenue[2023]); // 22000000

// Calculating profit for 2023
const profit2023 = company.financial.revenue[2023] -
company.financial.expenses[2023];
console.log(`2023 Profit:
$${profit2023.toLocaleString()}`); // "2023 Profit:
$5,000,000"
```

Arrays of Objects

Arrays containing objects create powerful data collections for managing similar entities:

#javascript

```
const movieDatabase = [
    {
        id: 1,
        title: "The Shawshank Redemption",
        director: "Frank Darabont",
        year: 1994,
        genre: ["Drama"],
        rating: 9.3,
        duration: 142,
        cast: [
            { name: "Tim Robbins", role: "Andy Dufresne"
},
            { name: "Morgan Freeman", role: "Ellis Boyd
'Red' Redding" }
        ],
        awards: {
            nominations: 7,
```

```
            wins: 0,
            categories: ["Best Picture", "Best Actor",
"Best Adapted Screenplay"]
        }
    },
    {
        id: 2,
        title: "The Godfather",
        director: "Francis Ford Coppola",
        year: 1972,
        genre: ["Crime", "Drama"],
        rating: 9.2,
        duration: 175,
        cast: [
            { name: "Marlon Brando", role: "Vito
Corleone" },
            { name: "Al Pacino", role: "Michael Corleone"
}
        ],
        awards: {
            nominations: 10,
            wins: 3,
            categories: ["Best Picture", "Best Actor",
"Best Adapted Screenplay"]
        }
    },
    {
        id: 3,
        title: "The Dark Knight",
        director: "Christopher Nolan",
        year: 2008,
        genre: ["Action", "Crime", "Drama"],
```

```
        rating: 9.0,
        duration: 152,
        cast: [
            { name: "Christian Bale", role: "Bruce Wayne
/ Batman" },
            { name: "Heath Ledger", role: "Joker" }
        ],
        awards: {
            nominations: 8,
            wins: 2,
            categories: ["Best Supporting Actor", "Best
Sound Editing"]
        }
    }
];

// Complex data manipulation
const highRatedMovies = movieDatabase.filter(movie =>
movie.rating >= 9.2);
const totalDuration = movieDatabase.reduce((total, movie)
=> total + movie.duration, 0);
const averageRating = movieDatabase.reduce((sum, movie)
=> sum + movie.rating, 0) / movieDatabase.length;

console.log(`High-rated movies:
${highRatedMovies.length}`);
console.log(`Total duration: ${totalDuration} minutes`);
console.log(`Average rating:
${averageRating.toFixed(1)}`);

// Finding movies by genre
const crimeMovies = movieDatabase.filter(movie =>
movie.genre.includes("Crime"));
```

```
console.log("Crime movies:", crimeMovies.map(movie =>
movie.title));
```

Objects in Arrays in Objects

Complex applications often require deeply nested structures combining objects and arrays:

#javascript

```
const university = {
    name: "Metropolitan University",
    established: 1995,
    location: "Chicago, IL",
    faculties: [
        {
            name: "Faculty of Engineering",
            dean: "Dr. Sarah Mitchell",
            departments: [
                {
                    name: "Computer Science",
                    head: "Prof. James Wilson",
                    courses: [
                        {
                            code: "CS101",
                            name: "Introduction to
Programming",
                            credits: 3,
                            prerequisites: [],
                            instructor: "Dr. Emily Chen",
                            students: [
```

```
                    { id: "S001", name: 
"Alice Johnson", grade: "A" },
                    { id: "S002", name: "Bob 
Smith", grade: "B+" },
                    { id: "S003", name: 
"Carol Davis", grade: "A-" }
                ]
            },
            {
                code: "CS201",
                name: "Data Structures",
                credits: 4,
                prerequisites: ["CS101"],
                instructor: "Prof. Michael 
Brown",
                students: [
                    { id: "S004", name: 
"David Wilson", grade: "B" },
                    { id: "S005", name: "Emma 
Taylor", grade: "A" }
                ]
            }
        ]
    },
    {
        name: "Electrical Engineering",
        head: "Prof. Lisa Anderson",
        courses: [
            {
                code: "EE101",
                name: "Circuit Analysis",
                credits: 4,
```

```
                              prerequisites: [],
                              instructor: "Dr. Robert Lee",
                              students: [
                                  { id: "S006", name:
"Frank Miller", grade: "B+" },
                                  { id: "S007", name:
"Grace White", grade: "A" }
                              ]
                          }
                      ]
                  }
              ]
          }
      ]
};

// Complex data access and manipulation
function getAllStudents(university) {
    const allStudents = [];
    university.faculties.forEach(faculty => {
        faculty.departments.forEach(department => {
            department.courses.forEach(course => {
                course.students.forEach(student => {
                    allStudents.push({
                        ...student,
                        course: course.code,
                        courseName: course.name,
                        department: department.name,
                        faculty: faculty.name
                    });
                });
```

```
            });
        });
    });
    return allStudents;
}

function calculateGPA(students) {
    const gradePoints = { "A": 4.0, "A-": 3.7, "B+": 3.3,
"B": 3.0, "B-": 2.7, "C+": 2.3, "C": 2.0 };
    const totalPoints = students.reduce((sum, student) =>
sum + gradePoints[student.grade], 0);
    return totalPoints / students.length;
}

const allStudents = getAllStudents(university);
const averageGPA = calculateGPA(allStudents);

console.log(`Total students: ${allStudents.length}`);
console.log(`Average GPA: ${averageGPA.toFixed(2)}`);
```

Deep Cloning Nested Objects

Working with nested objects requires understanding how to create deep copies:

#javascript

```
const originalData = {
    user: {
        name: "John Doe",
        preferences: {
            theme: "dark",
            notifications: {
```

```
                email: true,
                push: false,
                sms: true
            }
        },
        contacts: ["alice@email.com", "bob@email.com"]
    },
    settings: {
        language: "en",
        timezone: "UTC-5"
    }
};

// Shallow copy (only copies top level)
const shallowCopy = { ...originalData };
shallowCopy.user.name = "Jane Doe"; // This affects
original!

// Deep copy using JSON methods (limited)
const deepCopy1 =
JSON.parse(JSON.stringify(originalData));
deepCopy1.user.name = "Mike Johnson"; // This doesn't
affect original

// Custom deep clone function
function deepClone(obj) {
    if (obj === null || typeof obj !== "object") {
        return obj;
    }

    if (obj instanceof Date) {
```

```
        return new Date(obj.getTime());
    }

    if (obj instanceof Array) {
        return obj.map(item => deepClone(item));
    }

    if (typeof obj === "object") {
        const cloned = {};
        for (let key in obj) {
            if (obj.hasOwnProperty(key)) {
                cloned[key] = deepClone(obj[key]);
            }
        }
        return cloned;
    }
}

const deepCopy2 = deepClone(originalData);
deepCopy2.user.preferences.theme = "light"; // Safe
modification

console.log("Original theme:",
originalData.user.preferences.theme); // "dark"
console.log("Copy theme:",
deepCopy2.user.preferences.theme); // "light"
```

9.4 Introduction to JSON

Understanding JSON

JSON (JavaScript Object Notation) has become the universal standard for data exchange between web applications, APIs, and different programming languages. Despite its name suggesting a connection to JavaScript, JSON is language-independent and widely supported across all modern programming platforms.

JSON Syntax Rules

JSON follows strict formatting rules that distinguish it from JavaScript object literals:

#javascript

```
// Valid JSON structure
const validJSON = `{
    "name": "Sarah Johnson",
    "age": 30,
    "isEmployed": true,
    "spouse": null,
    "children": ["Emma", "Oliver"],
    "address": {
        "street": "123 Main St",
        "city": "Boston",
        "zipCode": "02101"
    },
    "hobbies": ["reading", "hiking", "photography"]
}`;

// JSON vs JavaScript Object differences
const jsObject = {
    name: "Sarah Johnson",        // No quotes around
keys in JS
    age: 30,
```

```
    isEmployed: true,
    spouse: undefined,              // undefined not
allowed in JSON
    getValue: function() {          // Functions not
allowed in JSON
        return this.name;
    },
    birthDate: new Date()           // Date objects become
strings in JSON
};
```

JSON Data Types

JSON supports six fundamental data types:

#javascript

```
const jsonDataTypes = `{
    "string": "Hello World",
    "number": 42.5,
    "boolean": true,
    "null": null,
    "array": [1, 2, 3, "mixed", true],
    "object": {
        "nested": "value",
        "count": 10
    }
}`;

// What JSON cannot represent:
const unsupportedTypes = {
    undefinedValue: undefined,    // Not supported
```

```
    functionValue: function() {}, // Not supported
    dateValue: new Date(),        // Becomes string
    regexValue: /pattern/g,       // Not supported
    symbolValue: Symbol('id')     // Not supported
};
```

Common JSON Use Cases

API Response Handling
#javascript

```javascript
// Simulated API response
const apiResponse = `{
    "status": "success",
    "data": {
        "users": [
            {
                "id": 1,
                "username": "johndoe",
                "email": "john@example.com",
                "profile": {
                    "firstName": "John",
                    "lastName": "Doe",
                    "avatar":
"https://example.com/avatar1.jpg",
                    "joinDate": "2023-01-15T10:30:00Z"
                },
                "permissions": ["read", "write"],
                "isActive": true
            },
            {
```

```
                "id": 2,
                "username": "janedoe",
                "email": "jane@example.com",
                "profile": {
                    "firstName": "Jane",
                    "lastName": "Doe",
                    "avatar":
"https://example.com/avatar2.jpg",
                    "joinDate": "2023-02-20T14:45:00Z"
                },
                "permissions": ["read"],
                "isActive": false
            }
        ],
        "pagination": {
            "currentPage": 1,
            "totalPages": 5,
            "itemsPerPage": 2,
            "totalItems": 10
        }
    },
    "timestamp": "2024-03-15T12:00:00Z"
}`;
```

Configuration Files
#javascript

```
const configJSON = `{
    "application": {
        "name": "MyWebApp",
        "version": "2.1.0",
```

```
        "environment": "production"
    },
    "database": {
        "host": "localhost",
        "port": 5432,
        "name": "myapp_db",
        "ssl": true,
        "connectionPool": {
            "min": 2,
            "max": 10,
            "idleTimeoutMillis": 30000
        }
    },
    "api": {
        "baseUrl": "https://api.myapp.com",
        "timeout": 5000,
        "retryAttempts": 3,
        "endpoints": {
            "users": "/api/v1/users",
            "products": "/api/v1/products",
            "orders": "/api/v1/orders"
        }
    },
    "features": {
        "enableLogging": true,
        "enableAnalytics": false,
        "maintenanceMode": false
    }
}`;
```

JSON Validation and Error Handling

#javascript

```
function validateJSON(jsonString) {
    try {
        const parsed = JSON.parse(jsonString);
        return {
            valid: true,
            data: parsed,
            error: null
        };
    } catch (error) {
        return {
            valid: false,
            data: null,
            error: {
                message: error.message,
                position: error.message.match(/position
(\d+)/)?.[1] || 'unknown'
            }
        };
    }
}

// Testing JSON validation
const validJSON = '{"name": "John", "age": 30}';
const invalidJSON = '{"name": "John", age: 30}'; //
Missing quotes around key

console.log(validateJSON(validJSON));   // { valid: true,
data: {...}, error: null }
```

```
console.log(validateJSON(invalidJSON)); // { valid:
false, data: null, error: {...} }
```

9.5 Converting Between JSON and JavaScript Objects

JSON.stringify() Method

The `JSON.stringify()` method converts JavaScript objects into JSON strings, enabling data serialization for storage and transmission:

#javascript

```
const userProfile = {
    id: 12345,
    username: "techexplorer",
    email: "explorer@tech.com",
    preferences: {
        theme: "dark",
        language: "en-US",
        notifications: {
            email: true,
            push: false,
            desktop: true
        }
    },
    tags: ["developer", "gamer", "reader"],
    lastLogin: new Date("2024-03-15T10:30:00Z"),
    isVerified: true
};

// Basic stringification
const jsonString = JSON.stringify(userProfile);
```

```
console.log(jsonString);

// Pretty-printed JSON with indentation
const prettyJSON = JSON.stringify(userProfile, null, 2);
console.log(prettyJSON);
/* Output:
{
  "id": 12345,
  "username": "techexplorer",
  "email": "explorer@tech.com",
  "preferences": {
    "theme": "dark",
    "language": "en-US",
    "notifications": {
      "email": true,
      "push": false,
      "desktop": true
    }
  },
  "tags": ["developer", "gamer", "reader"],
  "lastLogin": "2024-03-15T10:30:00.000Z",
  "isVerified": true
}
*/
```

Advanced JSON.stringify() Features

Replacer Function

The replacer parameter allows custom control over the stringification process:

#javascript

```
const sensitiveData = {
    username: "john_doe",
    email: "john@example.com",
    password: "secret123",
    creditCard: "1234-5678-9012-3456",
    profile: {
        name: "John Doe",
        age: 30,
        socialSecurity: "123-45-6789"
    }
};

// Replacer function to filter sensitive data
function secureReplacer(key, value) {
    const sensitiveKeys = ['password', 'creditCard',
'socialSecurity'];

    if (sensitiveKeys.includes(key)) {
        return '[REDACTED]';
    }

    if (typeof value === 'string' && value.includes('@'))
{
        // Mask part of email addresses
        return value.replace(/(.{2}).*(@.*)/, '$1***$2');
    }

    return value;
}
```

```
const secureJSON = JSON.stringify(sensitiveData,
secureReplacer, 2);
console.log(secureJSON);
/* Output:
{
  "username": "john_doe",
  "email": "jo***@example.com",
  "password": "[REDACTED]",
  "creditCard": "[REDACTED]",
  "profile": {
    "name": "John Doe",
    "age": 30,
    "socialSecurity": "[REDACTED]"
  }
}
*/
```

Replacer Array

Use an array to specify which properties to include:

#javascript

```
const productData = {
    id: "P001",
    name: "Wireless Headphones",
    price: 199.99,
    cost: 89.50,           // Internal cost - exclude
    profit: 110.49,        // Internal profit - exclude
    description: "High-quality wireless headphones",
    category: "Electronics",
    inStock: true,
```

```
    internalNotes: "Supplier: TechCorp" // Internal notes - exclude
};

// Only include public-facing properties
const publicProperties = ['id', 'name', 'price', 'description', 'category', 'inStock'];
const publicJSON = JSON.stringify(productData, publicProperties, 2);
console.log(publicJSON);
```

JSON.parse() Method

The `JSON.parse()` method converts JSON strings back into JavaScript objects:

#javascript

```
const jsonData = `{
    "order": {
        "id": "ORD-2024-001",
        "customer": {
            "name": "Alice Johnson",
            "email": "alice@email.com"
        },
        "items": [
            {
                "product": "Laptop",
                "quantity": 1,
                "price": 999.99
            },
            {
```

```
                "product": "Mouse",
                "quantity": 2,
                "price": 29.99
            }
        ],
        "orderDate": "2024-03-15T14:30:00Z",
        "total": 1059.97,
        "status": "processing"
    }
}`;

// Parse JSON string to JavaScript object
const orderData = JSON.parse(jsonData);

// Access parsed data
console.log(orderData.order.customer.name); // "Alice Johnson"
console.log(orderData.order.items[0].product); // "Laptop"
console.log(orderData.order.total); // 1059.97

// Calculate total items
const totalItems = orderData.order.items.reduce((sum, item) => sum + item.quantity, 0);
console.log(`Total items: ${totalItems}`); // "Total items: 3"
```

Advanced JSON.parse() with Reviver Function

The reviver function allows custom transformation during parsing:

#javascript

```
const complexJSON = `{
    "event": {
        "name": "Tech Conference 2024",
        "startDate": "2024-06-15T09:00:00Z",
        "endDate": "2024-06-17T17:00:00Z",
        "registrationDeadline": "2024-05-01T23:59:59Z",
        "attendees": [
            {
                "name": "John Smith",
                "registeredAt": "2024-03-10T14:30:00Z",
                "type": "speaker"
            },
            {
                "name": "Jane Doe",
                "registeredAt": "2024-03-12T10:15:00Z",
                "type": "attendee"
            }
        ],
        "pricing": {
            "earlyBird": "150.00",
            "regular": "200.00",
            "student": "75.00"
        }
    }
}`;

// Reviver function to transform specific values
function dateReviver(key, value) {
    // Convert ISO date strings to Date objects
    if (typeof value === 'string' && /^\d{4}-\d{2}-
\d{2}T\d{2}:\d{2}:\d{2}/.test(value)) {
```

```
        return new Date(value);
    }

    // Convert price strings to numbers
    if (key.includes('price') || key === 'earlyBird' ||
key === 'regular' || key === 'student') {
        return parseFloat(value);
    }

    return value;
}

const eventData = JSON.parse(complexJSON, dateReviver);

// Now dates are actual Date objects
console.log(eventData.event.startDate instanceof Date);
// true
console.log(eventData.event.startDate.getFullYear()); //
2024

// Prices are numbers
console.log(typeof eventData.event.pricing.regular); //
"number"
console.log(eventData.event.pricing.regular); // 150

// Calculate days until event
const daysUntilEvent =
Math.ceil((eventData.event.startDate - new Date()) /
(1000 * 60 * 60 * 24));
console.log(`Days until event: ${daysUntilEvent}`);
```

Error Handling for JSON Operations

Robust JSON handling requires proper error management:

#javascript

```javascript
class JSONHandler {
    static safeStringify(obj, replacer = null, space =
null) {
        try {
            return {
                success: true,
                result: JSON.stringify(obj, replacer,
space),
                error: null
            };
        } catch (error) {
            return {
                success: false,
                result: null,
                error: {
                    type: 'stringify',
                    message: error.message,
                    cause:
this.identifyStringifyError(error)
                }
            };
        }
    }

    static safeParse(jsonString, reviver = null) {
        try {
            return {
```

```
                success: true,
                result: JSON.parse(jsonString, reviver),
                error: null
            };
        } catch (error) {
            return {
                success: false,
                result: null,
                error: {
                    type: 'parse',
                    message: error.message,
                    position:
this.findErrorPosition(error.message),
                    suggestion:
this.suggestFix(jsonString, error)
                }
            };
        }
    }

    static identifyStringifyError(error) {
        if (error.message.includes('circular')) {
            return 'Circular reference detected';
        }
        if (error.message.includes('BigInt')) {
            return 'BigInt values cannot be serialized';
        }
        return 'Unknown stringify error';
    }

    static findErrorPosition(errorMessage) {
```

```
        const match = errorMessage.match(/position
(\d+)/);
        return match ? parseInt(match[1]) : null;
    }

    static suggestFix(jsonString, error) {
        if (error.message.includes('Unexpected token')) {
            return 'Check for missing quotes around
object keys or trailing commas';
        }
        if (error.message.includes('Unexpected end')) {
            return 'Check for missing closing brackets or
braces';
        }
        return 'Validate JSON syntax';
    }
}

// Testing error handling
const problematicData = {
    name: "Test",
    circular: null
};
problematicData.circular = problematicData; // Create
circular reference

const stringifyResult =
JSONHandler.safeStringify(problematicData);
console.log(stringifyResult);

const invalidJSON = '{"name": "Test", "age": 30,}'; //
Trailing comma
```

```
const parseResult = JSONHandler.safeParse(invalidJSON);
console.log(parseResult);
```

Real-World JSON Processing

API Data Processing
#javascript

```
class APIDataProcessor {
    static processUserData(jsonResponse) {
        const parseResult =
JSONHandler.safeParse(jsonResponse);

        if (!parseResult.success) {
            throw new Error(`Failed to parse API
response: ${parseResult.error.message}`);
        }

        const data = parseResult.result;

        // Transform and validate data
        return {
            users: data.users.map(user => ({
                id: user.id,
                name: `${user.profile.firstName}
${user.profile.lastName}`,
                email: user.email,
                joinDate: new
Date(user.profile.joinDate),
                isActive: user.isActive,
                permissions: user.permissions,
                avatar: user.profile.avatar
```

```
            })),
            pagination: {
                current: data.pagination.currentPage,
                total: data.pagination.totalPages,
                hasNext: data.pagination.currentPage <
data.pagination.totalPages,
                hasPrevious: data.pagination.currentPage
> 1
            },
            metadata: {
                totalUsers: data.pagination.totalItems,
                fetchedAt: new Date(data.timestamp)
            }
        };
    }

    static prepareRequestData(userData) {
        const requestData = {
            user: {
                profile: {
                    firstName: userData.firstName,
                    lastName: userData.lastName,
                    email: userData.email
                },
                preferences: userData.preferences || {},
                permissions: userData.permissions ||
['read']
            },
            metadata: {
                source: 'web-app',
                timestamp: new Date().toISOString(),
```

```
                version: '1.0'
            }
        };

        return JSONHandler.safeStringify(requestData);
    }
}

// Example usage
const apiResponse = `{
    "users": [
        {
            "id": 1,
            "email": "john@example.com",
            "profile": {
                "firstName": "John",
                "lastName": "Doe",
                "joinDate": "2023-01-15T10:30:00Z",
                "avatar": "avatar1.jpg"
            },
            "permissions": ["read", "write"],
            "isActive": true
        }
    ],
    "pagination": {
        "currentPage": 1,
        "totalPages": 1,
        "totalItems": 1
    },
    "timestamp": "2024-03-15T12:00:00Z"
}`;
```

```
const processedData =
APIDataProcessor.processUserData(apiResponse);
console.log(processedData);

// Prepare data for API request
const newUserData = {
    firstName: "Alice",
    lastName: "Johnson",
    email: "alice@example.com",
    preferences: { theme: "dark" },
    permissions: ["read", "write"]
};

const requestJSON =
APIDataProcessor.prepareRequestData(newUserData);
console.log(requestJSON.result);
```

Local Storage Integration

#javascript

```
class LocalStorageManager {
    static setItem(key, data) {
        const stringifyResult =
JSONHandler.safeStringify(data);

        if (stringifyResult.success) {
            localStorage.setItem(key,
stringifyResult.result);
            return { success: true, error: null };
        } else {
```

```
            return { success: false, error:
stringifyResult.error };
        }
    }

    static getItem(key, defaultValue = null) {
        try {
            const stored = localStorage.getItem(key);

            if (stored === null) {
                return { success: true, data:
defaultValue, error: null };
            }

            const parseResult =
JSONHandler.safeParse(stored);

            if (parseResult.success) {
                return { success: true, data:
parseResult.result, error: null };
            } else {
                return { success: false, data:
defaultValue, error: parseResult.error };
            }
        } catch (error) {
            return {
                success: false,
                data: defaultValue,
                error: { type: 'storage', message:
error.message }
            };
        }
```

```
    }

    static updateItem(key, updateFunction) {
        const current = this.getItem(key, {});

        if (current.success) {
            const updated = updateFunction(current.data);
            return this.setItem(key, updated);
        }

        return current;
    }
}

// Example usage
const userSettings = {
    theme: "dark",
    language: "en",
    notifications: {
        email: true,
        push: false
    },
    lastLogin: new Date().toISOString()
};

// Store settings
LocalStorageManager.setItem('userSettings',
userSettings);

// Retrieve settings
```

```
const retrieved =
LocalStorageManager.getItem('userSettings');
console.log(retrieved);

// Update specific setting
LocalStorageManager.updateItem('userSettings', (settings)
=> {
    settings.theme = "light";
    settings.notifications.push = true;
    return settings;
});
```

JSON Schema Validation

#javascript

```
class JSONValidator {
    static validateUserProfile(data) {
        const errors = [];

        // Required fields
        const requiredFields = ['name', 'email', 'age'];
        requiredFields.forEach(field => {
            if (!(field in data)) {
                errors.push(`Missing required field:
${field}`);
            }
        });

        // Type validation
        if (data.name && typeof data.name !== 'string') {
```

```
            errors.push('Name must be a string');
        }

        if (data.email && typeof data.email !== 'string')
{
            errors.push('Email must be a string');
        } else if (data.email &&
!this.isValidEmail(data.email)) {
            errors.push('Invalid email format');
        }

        if (data.age && typeof data.age !== 'number') {
            errors.push('Age must be a number');
        } else if (data.age && (data.age < 0 || data.age
> 150)) {
            errors.push('Age must be between 0 and 150');
        }

        // Optional fields validation
        if (data.preferences && typeof data.preferences
!== 'object') {
            errors.push('Preferences must be an object');
        }

        if (data.tags && !Array.isArray(data.tags)) {
            errors.push('Tags must be an array');
        }

        return {
            valid: errors.length === 0,
            errors: errors,
            data: errors.length === 0 ? data : null
```

```
        };
    }

    static isValidEmail(email) {
        const emailRegex = /^[^\s@]+@[^\s@]+\.[^\s@]+$/;
        return emailRegex.test(email);
    }

    static validateAndParse(jsonString, validator) {
        const parseResult =
JSONHandler.safeParse(jsonString);

        if (!parseResult.success) {
            return {
                valid: false,
                errors: [`JSON Parse Error:
${parseResult.error.message}`],
                data: null
            };
        }

        return validator(parseResult.result);
    }
}

// Example validation
const userJSON = `{
    "name": "John Doe",
    "email": "john@example.com",
    "age": 30,
    "preferences": {
```

```
        "theme": "dark"
    },
    "tags": ["developer", "javascript"]
}`;

const validationResult =
JSONValidator.validateAndParse(userJSON,
JSONValidator.validateUserProfile);
console.log(validationResult);
```

Essential Tips

- Always use consistent naming conventions for object properties to maintain code readability and reduce errors. Choose between camelCase or snake_case and stick with it throughout your project.
- Remember that object property access using bracket notation allows for dynamic property names, making it invaluable when working with user input or data that comes from external sources.
- When working with nested objects, implement defensive programming by checking if properties exist before accessing deeply nested values to prevent runtime errors.
- Use object destructuring to extract multiple properties efficiently and make your code more readable, especially when working with function parameters and API responses.
- Always validate JSON data before processing it in production applications, as malformed JSON can crash your application and corrupt data processing workflows.

Actionable Strategies

- Practice creating complex nested data structures that mirror real-world entities like e-commerce systems, social media platforms, or content management systems to build intuitive understanding.

- Build a personal utility library of JSON handling functions that include error handling, validation, and transformation capabilities for reuse across projects.
- Create object factories and constructor patterns that generate consistent object structures, making your code more maintainable and reducing the likelihood of property naming inconsistencies.
- Implement data transformation pipelines that convert between different object formats, helping you understand how to reshape data for different parts of your application.
- Develop debugging strategies for complex nested objects by creating utility functions that can safely traverse and display object structures without causing errors.
- Master the art of object composition by building larger objects from smaller, focused objects, promoting code reusability and separation of concerns.
- Create comprehensive test cases for your JSON parsing and stringifying operations, including edge cases like circular references, undefined values, and deeply nested structures to ensure robust error handling.

Chapter 10: Control Flow - If, Else, and Switch

Control flow statements form the backbone of decision-making in JavaScript applications. These powerful constructs allow your programs to execute different code paths based on specific conditions, making your applications dynamic and responsive to various scenarios. Understanding how to implement conditional logic effectively is crucial for creating robust, maintainable JavaScript code.

10.1 Writing `if` Statements

Understanding the Fundamentals of If Statements

The `if` statement represents the most basic form of conditional execution in JavaScript. This statement evaluates a condition and executes a block of code only when that condition evaluates to `true`. The syntax follows a straightforward pattern that makes it intuitive for developers to implement decision-making logic.

#javascript

```
if (condition) {
    // Code to execute when condition is true
}
```

The condition within the parentheses can be any expression that JavaScript can evaluate to either `true` or `false`. JavaScript automatically converts non-boolean values to boolean values through a process called type coercion.

Basic If Statement Examples

Let's examine practical implementations of `if` statements:

#javascript

```
let temperature = 25;
```

```
if (temperature > 20) {
    console.log("It's warm outside!");
}

let userAge = 18;

if (userAge >= 18) {
    console.log("User is eligible to vote");
}

let username = "admin";

if (username === "admin") {
    console.log("Welcome, administrator!");
}
```

Truthy and Falsy Values in Conditions

JavaScript considers certain values as "falsy" and others as "truthy" when evaluated in boolean contexts. Understanding this concept is essential for writing effective conditional statements.

Falsy values include:

- `false`
- `0`
- `-0`
- `0n` (BigInt)
- `""` (empty string)
- `null`
- `undefined`
- `NaN`

All other values are truthy, including:

- Non-empty strings
- Numbers other than 0
- Objects and arrays (even empty ones)
- Functions

#javascript

```
let userInput = "";

if (userInput) {
    console.log("User provided input");
} else {
    console.log("No input provided"); // This will
execute
}

let items = [];

if (items) {
    console.log("Items array exists"); // This will
execute (arrays are truthy)
}

let count = 0;

if (count) {
    console.log("Count is non-zero");
} else {
    console.log("Count is zero"); // This will execute
}
```

Complex Conditions in If Statements

You can create sophisticated conditions by combining multiple expressions using logical operators:

#javascript

```
let score = 85;
let attendance = 90;

if (score >= 80 && attendance >= 85) {
    console.log("Student receives honors");
}

let weather = "sunny";
let temperature = 22;

if (weather === "sunny" && temperature > 20) {
    console.log("Perfect day for outdoor activities");
}

let userRole = "editor";
let hasPermission = true;

if (userRole === "admin" || (userRole === "editor" &&
hasPermission)) {
    console.log("Access granted to edit content");
}
```

10.2 Using `else` and `else if`

The Power of Else Statements

The `else` statement provides an alternative execution path when the `if` condition evaluates to `false`. This creates a binary decision structure that ensures one of two code blocks will always execute.

#javascript

```
let isLoggedIn = false;

if (isLoggedIn) {
    console.log("Welcome back!");
} else {
    console.log("Please log in to continue");
}
```

Implementing Else If for Multiple Conditions

When you need to test multiple conditions in sequence, `else if` statements provide an elegant solution. JavaScript evaluates these conditions from top to bottom, executing the first block whose condition evaluates to `true`.

#javascript

```
let grade = 87;

if (grade >= 90) {
    console.log("Grade: A");
} else if (grade >= 80) {
    console.log("Grade: B");
} else if (grade >= 70) {
    console.log("Grade: C");
} else if (grade >= 60) {
    console.log("Grade: D");
} else {
```

```
    console.log("Grade: F");
}
```

Complex Multi-Condition Logic

Real-world applications often require sophisticated conditional logic that combines multiple `else if` statements with complex conditions:

#javascript

```
function determineShippingCost(weight, distance, isPriority) {
    let baseCost = 5;
    let cost = baseCost;

    if (weight > 10 && distance > 100) {
        cost += 15;
    } else if (weight > 10) {
        cost += 10;
    } else if (distance > 100) {
        cost += 8;
    }

    if (isPriority) {
        cost *= 1.5;
    }

    return cost;
}

let shippingCost = determineShippingCost(12, 150, true);
console.log(`Shipping cost: $${shippingCost}`);
```

Nested If Statements

Sometimes you need to check additional conditions only after an initial condition is met. Nested `if` statements allow you to create hierarchical decision structures:

#javascript

```
let user = {
    isLoggedIn: true,
    role: "admin",
    permissions: ["read", "write", "delete"]
};

if (user.isLoggedIn) {
    if (user.role === "admin") {
        if (user.permissions.includes("delete")) {
            console.log("Full administrative access
granted");
        } else {
            console.log("Limited administrative access");
        }
    } else {
        console.log("Standard user access");
    }
} else {
    console.log("Access denied - please log in");
}
```

Avoiding Deep Nesting with Guard Clauses

Deep nesting can make code difficult to read and maintain. Guard clauses provide an alternative approach by handling edge cases early:

#javascript

```
function processOrder(order) {
    // Guard clauses - handle invalid cases first
    if (!order) {
        console.log("Error: No order provided");
        return;
    }

    if (!order.items || order.items.length === 0) {
        console.log("Error: Order contains no items");
        return;
    }

    if (order.total <= 0) {
        console.log("Error: Invalid order total");
        return;
    }

    // Main logic - only executes if all conditions are
met
    console.log("Processing valid order");
    console.log(`Order total: $${order.total}`);
    console.log(`Items: ${order.items.length}`);
}
```

10.3 Comparison and Logical Operators in Conditions

Comparison Operators Deep Dive

Comparison operators form the foundation of conditional logic, allowing you to compare values and create boolean expressions.

Equality Operators

JavaScript provides two types of equality operators, each with distinct behavior:

#javascript

```
// Loose equality (==) - performs type coercion
console.log(5 == "5");      // true
console.log(true == 1);     // true
console.log(null == undefined); // true

// Strict equality (===) - no type coercion
console.log(5 === "5");     // false
console.log(true === 1);    // false
console.log(null === undefined); // false
```

Inequality Operators

#javascript

```
let a = 10;
let b = 20;

console.log(a != b);    // true (loose inequality)
console.log(a !== "10"); // true (strict inequality)
console.log(a < b);     // true
console.log(a > b);     // false
console.log(a <= 10);   // true
console.log(b >= 20);   // true
```

Relational Operators in Practice

#javascript

```
function validateAge(age) {
    if (age < 0) {
        return "Age cannot be negative";
    } else if (age < 13) {
        return "Child";
    } else if (age < 20) {
        return "Teenager";
    } else if (age < 65) {
        return "Adult";
    } else {
        return "Senior";
    }
}

console.log(validateAge(25)); // "Adult"
console.log(validateAge(-5)); // "Age cannot be negative"
```

Logical Operators for Complex Conditions

Logical AND (&&)

The AND operator returns `true` only when both operands are truthy:

#javascript

```
let hasAccount = true;
let isVerified = true;
let hasValidPayment = false;
```

```
if (hasAccount && isVerified && hasValidPayment) {
    console.log("User can make purchases");
} else {
    console.log("User cannot make purchases");
}

// Short-circuit evaluation
let user = { name: "John" };

if (user && user.name) {
    console.log(`Hello, ${user.name}`);
}
```

Logical OR (||)

The OR operator returns `true` when at least one operand is truthy:

#javascript

```
let isWeekend = false;
let isHoliday = true;

if (isWeekend || isHoliday) {
    console.log("No work today!");
}

// Default value assignment using OR
let username = "" || "Guest";
console.log(username); // "Guest"

let userPreference = null;
let theme = userPreference || "light";
```

```
console.log(theme); // "light"
```

Logical NOT (!)

The NOT operator inverts the boolean value of its operand:

#javascript

```
let isLoggedIn = false;

if (!isLoggedIn) {
    console.log("Please log in");
}

// Double negation to convert to boolean
let value = "hello";
let isValueTruthy = !!value;
console.log(isValueTruthy); // true
```

Advanced Logical Operator Patterns

Nullish Coalescing Operator (??)

#javascript

```
let userConfig = {
    theme: null,
    language: undefined,
    notifications: false
};

// Using nullish coalescing
let theme = userConfig.theme ?? "default";
```

```
let language = userConfig.language ?? "en";
let notifications = userConfig.notifications ?? true;

console.log(theme);         // "default"
console.log(language);      // "en"
console.log(notifications); // false (not null or
undefined)
```

Optional Chaining in Conditions
#javascript

```
let user = {
    profile: {
        settings: {
            darkMode: true
        }
    }
};

// Safe property access in conditions
if (user?.profile?.settings?.darkMode) {
    console.log("Dark mode is enabled");
}

// Checking array elements safely
let users = [
    { name: "Alice", permissions: ["read", "write"] },
    { name: "Bob" }
];

if (users[0]?.permissions?.includes("write")) {
```

```
    console.log("First user has write permission");
}
```

10.4 Switch Statements

Understanding Switch Statement Structure

The `switch` statement provides an efficient way to execute different code blocks based on the value of an expression. It's particularly useful when you need to compare a single variable against multiple possible values.

#javascript

```javascript
let dayOfWeek = 3;

switch (dayOfWeek) {
    case 1:
        console.log("Monday");
        break;
    case 2:
        console.log("Tuesday");
        break;
    case 3:
        console.log("Wednesday");
        break;
    case 4:
        console.log("Thursday");
        break;
    case 5:
        console.log("Friday");
        break;
    case 6:
```

```
        console.log("Saturday");
        break;
    case 7:
        console.log("Sunday");
        break;
    default:
        console.log("Invalid day");
}
```

The Importance of Break Statements

Without `break` statements, JavaScript will continue executing subsequent cases, a behavior known as "fall-through":

#javascript

```
let grade = "B";

switch (grade) {
    case "A":
        console.log("Excellent!");
        // No break - falls through
    case "B":
        console.log("Good job!");
        // No break - falls through
    case "C":
        console.log("You passed!");
        break;
    case "D":
        console.log("Need improvement");
        break;
    default:
```

```
        console.log("Invalid grade");
}
// Output: "Good job!" and "You passed!"
```

Intentional Fall-Through Patterns

Sometimes fall-through behavior is desirable for grouping related cases:

#javascript

```
function getSeasonFromMonth(month) {
    switch (month) {
        case 12:
        case 1:
        case 2:
            return "Winter";
        case 3:
        case 4:
        case 5:
            return "Spring";
        case 6:
        case 7:
        case 8:
            return "Summer";
        case 9:
        case 10:
        case 11:
            return "Fall";
        default:
            return "Invalid month";
    }
```

```
}

console.log(getSeasonFromMonth(7)); // "Summer"
```

Complex Switch Statement Examples

#javascript

```
function calculatePrice(product, quantity, customerType)
{
    let basePrice;

    // Determine base price
    switch (product) {
        case "laptop":
            basePrice = 999;
            break;
        case "mouse":
            basePrice = 29;
            break;
        case "keyboard":
            basePrice = 79;
            break;
        case "monitor":
            basePrice = 299;
            break;
        default:
            return "Product not found";
    }

    let totalPrice = basePrice * quantity;
```

```
    // Apply customer discount
    switch (customerType) {
        case "premium":
            totalPrice *= 0.8; // 20% discount
            break;
        case "regular":
            totalPrice *= 0.95; // 5% discount
            break;
        case "new":
            // No discount
            break;
        default:
            return "Invalid customer type";
    }

    return totalPrice;
}

console.log(calculatePrice("laptop", 2, "premium")); //
1598.4
```

Switch vs If-Else Performance Considerations

For multiple condition checks, `switch` statements can be more readable and potentially more performant:

#javascript

```
// Using if-else
function handleHttpStatus(status) {
    if (status === 200) {
```

```
        return "Success";
    } else if (status === 201) {
        return "Created";
    } else if (status === 400) {
        return "Bad Request";
    } else if (status === 401) {
        return "Unauthorized";
    } else if (status === 404) {
        return "Not Found";
    } else if (status === 500) {
        return "Server Error";
    } else {
        return "Unknown Status";
    }
}

// Using switch (more readable for this scenario)
function handleHttpStatusSwitch(status) {
    switch (status) {
        case 200:
            return "Success";
        case 201:
            return "Created";
        case 400:
            return "Bad Request";
        case 401:
            return "Unauthorized";
        case 404:
            return "Not Found";
        case 500:
            return "Server Error";
```

```
        default:
            return "Unknown Status";
    }
}
```

Modern Switch Alternatives

JavaScript doesn't have traditional switch expressions, but you can achieve similar functionality with objects or Map structures:

#javascript

```javascript
// Object-based switch alternative
const dayNames = {
    1: "Monday",
    2: "Tuesday",
    3: "Wednesday",
    4: "Thursday",
    5: "Friday",
    6: "Saturday",
    7: "Sunday"
};

function getDayName(dayNumber) {
    return dayNames[dayNumber] || "Invalid day";
}

// Map-based alternative
const httpStatusMessages = new Map([
    [200, "Success"],
    [201, "Created"],
    [400, "Bad Request"],
```

```
    [401, "Unauthorized"],
    [404, "Not Found"],
    [500, "Server Error"]
]);

function getStatusMessage(code) {
    return httpStatusMessages.get(code) || "Unknown
Status";
}
```

10.5 Best Practices for Conditional Logic

Writing Readable Conditions

Clarity should be your primary goal when writing conditional statements. Use descriptive variable names and avoid overly complex expressions:

#javascript

```
// Poor readability
if (u.a > 18 && u.s === "a" && u.p.includes("w")) {
    // Code here
}

// Better readability
let user = {
    age: 25,
    status: "active",
    permissions: ["read", "write"]
};

let isAdult = user.age > 18;
```

```
let isActiveUser = user.status === "active";
let hasWritePermission =
user.permissions.includes("write");

if (isAdult && isActiveUser && hasWritePermission) {
    // Grant write access
}
```

Extracting Complex Conditions

When conditions become complex, extract them into well-named functions:

#javascript

```
function isEligibleForLoan(applicant) {
    return applicant.age >= 18 &&
           applicant.income >= 30000 &&
           applicant.creditScore >= 650 &&
           !applicant.hasDefaultedLoans;
}

function isQualifiedForPremiumRate(applicant) {
    return applicant.creditScore >= 750 &&
           applicant.income >= 75000 &&
           applicant.employmentYears >= 2;
}

// Usage
if (isEligibleForLoan(applicant)) {
    if (isQualifiedForPremiumRate(applicant)) {
        console.log("Approved for premium rate loan");
    } else {
```

```
        console.log("Approved for standard rate loan");
    }
} else {
    console.log("Loan application rejected");
}
```

Avoiding Magic Numbers and Strings

Use constants to make your code more maintainable:

#javascript

```
// Constants for better maintainability
const MIN_VOTING_AGE = 18;
const MAX_RETIREMENT_AGE = 65;
const ADMIN_ROLE = "admin";
const EDITOR_ROLE = "editor";

const USER_STATUS = {
    ACTIVE: "active",
    INACTIVE: "inactive",
    SUSPENDED: "suspended"
};

function canAccessAdminPanel(user) {
    return user.age >= MIN_VOTING_AGE &&
           user.status === USER_STATUS.ACTIVE &&
           (user.role === ADMIN_ROLE || user.role ===
EDITOR_ROLE);
}
```

Error Handling in Conditional Logic

Always consider edge cases and potential errors:

#javascript

```
function processUserData(userData) {
    // Input validation
    if (!userData) {
        throw new Error("User data is required");
    }

    if (typeof userData !== "object") {
        throw new Error("User data must be an object");
    }

    // Safe property access
    const userName = userData.name?.trim();
    if (!userName) {
        throw new Error("Valid user name is required");
    }

    const userAge = userData.age;
    if (typeof userAge !== "number" || userAge < 0 ||
userAge > 150) {
        throw new Error("Valid user age is required");
    }

    // Process validated data
    if (userAge >= 18) {
        return `Adult user: ${userName}`;
    } else {
        return `Minor user: ${userName}`;
```

```
    }
}
```

Performance Optimization Strategies

Order conditions strategically to minimize unnecessary evaluations:

#javascript

```
// Optimize by putting most likely conditions first
function shouldShowDiscountBanner(user) {
    // Most users are not premium, check this first
    if (!user.isPremium) {
        return true;
    }

    // Premium users might still see banners under
certain conditions
    if (user.purchaseHistory.length < 5) {
        return true;
    }

    return false;
}

// Use short-circuit evaluation effectively
function isValidUser(user) {
    return user &&
           user.id &&
           user.email &&
           user.email.includes("@") &&
           user.isActive;
```

```
}
```

Testing Conditional Logic

Structure your conditions to make them easily testable:

#javascript

```
// Testable condition functions
function hasValidEmail(email) {
    return email &&
           typeof email === "string" &&
           email.includes("@") &&
           email.includes(".");
}

function isOfLegalAge(age, minimumAge = 18) {
    return typeof age === "number" &&
           age >= minimumAge;
}

function hasRequiredPermissions(user,
requiredPermissions) {
    if (!user || !user.permissions ||
!Array.isArray(user.permissions)) {
        return false;
    }

    return requiredPermissions.every(permission =>
        user.permissions.includes(permission)
    );
}
```

```
// Main logic becomes simpler and more testable
function canAccessFeature(user, feature) {
    const requiredPermissions =
getRequiredPermissions(feature);

    return hasValidEmail(user.email) &&
           isOfLegalAge(user.age) &&
           hasRequiredPermissions(user,
requiredPermissions);
}
```

Essential Tips

- Use strict equality (===) instead of loose equality (==) to avoid unexpected type coercion issues that can lead to bugs and unpredictable behavior in your applications.
- Extract complex conditions into well-named boolean variables or functions to improve code readability and make your intentions clear to other developers.
- Consider using guard clauses at the beginning of functions to handle edge cases early, reducing nesting levels and making the main logic flow more apparent.
- When working with object properties that might not exist, use optional chaining (?.) and nullish coalescing (??) operators to write safer, more robust conditional code.
- Always include a default case in switch statements to handle unexpected values gracefully, even if you believe all possible cases are covered.

Actionable Strategies

- Implement consistent error handling patterns throughout your conditional logic by checking for null, undefined, and invalid values before processing data.

- Create reusable condition functions that can be easily tested in isolation, making your codebase more maintainable and reducing duplication across your application.
- Use constants and enums instead of magic strings and numbers in your conditions to make your code more maintainable and reduce the risk of typos.
- Apply the principle of early returns and guard clauses to flatten nested if-else structures, making your code easier to read and understand.
- Leverage short-circuit evaluation in logical operators to optimize performance by placing the most likely-to-fail conditions first in AND operations.
- Organize related conditions using switch statements when comparing a single value against multiple possibilities, as this often provides better readability than long if-else chains.
- Document complex conditional logic with comments that explain the business rules and reasoning behind the conditions, not just what the code does but why it exists.

Chapter 11: Loops in JavaScript

11.1 Introduction to Loops: `for`, `while`, `do...while`

Understanding Loop Fundamentals

Loops represent one of the most powerful programming constructs in JavaScript, enabling developers to execute blocks of code repeatedly based on specific conditions. Rather than writing the same code multiple times, loops provide an elegant solution for automating repetitive tasks, processing collections of data, and creating dynamic applications.

JavaScript provides three primary loop types: `for`, `while`, and `do...while`. Each serves different purposes and excels in particular scenarios. Understanding when and how to use each loop type forms the foundation of efficient JavaScript programming.

The `for` Loop

The `for` loop stands as the most commonly used loop in JavaScript due to its clear structure and versatility. It consists of three main components: initialization, condition, and increment/decrement.

Syntax Structure

#javascript

```
for (initialization; condition; increment/decrement) {
    // Code to be executed
}
```

Basic `for` Loop Examples

#javascript

```
// Basic counting loop
for (let i = 0; i < 5; i++) {
```

```
    console.log("Iteration number: " + i);
}

// Output:
// Iteration number: 0
// Iteration number: 1
// Iteration number: 2
// Iteration number: 3
// Iteration number: 4
javascript
// Counting backwards
for (let i = 10; i >= 1; i--) {
    console.log("Countdown: " + i);
}

// Output:
// Countdown: 10
// Countdown: 9
// ... (continues until 1)
```

Advanced `for` Loop Patterns
#javascript

```
// Incrementing by different values
for (let i = 0; i <= 20; i += 2) {
    console.log("Even number: " + i);
}

// Multiple variables in initialization
for (let i = 0, j = 10; i < 5; i++, j--) {
    console.log(`i = ${i}, j = ${j}`);
```

```
}

// Using for loop with strings
const message = "JavaScript";
for (let i = 0; i < message.length; i++) {
    console.log(`Character at position ${i}:
${message[i]}`);
}
```

The `while` Loop

The `while` loop executes code as long as a specified condition remains true. It's particularly useful when the number of iterations is unknown beforehand.

Syntax Structure

#javascript

```
while (condition) {
    // Code to be executed
}
```

Basic `while` Loop Examples

#javascript

```
let count = 0;
while (count < 5) {
    console.log("Count is: " + count);
    count++;
}

// User input simulation
let userInput = "";
```

```
while (userInput !== "quit") {
    userInput = prompt("Enter a command (type 'quit' to
exit):");
    console.log("You entered: " + userInput);
}
```

Practical **while** Loop Applications

#javascript

```
// Finding the first power of 2 greater than 1000
let power = 1;
let exponent = 0;
while (power <= 1000) {
    power *= 2;
    exponent++;
}
console.log(`2^${exponent} = ${power} is the first power
of 2 greater than 1000`);

// Processing array elements until a condition is met
const numbers = [1, 3, 5, 7, 9, 12, 15, 18];
let index = 0;
while (index < numbers.length && numbers[index] % 2 !==
0) {
    console.log(`Odd number found: ${numbers[index]}`);
    index++;
}
```

The do...while Loop

The `do...while` loop executes the code block at least once before checking the condition. This guarantees that the loop body runs at minimum one time, regardless of the initial condition.

Syntax Structure

#javascript

```
do {
    // Code to be executed
} while (condition);
```

Basic **do...while** Loop Examples

#javascript

```
let attempts = 0;
do {
    attempts++;
    console.log(`Attempt number: ${attempts}`);
} while (attempts < 3);

// Menu system example
let choice;
do {
    choice = prompt("Choose an option:\n1. View
Profile\n2. Settings\n3. Exit");
    switch(choice) {
        case "1":
            console.log("Viewing profile...");
            break;
        case "2":
            console.log("Opening settings...");
            break;
        case "3":
```

```
            console.log("Exiting...");
            break;
        default:
            console.log("Invalid choice. Please try again.");
    }
} while (choice !== "3");
```

Loop Selection Guidelines

When to Use `for` Loops

- When you know the exact number of iterations needed
- When working with arrays or strings where you need index access
- When you need to increment/decrement by specific values
- For mathematical calculations requiring precise control

When to Use `while` Loops

- When the number of iterations depends on user input or external conditions
- When implementing search algorithms or data processing
- When the loop condition is complex and doesn't fit the `for` loop pattern
- For event-driven programming scenarios

When to Use `do...while` Loops

- When you need to ensure the loop body executes at least once
- For menu systems or user interaction scenarios
- When validating user input
- For game loops or animation frames

11.2 Breaking and Continuing Loops

Understanding Loop Control Statements

Loop control statements provide mechanisms to alter the normal flow of loop execution. JavaScript offers two primary control statements: `break` and `continue`. These statements allow developers to create more sophisticated loop behaviors and handle exceptional conditions within iterations.

The `break` Statement

The `break` statement immediately terminates the current loop and transfers control to the statement following the loop. It's particularly useful for exiting loops when specific conditions are met, preventing unnecessary iterations.

Basic `break` Usage
#javascript

```javascript
// Finding the first even number in an array
const numbers = [1, 3, 5, 8, 9, 11, 14];
for (let i = 0; i < numbers.length; i++) {
    if (numbers[i] % 2 === 0) {
        console.log(`First even number found:
${numbers[i]} at index ${i}`);
        break;
    }
}
```

Advanced `break` Applications
#javascript

```javascript
// Search with break condition
const products = [
    { name: "Laptop", price: 999 },
    { name: "Phone", price: 699 },
    { name: "Tablet", price: 399 },
```

```
    { name: "Watch", price: 299 }
];

for (let i = 0; i < products.length; i++) {
    if (products[i].price < 500) {
        console.log(`Affordable product found:
${products[i].name} - $${products[i].price}`);
        break;
    }
}

// User authentication with attempts limit
let attempts = 0;
const maxAttempts = 3;
while (attempts < maxAttempts) {
    const password = prompt("Enter password:");
    if (password === "secretpass") {
        console.log("Access granted!");
        break;
    } else {
        attempts++;
        console.log(`Incorrect password. ${maxAttempts -
attempts} attempts remaining.`);
    }
}

if (attempts === maxAttempts) {
    console.log("Account locked due to multiple failed
attempts.");
}
```

The `continue` Statement

The `continue` statement skips the remaining code in the current iteration and moves to the next iteration of the loop. Unlike `break`, it doesn't terminate the entire loop but only the current cycle.

Basic `continue` Usage

#javascript

```
// Printing only odd numbers
for (let i = 1; i <= 10; i++) {
    if (i % 2 === 0) {
        continue; // Skip even numbers
    }
    console.log(`Odd number: ${i}`);
}

// Output: 1, 3, 5, 7, 9
```

Advanced `continue` Applications

#javascript

```
// Processing valid data only
const userData = [
    { name: "John", age: 25, email: "john@email.com" },
    { name: "", age: 30, email: "invalid-email" },
    { name: "Jane", age: -5, email: "jane@email.com" },
    { name: "Bob", age: 35, email: "bob@email.com" }
];

for (let i = 0; i < userData.length; i++) {
    const user = userData[i];
```

```
    // Skip invalid records
    if (!user.name || user.age < 0 ||
!user.email.includes("@")) {
        console.log(`Skipping invalid user record at
index ${i}`);
        continue;
    }

    // Process valid user
    console.log(`Processing user: ${user.name}, Age:
${user.age}, Email: ${user.email}`);
}
```

Loop Labels and Advanced Control

JavaScript supports labeled statements, which allow for more precise control in nested loop scenarios.

Labeled Break and Continue

#javascript

```
// Breaking out of nested loops
outerLoop: for (let i = 0; i < 3; i++) {
    console.log(`Outer loop iteration: ${i}`);

    for (let j = 0; j < 3; j++) {
        if (i === 1 && j === 1) {
            console.log("Breaking out of both loops");
            break outerLoop;
        }
        console.log(`  Inner loop iteration: ${j}`);
    }
}
```

```javascript
// Continuing outer loop from inner loop
outerContinue: for (let i = 0; i < 3; i++) {
    console.log(`Outer loop iteration: ${i}`);

    for (let j = 0; j < 3; j++) {
        if (j === 1) {
            console.log("Continuing to next outer
iteration");
            continue outerContinue;
        }
        console.log(`  Inner loop iteration: ${j}`);
    }
}
```

Error Handling in Loops

Combining loop control statements with error handling creates robust loop structures that can handle unexpected conditions gracefully.

#javascript

```javascript
// Safe array processing with error handling
const mixedData = [1, "hello", null, 42, undefined,
"world", 0];

for (let i = 0; i < mixedData.length; i++) {
    try {
        const item = mixedData[i];

        // Skip null or undefined values
        if (item == null) {
```

```
            continue;
        }

        // Skip non-numeric strings
        if (typeof item === "string" &&
isNaN(Number(item))) {
            continue;
        }

        const result = Number(item) * 2;
        console.log(`${item} * 2 = ${result}`);

    } catch (error) {
        console.log(`Error processing item at index ${i}:
${error.message}`);
        continue;
    }
}
```

11.3 Looping Through Arrays

Array Iteration Fundamentals

Arrays represent ordered collections of data, and JavaScript provides multiple approaches for iterating through array elements. Understanding different iteration methods enables developers to choose the most appropriate technique for specific scenarios, optimizing both performance and code readability.

Traditional `for` Loop with Arrays

The traditional `for` loop offers complete control over array iteration, providing access to both index and value.

Basic Array Iteration
#javascript

```
const fruits = ["apple", "banana", "orange", "grape", "mango"];

// Standard forward iteration
for (let i = 0; i < fruits.length; i++) {
    console.log(`Index ${i}: ${fruits[i]}`);
}

// Reverse iteration
for (let i = fruits.length - 1; i >= 0; i--) {
    console.log(`Reverse index ${i}: ${fruits[i]}`);
}

// Iterating with step increment
for (let i = 0; i < fruits.length; i += 2) {
    console.log(`Every other fruit: ${fruits[i]}`);
}
```

Complex Array Processing
#javascript

```
const students = [
    { name: "Alice", grade: 85, subject: "Math" },
    { name: "Bob", grade: 78, subject: "Science" },
    { name: "Charlie", grade: 92, subject: "Math" },
    { name: "Diana", grade: 88, subject: "Science" }
];

// Finding high-performing students
```

```
for (let i = 0; i < students.length; i++) {
    if (students[i].grade >= 85) {
        console.log(`High performer: ${students[i].name}
scored ${students[i].grade} in ${students[i].subject}`);
    }
}

// Calculating subject averages
const subjects = {};
for (let i = 0; i < students.length; i++) {
    const student = students[i];
    if (!subjects[student.subject]) {
        subjects[student.subject] = { total: 0, count: 0
};
    }
    subjects[student.subject].total += student.grade;
    subjects[student.subject].count++;
}

for (const subject in subjects) {
    const average = subjects[subject].total /
subjects[subject].count;
    console.log(`${subject} average:
${average.toFixed(2)}`);
}
```

`for...of` Loop for Array Values

The `for...of` loop provides a clean syntax for iterating through array values without requiring index management.

Basic `for...of` Usage

#javascript

```javascript
const colors = ["red", "green", "blue", "yellow"];

for (const color of colors) {
    console.log(`Color: ${color}`);
}

// Working with array of objects
const books = [
    { title: "JavaScript Guide", pages: 450 },
    { title: "Web Development", pages: 320 },
    { title: "Node.js Handbook", pages: 280 }
];

for (const book of books) {
    console.log(`${book.title} has ${book.pages} pages`);
}
```

Advanced `for...of` Applications

#javascript

```javascript
// Processing arrays with destructuring
const coordinates = [[10, 20], [30, 40], [50, 60]];

for (const [x, y] of coordinates) {
    console.log(`Point: (${x}, ${y})`);
    console.log(`Distance from origin: ${Math.sqrt(x*x +
y*y).toFixed(2)}`);
}
```

```
// Working with strings as iterable
const message = "Hello World";
for (const char of message) {
    if (char !== ' ') {
        console.log(`Character: ${char}`);
    }
}
```

`for...in` Loop for Array Indices

The `for...in` loop iterates over enumerable properties of an object, including array indices. However, it's generally not recommended for arrays due to potential issues with inherited properties.

#javascript

```
const numbers = [10, 20, 30, 40, 50];

// Using for...in (not recommended for arrays)
for (const index in numbers) {
    console.log(`Index ${index}: ${numbers[index]}`);
}

// Better approach for arrays
for (let i = 0; i < numbers.length; i++) {
    console.log(`Index ${i}: ${numbers[i]}`);
}
```

Array Method Alternatives

JavaScript provides several array methods that can replace traditional loops for specific operations.

forEach() Method

#javascript

```
const prices = [19.99, 29.99, 39.99, 49.99];

// Using forEach for simple iteration
prices.forEach((price, index) => {
    console.log(`Item ${index + 1}:
$${price.toFixed(2)}`);
});

// Using forEach with array of objects
const employees = [
    { name: "John", department: "IT", salary: 50000 },
    { name: "Jane", department: "HR", salary: 45000 },
    { name: "Mike", department: "Finance", salary: 55000
}
];

employees.forEach((employee, index) => {
    const bonus = employee.salary * 0.1;
    console.log(`${employee.name}
(${employee.department}) receives $${bonus} bonus`);
});
```

map() Method for Transformation

#javascript

```
const temperatures = [0, 10, 20, 30, 40];
```

```
// Converting Celsius to Fahrenheit
const fahrenheit = temperatures.map(celsius => (celsius *
9/5) + 32);
console.log("Celsius:", temperatures);
console.log("Fahrenheit:", fahrenheit);

// Transforming array of objects
const products = [
    { name: "Laptop", price: 999 },
    { name: "Phone", price: 699 },
    { name: "Tablet", price: 399 }
];

const discountedProducts = products.map(product => ({
    ...product,
    discountedPrice: product.price * 0.8,
    savings: product.price * 0.2
}));

console.log("Discounted products:", discountedProducts);
```

`filter()` Method for Conditional Selection
#javascript

```
const ages = [16, 18, 21, 25, 17, 30, 15, 22];

// Filtering adults (18 and older)
const adults = ages.filter(age => age >= 18);
console.log("Adult ages:", adults);

// Complex filtering with objects
```

```
const inventory = [
    { item: "Laptop", quantity: 5, price: 999 },
    { item: "Phone", quantity: 0, price: 699 },
    { item: "Tablet", quantity: 3, price: 399 },
    { item: "Watch", quantity: 8, price: 299 }
];

const availableExpensiveItems = inventory.filter(product
=>
    product.quantity > 0 && product.price > 400
);

console.log("Available expensive items:",
availableExpensiveItems);
```

Performance Considerations for Array Loops

Different loop types have varying performance characteristics, especially with large datasets.

#javascript

```
// Performance comparison example
const largeArray = new Array(1000000).fill(0).map((_, i)
=> i);

// Traditional for loop (fastest)
console.time('Traditional for loop');
let sum1 = 0;
for (let i = 0; i < largeArray.length; i++) {
    sum1 += largeArray[i];
}
```

```
console.timeEnd('Traditional for loop');

// for...of loop
console.time('for...of loop');
let sum2 = 0;
for (const num of largeArray) {
    sum2 += num;
}
console.timeEnd('for...of loop');

// forEach method
console.time('forEach method');
let sum3 = 0;
largeArray.forEach(num => {
    sum3 += num;
});
console.timeEnd('forEach method');
```

11.4 Nested Loops

Understanding Nested Loop Structures

Nested loops consist of one loop placed inside another loop, creating a powerful mechanism for handling multi-dimensional data structures and complex algorithmic problems. The outer loop controls the major iterations, while the inner loop completes all its iterations for each single iteration of the outer loop.

Basic Nested Loop Patterns

Simple Nested Loops
#javascript

```javascript
// Basic nested loop structure
for (let i = 1; i <= 3; i++) {
    console.log(`Outer loop iteration: ${i}`);
    for (let j = 1; j <= 3; j++) {
        console.log(`  Inner loop iteration: ${j}`);
    }
}

// Output:
// Outer loop iteration: 1
//   Inner loop iteration: 1
//   Inner loop iteration: 2
//   Inner loop iteration: 3
// Outer loop iteration: 2
//   Inner loop iteration: 1
//   Inner loop iteration: 2
//   Inner loop iteration: 3
// Outer loop iteration: 3
//   Inner loop iteration: 1
//   Inner loop iteration: 2
//   Inner loop iteration: 3
```

Multiplication Table Generation
javascript

```javascript
// Creating a multiplication table
console.log("Multiplication Table (1-10):");
console.log("    ", end="");

// Print header row
```

```
for (let i = 1; i <= 10; i++) {
    process.stdout.write(`${i.toString().padStart(4)}`);
}
console.log();

// Print table rows
for (let i = 1; i <= 10; i++) {
    process.stdout.write(`${i.toString().padStart(4)}:
`);
    for (let j = 1; j <= 10; j++) {
        process.stdout.write(`${(i *
j).toString().padStart(4)}`);
    }
    console.log();
}
```

Working with Two-Dimensional Arrays

Nested loops excel at processing two-dimensional arrays (arrays of arrays), enabling matrix operations and grid-based calculations.

Matrix Processing

#javascript

```
// Creating and processing a 2D array
const matrix = [
    [1, 2, 3, 4],
    [5, 6, 7, 8],
    [9, 10, 11, 12]
];

// Displaying matrix elements
```

```
console.log("Matrix elements:");
for (let row = 0; row < matrix.length; row++) {
    for (let col = 0; col < matrix[row].length; col++) {
        process.stdout.write(`${matrix[row][col]}\t`);
    }
    console.log();
}

// Calculating row sums
console.log("\nRow sums:");
for (let row = 0; row < matrix.length; row++) {
    let rowSum = 0;
    for (let col = 0; col < matrix[row].length; col++) {
        rowSum += matrix[row][col];
    }
    console.log(`Row ${row + 1}: ${rowSum}`);
}

// Calculating column sums
console.log("\nColumn sums:");
for (let col = 0; col < matrix[0].length; col++) {
    let colSum = 0;
    for (let row = 0; row < matrix.length; row++) {
        colSum += matrix[row][col];
    }
    console.log(`Column ${col + 1}: ${colSum}`);
}
```

Game Board Creation

#javascript

```
// Creating a game board (tic-tac-toe example)
const boardSize = 3;
const gameBoard = [];

// Initialize empty board
for (let row = 0; row < boardSize; row++) {
    gameBoard[row] = [];
    for (let col = 0; col < boardSize; col++) {
        gameBoard[row][col] = '-';
    }
}

// Place some game pieces
gameBoard[0][0] = 'X';
gameBoard[1][1] = 'O';
gameBoard[2][2] = 'X';

// Display the board
console.log("Game Board:");
for (let row = 0; row < boardSize; row++) {
    let rowString = "";
    for (let col = 0; col < boardSize; col++) {
        rowString += gameBoard[row][col] + " ";
    }
    console.log(rowString);
}
```

Complex Nested Loop Applications

Pattern Generation
#javascript

```
// Creating various patterns with nested loops

// Right triangle pattern
console.log("Right Triangle Pattern:");
for (let i = 1; i <= 5; i++) {
    let pattern = "";
    for (let j = 1; j <= i; j++) {
        pattern += "* ";
    }
    console.log(pattern);
}

// Diamond pattern
console.log("\nDiamond Pattern:");
const size = 5;

// Upper half of diamond
for (let i = 1; i <= size; i++) {
    let spaces = "";
    let stars = "";

    // Add spaces
    for (let j = 1; j <= size - i; j++) {
        spaces += " ";
    }

    // Add stars
    for (let k = 1; k <= 2 * i - 1; k++) {
```

```
        stars += "*";
    }

    console.log(spaces + stars);
}

// Lower half of diamond
for (let i = size - 1; i >= 1; i--) {
    let spaces = "";
    let stars = "";

    for (let j = 1; j <= size - i; j++) {
        spaces += " ";
    }

    for (let k = 1; k <= 2 * i - 1; k++) {
        stars += "*";
    }

    console.log(spaces + stars);
}
```

Data Analysis with Nested Loops
#javascript

```
// Analyzing sales data across multiple regions and
months
const salesData = [
    { region: "North", months: [120, 150, 180, 200, 160,
140] },
    { region: "South", months: [100, 130, 160, 190, 170,
150] },
```

```
    { region: "East", months: [110, 140, 170, 180, 155,
135] },
    { region: "West", months: [90, 120, 150, 170, 160,
145] }
];

// Calculate regional totals and averages
console.log("Regional Sales Analysis:");
let grandTotal = 0;

for (let i = 0; i < salesData.length; i++) {
    const region = salesData[i];
    let regionalTotal = 0;

    for (let j = 0; j < region.months.length; j++) {
        regionalTotal += region.months[j];
    }

    const average = regionalTotal / region.months.length;
    grandTotal += regionalTotal;

    console.log(`${region.region}: Total =
${regionalTotal}, Average = ${average.toFixed(2)}`);
}

console.log(`Grand Total: ${grandTotal}`);
console.log(`Overall Average: ${(grandTotal /
(salesData.length *
salesData[0].months.length)).toFixed(2)}`);
```

Nested Loop Optimization Strategies

Breaking Out of Nested Loops
#javascript

```
// Finding the first occurrence in a 2D array
const searchMatrix = [
    [1, 3, 5, 7],
    [10, 11, 16, 20],
    [23, 30, 34, 60]
];

const target = 16;
let found = false;

outerLoop: for (let row = 0; row < searchMatrix.length; row++) {
    for (let col = 0; col < searchMatrix[row].length; col++) {
        if (searchMatrix[row][col] === target) {
            console.log(`Found ${target} at position [${row}, ${col}]`);
            found = true;
            break outerLoop;
        }
    }
}

if (!found) {
    console.log(`${target} not found in the matrix`);
}
```

Avoiding Unnecessary Iterations
#javascript

```javascript
// Optimized nested loop for finding duplicates
const numbers = [1, 2, 3, 4, 5, 2, 6, 7, 8, 1];
const duplicates = [];

for (let i = 0; i < numbers.length - 1; i++) {
    // Start inner loop from i+1 to avoid checking same
pairs twice
    for (let j = i + 1; j < numbers.length; j++) {
        if (numbers[i] === numbers[j]) {
            if (!duplicates.includes(numbers[i])) {
                duplicates.push(numbers[i]);
            }
        }
    }
}

console.log("Duplicate numbers found:", duplicates);
```

11.5 Loop Performance Tips

Understanding Loop Performance Fundamentals

Loop performance significantly impacts application efficiency, especially when dealing with large datasets or complex calculations. Optimizing loops involves understanding how JavaScript engines execute code, memory management principles, and algorithmic complexity considerations.

Variable Declaration and Scope Optimization

Efficient Variable Management
#javascript

```javascript
// Inefficient: Variable declared inside loop
console.time('Variable inside loop');
for (let i = 0; i < 1000000; i++) {
    let temp = i * 2; // Declared every iteration
    // Some processing
}
console.timeEnd('Variable inside loop');

// Efficient: Variable declared outside loop
console.time('Variable outside loop');
let temp;
for (let i = 0; i < 1000000; i++) {
    temp = i * 2; // Reused variable
    // Some processing
}
console.timeEnd('Variable outside loop');
```

Array Length Caching

#javascript

```javascript
const largeArray = new Array(1000000).fill(0);

// Inefficient: Array length calculated every iteration
console.time('Length not cached');
for (let i = 0; i < largeArray.length; i++) {
    // Processing
}
console.timeEnd('Length not cached');

// Efficient: Array length cached
```

```
console.time('Length cached');
const arrayLength = largeArray.length;
for (let i = 0; i < arrayLength; i++) {
    // Processing
}
console.timeEnd('Length cached');

// Alternative efficient approach
console.time('Reverse loop');
for (let i = largeArray.length - 1; i >= 0; i--) {
    // Processing
}
console.timeEnd('Reverse loop');
```

Loop Type Selection for Performance

Comparing Different Loop Types
#javascript

```
const testArray = new Array(1000000).fill(0).map((_, i)
=> i);

// Traditional for loop (usually fastest)
console.time('Traditional for loop');
let sum1 = 0;
for (let i = 0; i < testArray.length; i++) {
    sum1 += testArray[i];
}
console.timeEnd('Traditional for loop');

// While loop
```

```
console.time('While loop');
let sum2 = 0;
let j = 0;
while (j < testArray.length) {
    sum2 += testArray[j];
    j++;
}
console.timeEnd('While loop');

// for...of loop
console.time('for...of loop');
let sum3 = 0;
for (const num of testArray) {
    sum3 += num;
}
console.timeEnd('for...of loop');

// forEach method
console.time('forEach method');
let sum4 = 0;
testArray.forEach(num => sum4 += num);
console.timeEnd('forEach method');
```

Minimizing Function Calls in Loops

Avoiding Repeated Calculations
#javascript

```
// Inefficient: Repeated calculations
const coordinates = [[1, 2], [3, 4], [5, 6], [7, 8]];
```

```
console.time('Repeated calculations');
for (let i = 0; i < coordinates.length; i++) {
    const distance =
Math.sqrt(Math.pow(coordinates[i][0], 2) +
Math.pow(coordinates[i][1], 2));
    console.log(`Distance: ${distance}`);
}
console.timeEnd('Repeated calculations');

// Efficient: Minimize function calls
console.time('Optimized calculations');
for (let i = 0; i < coordinates.length; i++) {
    const x = coordinates[i][0];
    const y = coordinates[i][1];
    const distance = Math.sqrt(x * x + y * y); // Avoid
Math.pow for simple squares
    console.log(`Distance: ${distance}`);
}
console.timeEnd('Optimized calculations');
```

Hoisting Expensive Operations
#javascript

```
// Inefficient: Expensive operations inside loop
const data = ['apple', 'banana', 'cherry', 'date'];
const pattern = /^[a-c]/i;

console.time('Regex in loop');
for (let i = 0; i < data.length; i++) {
    if (/^[a-c]/i.test(data[i])) { // Regex created every
iteration
        console.log(`Matches: ${data[i]}`);
```

```
    }
}
console.timeEnd('Regex in loop');

// Efficient: Regex created once
console.time('Regex outside loop');
const regexPattern = /^[a-c]/i;
for (let i = 0; i < data.length; i++) {
    if (regexPattern.test(data[i])) {
        console.log(`Matches: ${data[i]}`);
    }
}
console.timeEnd('Regex outside loop');
```

Memory Management and Loop Optimization

Avoiding Memory Leaks in Loops

#javascript

```
// Potential memory leak with closures
function createHandlers() {
    const handlers = [];
    const largeData = new Array(1000000).fill('data');

    // Inefficient: Each closure retains reference to
largeData
    for (let i = 0; i < 10; i++) {
        handlers.push(function() {
            console.log(`Handler ${i} with data length:
${largeData.length}`);
        });
```

```
    }

    return handlers;
}

// Efficient: Break closure chain when possible
function createOptimizedHandlers() {
    const handlers = [];
    const dataLength = new Array(1000000).length; // Only
store what's needed

    for (let i = 0; i < 10; i++) {
        handlers.push(function() {
            console.log(`Handler ${i} with data length:
${dataLength}`);
        });
    }

    return handlers;
}
```

Efficient Array Operations in Loops
#javascript

```
// Inefficient: Growing arrays inside loops
console.time('Array push in loop');
const result1 = [];
for (let i = 0; i < 100000; i++) {
    result1.push(i * 2);
}
console.timeEnd('Array push in loop');
```

```
// Efficient: Pre-allocate array size
console.time('Pre-allocated array');
const result2 = new Array(100000);
for (let i = 0; i < 100000; i++) {
    result2[i] = i * 2;
}
console.timeEnd('Pre-allocated array');

// Most efficient for transformations: Use map
console.time('Array map');
const sourceArray = new Array(100000).fill(0).map((_, i)
=> i);
const result3 = sourceArray.map(i => i * 2);
console.timeEnd('Array map');
```

Advanced Performance Techniques

Loop Unrolling for Small Fixed Iterations
#javascript

```
// Standard loop
function processArrayStandard(arr) {
    let sum = 0;
    for (let i = 0; i < arr.length; i++) {
        sum += arr[i] * arr[i];
    }
    return sum;
}

// Unrolled loop (for small, known sizes)
```

```
function processArrayUnrolled(arr) {
    let sum = 0;
    let i = 0;

    // Process 4 elements at a time
    for (; i < arr.length - 3; i += 4) {
        sum += arr[i] * arr[i] +
               arr[i + 1] * arr[i + 1] +
               arr[i + 2] * arr[i + 2] +
               arr[i + 3] * arr[i + 3];
    }

    // Handle remaining elements
    for (; i < arr.length; i++) {
        sum += arr[i] * arr[i];
    }

    return sum;
}

// Performance comparison
const testData = new Array(1000000).fill(0).map(() =>
Math.random() * 100);

console.time('Standard loop');
const result1 = processArrayStandard(testData);
console.timeEnd('Standard loop');

console.time('Unrolled loop');
const result2 = processArrayUnrolled(testData);
console.timeEnd('Unrolled loop');
```

Conditional Logic Optimization

#javascript

```
// Inefficient: Complex conditions checked every
iteration
const items = new Array(100000).fill(0).map(() => ({
    type: Math.random() > 0.5 ? 'premium' : 'standard',
    value: Math.random() * 100,
    active: Math.random() > 0.3
}));

console.time('Complex conditions in loop');
let expensiveItems = 0;
for (let i = 0; i < items.length; i++) {
    if (items[i].active && items[i].type === 'premium' &&
items[i].value > 50) {
        expensiveItems++;
    }
}
console.timeEnd('Complex conditions in loop');

// Efficient: Separate loops for different conditions
console.time('Optimized conditions');
let expensiveItemsOpt = 0;
for (let i = 0; i < items.length; i++) {
    const item = items[i];
    if (!item.active) continue;
    if (item.type !== 'premium') continue;
    if (item.value <= 50) continue;
    expensiveItemsOpt++;
```

```
}
console.timeEnd('Optimized conditions');
```

Debugging and Profiling Loop Performance

Performance Measurement Utilities

#javascript

```
// Custom performance measurement function
function measureLoopPerformance(loopFunction, iterations = 1000000, description = 'Loop') {
    const startTime = performance.now();
    const startMemory = performance.memory ? performance.memory.usedJSHeapSize : 0;

    loopFunction(iterations);

    const endTime = performance.now();
    const endMemory = performance.memory ? performance.memory.usedJSHeapSize : 0;

    console.log(`${description}:`);
    console.log(`  Time: ${(endTime - startTime).toFixed(2)}ms`);
    if (performance.memory) {
        console.log(`  Memory change: ${((endMemory - startMemory) / 1024 / 1024).toFixed(2)}MB`);
    }
    console.log('---');
}

// Example usage
```

```
measureLoopPerformance((n) => {
    let sum = 0;
    for (let i = 0; i < n; i++) {
        sum += i;
    }
}, 1000000, 'Simple Addition Loop');

measureLoopPerformance((n) => {
    const arr = [];
    for (let i = 0; i < n; i++) {
        arr.push(i);
    }
}, 100000, 'Array Building Loop');
```

Memory-Efficient Large Dataset Processing
#javascript

```
// Processing large datasets in chunks
function processLargeDataset(dataset, chunkSize = 1000) {
    console.time('Chunked processing');

    for (let i = 0; i < dataset.length; i += chunkSize) {
        const chunk = dataset.slice(i, i + chunkSize);

        // Process chunk
        const processedChunk = chunk.map(item => ({
            ...item,
            processed: true,
            timestamp: Date.now()
        }));
```

```
        // Optional: Clear chunk from memory if not
needed
        chunk.length = 0;

        // Yield control occasionally to prevent blocking
        if (i % (chunkSize * 10) === 0) {
            // In real applications, you might use
setTimeout or requestIdleCallback
            console.log(`Processed ${i + chunkSize}
items...`);
        }
    }

    console.timeEnd('Chunked processing');
}

// Example with large dataset
const largeDataset = new Array(50000).fill(0).map((_, i)
=> ({
    id: i,
    value: Math.random() * 1000,
    category: `category_${i % 10}`
}));

processLargeDataset(largeDataset);
```

Browser-Specific Optimizations

Optimizing for Different JavaScript Engines
#javascript

```
// V8 (Chrome/Node.js) optimizations
```

```
function v8OptimizedLoop(arr) {
    // V8 optimizes for consistent types and predictable
patterns
    const length = arr.length;  // Cache length
    let result = 0;             // Initialize with
correct type

    for (let i = 0; i < length; i++) {
        result += arr[i];       // Consistent operation
    }

    return result;
}

// General cross-browser optimization
function crossBrowserOptimizedLoop(arr) {
    // Use traditional for loop for maximum compatibility
    const len = arr.length;
    let sum = 0;

    // Minimize array access
    for (let i = 0; i < len; i++) {
        const current = arr[i];
        if (typeof current === 'number') {
            sum += current;
        }
    }

    return sum;
}
```

Essential Tips

- **Cache frequently accessed values outside loops** - Store array lengths, object properties, and expensive calculations before entering loop iterations to avoid repeated computations.
- **Choose the right loop type for your use case** - Traditional for loops offer the best performance for index-based operations, while for...of provides cleaner syntax with acceptable performance for value-based iterations.
- **Minimize function calls within loops** - Move object method calls, regular expression creation, and complex calculations outside the loop body whenever possible to reduce overhead.
- **Pre-allocate arrays when final size is known** - Creating arrays with predetermined size using `new Array(size)` performs better than dynamically growing arrays with push operations.
- **Use early termination strategies** - Implement break and continue statements strategically to avoid unnecessary iterations and computations when conditions are met.

Actionable Strategies

- **Implement loop unrolling for performance-critical small loops** - Process multiple elements per iteration when dealing with fixed-size datasets to reduce loop overhead and improve cache performance.
- **Profile your loops with browser developer tools** - Use performance tabs and timing functions to identify bottlenecks and measure the impact of optimizations on real-world data.
- **Separate filtering logic from processing logic** - Use multiple simple loops instead of one complex loop with multiple conditions to improve readability and potentially enhance performance.
- **Consider using array methods for functional operations** - Replace traditional loops with map, filter, and reduce when performing transformations to leverage browser optimizations for these native functions.
- **Implement pagination or chunking for large datasets** - Break large data processing into smaller batches to prevent UI blocking and reduce memory pressure in browser environments.

- **Optimize nested loops by restructuring algorithms** - Look for opportunities to reduce time complexity by changing the approach, such as using hash maps for lookups instead of nested searches.
- **Use consistent data types within loops** - Maintain type consistency for variables and array elements to help JavaScript engines optimize execution paths and improve performance.

Chapter 12: Functions

Functions are the fundamental building blocks of JavaScript programming. They allow you to group code into reusable units, making your programs more organized, maintainable, and efficient. Understanding functions is crucial for writing clean, professional JavaScript code that follows best practices and modern development patterns.

12.1 Defining and Calling Functions

Function Declaration Syntax

The most straightforward way to create a function in JavaScript is through function declaration. This method uses the `function` keyword followed by the function name, parentheses for parameters, and curly braces containing the function body.

#javascript

```
function greetUser() {
    console.log("Hello, welcome to our application!");
}

// Calling the function
greetUser();
```

Function Naming Conventions

Function names should be descriptive and follow camelCase convention. They typically start with a verb since functions perform actions.

#javascript

```
function calculateTotalPrice(price, tax) {
    return price * (1 + tax);
```

```
}

function validateEmailAddress(email) {
    const emailPattern = /^[^\s@]+@[^\s@]+\.[^\s@]+$/;
    return emailPattern.test(email);
}

function displayUserProfile(user) {
    console.log(`Name: ${user.name}`);
    console.log(`Age: ${user.age}`);
    console.log(`Email: ${user.email}`);
}
```

Function Hoisting

JavaScript hoists function declarations, meaning you can call a function before it's defined in your code. This behavior is unique to function declarations and doesn't apply to other function types.

#javascript

```
// This works due to hoisting
sayHello();

function sayHello() {
    console.log("Hello from a hoisted function!");
}

// Another example
console.log(addNumbers(5, 3)); // Output: 8

function addNumbers(a, b) {
```

```
    return a + b;
}
```

Best Practices for Function Definition

When defining functions, consider readability and maintainability. Keep functions focused on a single responsibility and use clear, descriptive names.

#javascript

```
// Good: Clear purpose and descriptive name
function convertCelsiusToFahrenheit(celsius) {
    return (celsius * 9/5) + 32;
}

// Good: Single responsibility
function formatCurrency(amount, currency = 'USD') {
    return new Intl.NumberFormat('en-US', {
        style: 'currency',
        currency: currency
    }).format(amount);
}

// Good: Input validation
function divideNumbers(dividend, divisor) {
    if (divisor === 0) {
        throw new Error("Division by zero is not
allowed");
    }
    return dividend / divisor;
}
```

12.2 Parameters and Return Values

Understanding Parameters

Parameters are variables that act as placeholders for values passed to functions. They allow functions to work with different data each time they're called.

#javascript

```
function createWelcomeMessage(name, age, city) {
    return `Welcome ${name}! You are ${age} years old and live in ${city}.`;
}

console.log(createWelcomeMessage("Alice", 25, "New York"));
console.log(createWelcomeMessage("Bob", 30, "London"));
```

Default Parameters

ES6 introduced default parameters, allowing you to specify default values for parameters when no argument is provided.

#javascript

```
function calculateDiscount(price, discountRate = 0.1) {
    return price * (1 - discountRate);
}

console.log(calculateDiscount(100)); // Uses default 10% discount
console.log(calculateDiscount(100, 0.2)); // Uses 20% discount
```

```
function createUserAccount(username, role = 'user',
isActive = true) {
    return {
        username: username,
        role: role,
        isActive: isActive,
        createdAt: new Date()
    };
}
```

Rest Parameters

Rest parameters allow functions to accept an indefinite number of arguments as an array.

#javascript

```
function calculateSum(...numbers) {
    return numbers.reduce((total, num) => total + num,
0);
}

console.log(calculateSum(1, 2, 3)); // 6
console.log(calculateSum(1, 2, 3, 4, 5)); // 15

function logMessages(level, ...messages) {
    const timestamp = new Date().toISOString();
    messages.forEach(message => {
        console.log(`[${timestamp}] ${level}:
${message}`);
    });
}
```

```
logMessages('INFO', 'User logged in', 'Session started',
'Dashboard loaded');
```

Return Values and Early Returns

Functions can return values using the `return` statement. Once a return statement is executed, the function exits immediately.

#javascript

```javascript
function processAge(age) {
    // Early return for invalid input
    if (age < 0 || age > 150) {
        return "Invalid age provided";
    }

    // Early return for specific conditions
    if (age < 18) {
        return "Minor";
    }

    if (age >= 65) {
        return "Senior";
    }

    return "Adult";
}

function findLargestNumber(numbers) {
    if (!Array.isArray(numbers) || numbers.length === 0)
{
```

```
        return null;
    }

    return Math.max(...numbers);
}
```

Multiple Return Values Using Objects

JavaScript functions can return only one value, but you can return objects or arrays to effectively return multiple values.

#javascript

```
function analyzeText(text) {
    const words = text.split(' ');
    const characters = text.length;
    const wordsCount = words.length;
    const averageWordLength = words.reduce((sum, word) =>
sum + word.length, 0) / wordsCount;

    return {
        totalCharacters: characters,
        totalWords: wordsCount,
        averageWordLength: Math.round(averageWordLength *
100) / 100,
        longestWord: words.reduce((longest, current) =>
            current.length > longest.length ? current :
longest, '')
    };
}

const analysis = analyzeText("JavaScript functions are
powerful and flexible");
```

```
console.log(analysis);
```

12.3 Function Expressions and Arrow Functions

Function Expressions

Function expressions create functions as part of a larger expression. Unlike function declarations, they are not hoisted.

#javascript

```
// Function expression assigned to a variable
const multiply = function(a, b) {
    return a * b;
};

// Anonymous function expression used as callback
setTimeout(function() {
    console.log("This runs after 2 seconds");
}, 2000);

// Named function expression (useful for debugging)
const factorial = function calculateFactorial(n) {
    if (n <= 1) return 1;
    return n * calculateFactorial(n - 1);
};
```

Arrow Functions Syntax

Arrow functions provide a concise syntax for writing functions and have different behavior regarding the `this` keyword.

#javascript

```
// Basic arrow function syntax
const add = (a, b) => a + b;

// Arrow function with single parameter (parentheses
optional)
const square = x => x * x;

// Arrow function with no parameters
const getCurrentTime = () => new
Date().toLocaleTimeString();

// Arrow function with multiple statements
const processOrder = (order) => {
    const tax = order.amount * 0.08;
    const total = order.amount + tax;

    return {
        orderId: order.id,
        subtotal: order.amount,
        tax: tax,
        total: total
    };
};
```

When to Use Arrow Functions vs Regular Functions

Arrow functions are ideal for short, simple functions and callbacks, while regular functions are better for methods and when you need `this` binding.

#javascript

```
// Good use of arrow functions - array methods
const numbers = [1, 2, 3, 4, 5];
const doubled = numbers.map(n => n * 2);
const evens = numbers.filter(n => n % 2 === 0);
const sum = numbers.reduce((acc, n) => acc + n, 0);

// Good use of regular functions - object methods
const calculator = {
    result: 0,
    add: function(value) {
        this.result += value;
        return this;
    },
    multiply: function(value) {
        this.result *= value;
        return this;
    },
    getResult: function() {
        return this.result;
    }
};

// Chaining methods
const finalResult =
calculator.add(5).multiply(3).getResult();
```

Immediately Invoked Function Expressions (IIFE)

IIFEs are functions that execute immediately after being defined, useful for creating isolated scopes.

#javascript

```javascript
// Basic IIFE
(function() {
    const privateVariable = "This is private";
    console.log("IIFE executed!");
})();

// IIFE with parameters
(function(name, version) {
    console.log(`Initializing ${name} version
${version}`);
})("MyApp", "1.0.0");

// IIFE with return value
const moduleResult = (function() {
    let counter = 0;

    return {
        increment: () => ++counter,
        decrement: () => --counter,
        getValue: () => counter
    };
})();

console.log(moduleResult.increment()); // 1
console.log(moduleResult.getValue()); // 1
```

12.4 Scope and Closures

Understanding Scope

Scope determines where variables can be accessed in your code. JavaScript has function scope, block scope, and global scope.

#javascript

```
// Global scope
let globalVariable = "I'm accessible everywhere";

function demonstrateScope() {
    // Function scope
    let functionVariable = "I'm only accessible within
this function";

    if (true) {
        // Block scope
        let blockVariable = "I'm only accessible within
this block";
        const anotherBlockVariable = "Me too!";

        console.log(globalVariable); // Accessible
        console.log(functionVariable); // Accessible
        console.log(blockVariable); // Accessible
    }

    // console.log(blockVariable); // Error: not
accessible
    console.log(functionVariable); // Accessible
}

// Scope chain example
function outerFunction(x) {
    function innerFunction(y) {
        function deepInnerFunction(z) {
```

```
            return x + y + z; // Can access all outer
variables
        }
        return deepInnerFunction;
    }
    return innerFunction;
}

const result = outerFunction(1)(2)(3); // 6
```

Variable Hoisting and Temporal Dead Zone

Understanding how JavaScript handles variable declarations is crucial for avoiding common pitfalls.

#javascript

```
// Var hoisting example
console.log(hoistedVar); // undefined (not an error)
var hoistedVar = "I'm hoisted";

// Let and const temporal dead zone
function demonstrateTDZ() {
    console.log(typeof notDeclaredYet); // "undefined"

    // console.log(letVariable); // ReferenceError
    // console.log(constVariable); // ReferenceError

    let letVariable = "Let variable";
    const constVariable = "Const variable";

    console.log(letVariable);
```

```
    console.log(constVariable);
}
```

Introduction to Closures

Closures occur when inner functions have access to variables from their outer function even after the outer function has returned.

#javascript

```
function createCounter() {
    let count = 0;

    return function() {
        count++;
        return count;
    };
}

const counter1 = createCounter();
const counter2 = createCounter();

console.log(counter1()); // 1
console.log(counter1()); // 2
console.log(counter2()); // 1 (independent counter)
```

Practical Closure Examples

Closures are powerful for creating private variables, factory functions, and maintaining state.

#javascript

```
// Private variables with closures
function createBankAccount(initialBalance) {
    let balance = initialBalance;
    let transactionHistory = [];

    return {
        deposit: function(amount) {
            if (amount > 0) {
                balance += amount;
                transactionHistory.push({ type:
'deposit', amount, date: new Date() });
                return balance;
            }
            throw new Error("Deposit amount must be
positive");
        },

        withdraw: function(amount) {
            if (amount > 0 && amount <= balance) {
                balance -= amount;
                transactionHistory.push({ type:
'withdrawal', amount, date: new Date() });
                return balance;
            }
            throw new Error("Invalid withdrawal amount");
        },

        getBalance: function() {
            return balance;
        },
```

```
        getHistory: function() {
            return [...transactionHistory]; // Return
copy to prevent mutation
        }
    };
}

const account = createBankAccount(1000);
account.deposit(500);
account.withdraw(200);
console.log(account.getBalance()); // 1300

// Factory function with closures
function createValidator(rules) {
    return function(value) {
        const errors = [];

        rules.forEach(rule => {
            if (!rule.test(value)) {
                errors.push(rule.message);
            }
        });

        return {
            isValid: errors.length === 0,
            errors: errors
        };
    };
}

const emailValidator = createValidator([
```

```
    {
        test: value => value.length > 0,
        message: "Email is required"
    },
    {
        test: value => value.includes('@'),
        message: "Email must contain @ symbol"
    },
    {
        test: value =>
/^[^\s@]+@[^\s@]+\.[^\s@]+$/.test(value),
        message: "Email format is invalid"
    }
]);

console.log(emailValidator("user@example.com"));
```

12.5 Callback Functions

Understanding Callbacks

Callback functions are functions passed as arguments to other functions, allowing for asynchronous behavior and flexible code design.

#javascript

```
function processUserData(userData, successCallback,
errorCallback) {
    // Simulate processing time
    setTimeout(() => {
        if (userData && userData.name) {
            successCallback(`User ${userData.name}
processed successfully`);
```

```
        } else {
            errorCallback("Invalid user data provided");
        }
    }, 1000);
}

// Using the callback function
processUserData(
    { name: "Alice", age: 30 },
    (message) => console.log("Success:", message),
    (error) => console.log("Error:", error)
);
```

Higher-Order Functions

Functions that take other functions as parameters or return functions are called higher-order functions.

#javascript

```
function createMultiplier(factor) {
    return function(number) {
        return number * factor;
    };
}

const double = createMultiplier(2);
const triple = createMultiplier(3);

function applyOperation(numbers, operation) {
    return numbers.map(operation);
}
```

```javascript
const numbers = [1, 2, 3, 4, 5];
console.log(applyOperation(numbers, double)); // [2, 4,
6, 8, 10]
console.log(applyOperation(numbers, triple)); // [3, 6,
9, 12, 15]

// Function composition
function compose(f, g) {
    return function(x) {
        return f(g(x));
    };
}

const addOne = x => x + 1;
const multiplyByTwo = x => x * 2;

const addOneThenDouble = compose(multiplyByTwo, addOne);
console.log(addOneThenDouble(3)); // 8 (3 + 1 = 4, 4 * 2
= 8)
```

Array Methods as Callback Examples

JavaScript's built-in array methods extensively use callbacks, making them excellent examples of callback usage.

#javascript

```javascript
const products = [
    { name: "Laptop", price: 999, category: "Electronics"
},
    { name: "Book", price: 15, category: "Education" },
```

```
    { name: "Headphones", price: 199, category:
"Electronics" },
    { name: "Coffee Mug", price: 12, category: "Home" }
];

// Filter with callback
const expensiveProducts = products.filter(product =>
product.price > 50);

// Map with callback
const productNames = products.map(product =>
product.name.toUpperCase());

// Reduce with callback
const totalValue = products.reduce((sum, product) => sum
+ product.price, 0);

// Find with callback
const electronicProduct = products.find(product =>
product.category === "Electronics");

// Sort with callback
const sortedByPrice = [...products].sort((a, b) =>
a.price - b.price);

console.log("Expensive products:", expensiveProducts);
console.log("Product names:", productNames);
console.log("Total value:", totalValue);
```

Event Handling with Callbacks

Callbacks are fundamental in event-driven programming, especially in web development.

#javascript

```
// Simulating event handling (in browser environment)
function setupEventHandlers() {
    // Button click handler
    function handleButtonClick(event) {
        console.log("Button clicked!",
event.target.textContent);
    }

    // Form submission handler
    function handleFormSubmit(event) {
        event.preventDefault();
        const formData = new FormData(event.target);

        // Process form data
        for (let [key, value] of formData.entries()) {
            console.log(`${key}: ${value}`);
        }
    }

    // Custom event system
    function createEventEmitter() {
        const events = {};

        return {
            on: function(eventName, callback) {
                if (!events[eventName]) {
                    events[eventName] = [];
```

```
            }
            events[eventName].push(callback);
        },

        emit: function(eventName, data) {
            if (events[eventName]) {
                events[eventName].forEach(callback =>
callback(data));
            }
        },

        off: function(eventName, callback) {
            if (events[eventName]) {
                events[eventName] =
events[eventName].filter(cb => cb !== callback);
            }
        }
    };
}

const emitter = createEventEmitter();

// Register event listeners
emitter.on('userLogin', (user) => console.log(`User
${user.name} logged in`));
emitter.on('userLogin', (user) =>
console.log(`Welcome ${user.name}!`));

// Emit event
emitter.emit('userLogin', { name: 'Alice', id: 123
});
}
```

Asynchronous Callbacks

Callbacks are essential for handling asynchronous operations, though modern JavaScript often uses Promises and async/await.

#javascript

```
// File reading simulation
function readFile(filename, callback) {
    console.log(`Starting to read ${filename}...`);

    // Simulate async file reading
    setTimeout(() => {
        if (filename.endsWith('.txt')) {
            callback(null, `Content of ${filename}`);
        } else {
            callback(new Error('File format not
supported'));
        }
    }, Math.random() * 2000);
}

// Using the async callback
readFile('document.txt', (error, content) => {
    if (error) {
        console.error('Error reading file:',
error.message);
    } else {
        console.log('File content:', content);
    }
});
```

```
// Multiple async operations with callbacks
function fetchUserData(userId, callback) {
    setTimeout(() => {
        callback(null, { id: userId, name:
`User${userId}`, email: `user${userId}@example.com` });
    }, 500);
}

function fetchUserPosts(userId, callback) {
    setTimeout(() => {
        callback(null, [
            { id: 1, title: 'First Post', content: 'Hello
World!' },
            { id: 2, title: 'Second Post', content:
'Learning JavaScript!' }
        ]);
    }, 800);
}

// Nested callbacks (callback hell example)
fetchUserData(123, (error, user) => {
    if (error) {
        console.error('Error fetching user:', error);
        return;
    }

    console.log('User:', user);

    fetchUserPosts(user.id, (error, posts) => {
        if (error) {
```

```
            console.error('Error fetching posts:',
error);
            return;
        }

        console.log('Posts:', posts);
    });
});
```

Essential Tips

- Always use descriptive function names that clearly indicate what the function does - `calculateTotalPrice()` is better than `calc()` or `doStuff()`
- Keep functions small and focused on a single responsibility; if a function is doing multiple things, consider breaking it into smaller functions
- Use default parameters to make your functions more flexible and reduce the need for conditional checks inside the function body
- Take advantage of arrow functions for short, simple operations and callbacks, but use regular functions when you need `this` binding or hoisting behavior
- Always validate input parameters at the beginning of your functions to prevent errors and make your code more robust and predictable

Actionable Strategies

- Practice writing pure functions that don't modify external state and always return the same output for the same input - this makes testing and debugging much easier
- Master the array methods (map, filter, reduce, forEach) as they use callbacks extensively and are fundamental to functional programming patterns in JavaScript
- Create reusable utility functions for common operations in your projects, such as formatting dates, validating emails, or converting data formats

- Use closures to create private variables and maintain state in your applications without polluting the global scope
- Implement proper error handling in your functions using try-catch blocks and meaningful error messages to help with debugging
- Learn to recognize when callback hell is forming in your code and research Promises and async/await as modern alternatives for handling asynchronous operations
- Build a personal library of commonly used functions that you can reuse across different projects, focusing on input validation, data transformation, and utility operations

Chapter 13: Events and DOM Interaction

The Document Object Model (DOM) serves as the bridge between JavaScript and HTML, enabling dynamic web pages that respond to user interactions. This chapter covers the fundamental concepts of DOM manipulation and event handling, providing you with the skills to create interactive web applications.

13.1 Introduction to the DOM

Understanding the Document Object Model

The DOM represents your HTML document as a tree-like structure where each HTML element becomes a node that JavaScript can access and modify. When a web page loads, the browser creates a DOM representation of the page, transforming static HTML into a dynamic, programmable interface.

The DOM tree consists of different node types:

- **Element nodes**: HTML tags like `<div>`, `<p>`, `<button>`
- **Text nodes**: The actual text content within elements
- **Attribute nodes**: Element attributes like `class`, `id`, `src`
- **Document node**: The root node representing the entire document

The Global Document Object

JavaScript provides access to the DOM through the global `document` object. This object contains methods and properties that allow you to interact with every aspect of your HTML page.

#javascript

```
// Access the document object
console.log(document); // Displays the entire HTML
document
console.log(document.title); // Gets the page title
console.log(document.URL); // Gets the current URL
```

```
// Modify document properties
document.title = "New Page Title";
```

DOM Tree Navigation

Understanding how to navigate the DOM tree is crucial for effective manipulation. Each element has properties that reference its relationships with other elements:

#javascript

```
// Parent-child relationships
const parentElement =
document.getElementById('container');
console.log(parentElement.children); // All child
elements
console.log(parentElement.firstElementChild); // First
child element
console.log(parentElement.lastElementChild); // Last
child element

// Sibling relationships
const element = document.getElementById('item');
console.log(element.nextElementSibling); // Next sibling
element
console.log(element.previousElementSibling); // Previous
sibling element
```

Node Properties and Methods

Every DOM node has properties that describe its characteristics and methods to manipulate its content:

#javascript

```
const element = document.getElementById('myElement');

// Content manipulation
element.innerHTML = '<strong>Bold text</strong>'; // Sets
HTML content
element.textContent = 'Plain text only'; // Sets text
content only
element.innerText = 'Visible text only'; // Sets visible
text

// Attribute manipulation
element.setAttribute('class', 'highlight');
element.getAttribute('id'); // Returns the id attribute
element.removeAttribute('data-info');

// Style manipulation
element.style.color = 'blue';
element.style.backgroundColor = 'yellow';
element.style.fontSize = '18px';
```

13.2 Selecting Elements with getElementById and querySelector

Using getElementById for Single Element Selection

The `getElementById` method returns the first element with the specified ID attribute. Since IDs should be unique within a document, this method always returns a single element or null.

#javascript

```
// HTML: <div id="header">Welcome</div>
```

```
const headerElement = document.getElementById('header');

if (headerElement) {
    headerElement.style.color = 'red';
    headerElement.textContent = 'Welcome, User!';
} else {
    console.log('Element not found');
}

// Common use case: form validation
const emailInput = document.getElementById('email');
const submitButton = document.getElementById('submit-
btn');

submitButton.addEventListener('click', function() {
    if (emailInput.value.includes('@')) {
        console.log('Valid email');
    } else {
        console.log('Invalid email');
    }
});
```

Modern Element Selection with querySelector

The `querySelector` method uses CSS selectors to find elements, making it more flexible than `getElementById`. It returns the first element that matches the specified selector.

#javascript

```
// Select by ID (equivalent to getElementById)
const header = document.querySelector('#header');
```

```
// Select by class
const firstButton = document.querySelector('.btn');

// Select by element type
const firstParagraph = document.querySelector('p');

// Complex selectors
const nestedSpan = document.querySelector('div.container
span.highlight');
const lastListItem = document.querySelector('ul li:last-
child');
const checkedInput =
document.querySelector('input[type="checkbox"]:checked');

// Attribute selectors
const requiredInputs =
document.querySelector('input[required]');
const dataElements = document.querySelector('[data-
role="button"]');
```

Selecting Multiple Elements with querySelectorAll

When you need to work with multiple elements, `querySelectorAll` returns a NodeList containing all matching elements:

#javascript

```
// Select all elements with a specific class
const allButtons = document.querySelectorAll('.btn');

// Convert NodeList to Array for easier manipulation
const buttonArray = Array.from(allButtons);
```

```javascript
// Iterate through multiple elements
allButtons.forEach(function(button, index) {
    button.textContent = `Button ${index + 1}`;
    button.addEventListener('click', function() {
        console.log(`Button ${index + 1} clicked`);
    });
});

// Select all checked checkboxes
const checkedBoxes =
document.querySelectorAll('input[type="checkbox"]:checked
');
console.log(`${checkedBoxes.length} checkboxes are
selected`);

// Select all paragraphs within a specific container
const containerParagraphs =
document.querySelectorAll('#content p');
containerParagraphs.forEach(p => {
    p.style.lineHeight = '1.6';
});
```

Performance Considerations and Best Practices

Different selection methods have varying performance characteristics:

#javascript

```javascript
// Most efficient for single elements with IDs
const fastSelection = document.getElementById('unique-
id');
```

```
// Efficient for simple selectors
const goodSelection = document.querySelector('.simple-class');

// Less efficient for complex selectors
const slowSelection = document.querySelector('div > ul > li:nth-child(3) span.highlight');

// Cache selections when using them multiple times
const expensiveElement = document.querySelector('.complex-selector');
// Use expensiveElement multiple times instead of re-querying

// Avoid repeated queries in loops
const items = document.querySelectorAll('.item');
for (let i = 0; i < items.length; i++) {
    // Good: using cached selection
    items[i].style.color = 'blue';
}
```

Alternative Selection Methods

While `querySelector` and `getElementById` are most commonly used, other selection methods remain useful in specific scenarios:

#javascript

```
// getElementsByClassName returns a live HTMLCollection
const liveButtons = document.getElementsByClassName('btn');
console.log(liveButtons.length); // Current count
```

```
// Add a new button to the DOM
const newButton = document.createElement('button');
newButton.className = 'btn';
document.body.appendChild(newButton);

console.log(liveButtons.length); // Count automatically
updated

// getElementsByTagName for selecting by tag type
const allImages = document.getElementsByTagName('img');
const allLinks = document.getElementsByTagName('a');

// Convert HTMLCollection to Array for modern methods
const imageArray = Array.from(allImages);
imageArray.filter(img => img.src.includes('thumbnail'));
```

13.3 Handling Events with addEventListener

Understanding Event-Driven Programming

Events are actions that occur in the browser, such as user interactions, page loading, or data changes. Event-driven programming responds to these events by executing specific functions called event handlers.

The addEventListener Method

The `addEventListener` method is the modern standard for attaching event handlers to elements. It offers several advantages over older methods like inline event handlers or property-based handlers.

#javascript

```
// Basic syntax
```

```
element.addEventListener('eventType', handlerFunction,
options);

// Simple click handler
const button = document.getElementById('myButton');
button.addEventListener('click', function() {
    console.log('Button was clicked!');
});

// Using arrow functions
button.addEventListener('click', () => {
    console.log('Arrow function handler');
});

// Named function handlers
function handleButtonClick() {
    console.log('Named function handler');
}
button.addEventListener('click', handleButtonClick);
```

Event Handler Functions and Parameters

Event handlers receive an event object containing information about the triggered event:

#javascript

```
const input = document.getElementById('textInput');

input.addEventListener('input', function(event) {
    console.log('Event type:', event.type);
    console.log('Target element:', event.target);
```

```
    console.log('Current value:', event.target.value);
    console.log('Key pressed:', event.key);
});

// Accessing event properties
button.addEventListener('click', function(event) {
    console.log('Mouse position:', event.clientX,
event.clientY);
    console.log('Ctrl key pressed:', event.ctrlKey);
    console.log('Shift key pressed:', event.shiftKey);

    // Prevent default behavior
    event.preventDefault();

    // Stop event propagation
    event.stopPropagation();
});
```

Multiple Event Listeners

You can attach multiple event listeners to the same element for the same event type:

#javascript

```
const button = document.getElementById('multiButton');

// First listener
button.addEventListener('click', function() {
    console.log('First handler executed');
});
```

```
// Second listener
button.addEventListener('click', function() {
    console.log('Second handler executed');
});

// Third listener with different functionality
button.addEventListener('click', function(event) {
    event.target.style.backgroundColor = 'lightblue';
});

// All three handlers will execute when the button is clicked
```

Removing Event Listeners

Sometimes you need to remove event listeners to prevent memory leaks or change behavior:

#javascript

```
// Define a named function for removal
function temporaryHandler() {
    console.log('This handler will be removed');
}

// Add the listener
button.addEventListener('click', temporaryHandler);

// Remove the listener later
button.removeEventListener('click', temporaryHandler);

// Anonymous functions cannot be removed
```

```
button.addEventListener('click', function() {
    // This cannot be removed because we don't have a
reference
});

// Solution: Store the function reference
const removableHandler = function() {
    console.log('This can be removed');
};

button.addEventListener('click', removableHandler);
// Later: button.removeEventListener('click',
removableHandler);
```

Event Listener Options

The third parameter of `addEventListener` can be an options object providing additional control:

#javascript

```
// Once option: listener executes only once
button.addEventListener('click', function() {
    console.log('This will only run once');
}, { once: true });

// Passive option: improves performance for touch/scroll
events
document.addEventListener('touchstart', function(event) {
    // Cannot call preventDefault() with passive: true
}, { passive: true });
```

```
// Capture option: handle event during capture phase
document.addEventListener('click', function() {
    console.log('Captured during capture phase');
}, { capture: true });

// Combined options
element.addEventListener('scroll', scrollHandler, {
    passive: true,
    once: false,
    capture: false
});
```

13.4 Common Event Types: click, mouseover, keydown

Click Events

Click events are the most common form of user interaction, triggered when users click on elements:

#javascript

```
// Basic click handling
const clickButton = document.getElementById('clickMe');
clickButton.addEventListener('click', function(event) {
    console.log('Element clicked!');
    console.log('Click coordinates:', event.clientX,
event.clientY);
});

// Double-click events
clickButton.addEventListener('dblclick', function() {
    console.log('Double-clicked!');
```

```
});

// Right-click context menu
clickButton.addEventListener('contextmenu',
function(event) {
    event.preventDefault(); // Prevent default context
menu
    console.log('Right-clicked!');
});

// Practical click example: toggle visibility
const toggleButton = document.getElementById('toggle');
const contentDiv = document.getElementById('content');

toggleButton.addEventListener('click', function() {
    if (contentDiv.style.display === 'none') {
        contentDiv.style.display = 'block';
        this.textContent = 'Hide Content';
    } else {
        contentDiv.style.display = 'none';
        this.textContent = 'Show Content';
    }
});
```

Mouse Events

Mouse events provide rich interaction possibilities beyond simple clicks:

#javascript

```
const mouseArea = document.getElementById('mouseArea');
```

```
// Mouse enter and leave
mouseArea.addEventListener('mouseenter', function() {
    this.style.backgroundColor = 'lightblue';
    console.log('Mouse entered the area');
});

mouseArea.addEventListener('mouseleave', function() {
    this.style.backgroundColor = 'white';
    console.log('Mouse left the area');
});

// Mouse over and out (with event bubbling)
mouseArea.addEventListener('mouseover', function(event) {
    event.target.style.border = '2px solid red';
});

mouseArea.addEventListener('mouseout', function(event) {
    event.target.style.border = 'none';
});

// Mouse movement tracking
mouseArea.addEventListener('mousemove', function(event) {
    const rect = this.getBoundingClientRect();
    const x = event.clientX - rect.left;
    const y = event.clientY - rect.top;

    this.textContent = `Mouse position: (${x}, ${y})`;
});

// Mouse button events
mouseArea.addEventListener('mousedown', function(event) {
```

```
    console.log('Mouse button pressed:', event.button);
    // 0 = left, 1 = middle, 2 = right
});

mouseArea.addEventListener('mouseup', function(event) {
    console.log('Mouse button released:', event.button);
});
```

Keyboard Events

Keyboard events enable text input handling and keyboard shortcuts:

#javascript

```
const textInput = document.getElementById('textInput');

// Keydown: fired when key is first pressed
textInput.addEventListener('keydown', function(event) {
    console.log('Key pressed:', event.key);
    console.log('Key code:', event.code);

    // Handle special keys
    if (event.key === 'Enter') {
        console.log('Enter key pressed');
        event.preventDefault(); // Prevent default form
submission
    }

    if (event.key === 'Escape') {
        this.value = ''; // Clear input
    }
```

```
    // Keyboard shortcuts
    if (event.ctrlKey && event.key === 's') {
        event.preventDefault();
        console.log('Save shortcut triggered');
    }
});

// Keyup: fired when key is released
textInput.addEventListener('keyup', function(event) {
    console.log('Key released:', event.key);

    // Real-time input validation
    if (this.value.length < 5) {
        this.style.borderColor = 'red';
    } else {
        this.style.borderColor = 'green';
    }
});

// Input event: fired when input value changes
textInput.addEventListener('input', function(event) {
    const charCount = this.value.length;
    const maxLength = 100;
    const remaining = maxLength - charCount;

    console.log(`Characters remaining: ${remaining}`);

    if (remaining < 10) {
        this.style.backgroundColor = 'lightyellow';
    } else {
        this.style.backgroundColor = 'white';
```

```
    }
});

// Keypress: fired for printable characters (deprecated
but still used)
textInput.addEventListener('keypress', function(event) {
    // Only allow numbers
    if (!/[0-9]/.test(event.key) && event.key !==
'Backspace') {
        event.preventDefault();
    }
});
```

Form Events

Form-specific events handle user interactions with form elements:

#javascript

```
const form = document.getElementById('myForm');
const emailInput = document.getElementById('email');
const passwordInput =
document.getElementById('password');

// Form submission
form.addEventListener('submit', function(event) {
    event.preventDefault(); // Prevent default form
submission

    // Custom validation
    const email = emailInput.value;
    const password = passwordInput.value;
```

```
    if (!email.includes('@')) {
        alert('Please enter a valid email');
        return;
    }

    if (password.length < 8) {
        alert('Password must be at least 8 characters');
        return;
    }

    console.log('Form is valid, submitting...');
    // Perform actual submission here
});

// Input focus and blur events
emailInput.addEventListener('focus', function() {
    this.style.backgroundColor = 'lightyellow';
});

emailInput.addEventListener('blur', function() {
    this.style.backgroundColor = 'white';

    // Validate email on blur
    if (this.value && !this.value.includes('@')) {
        this.style.borderColor = 'red';
    } else {
        this.style.borderColor = '';
    }
});
```

```
// Change event for select elements
const selectElement = document.getElementById('country');
selectElement.addEventListener('change', function() {
    console.log('Selected country:', this.value);
});

// Checkbox and radio button events
const checkbox = document.getElementById('newsletter');
checkbox.addEventListener('change', function() {
    if (this.checked) {
        console.log('User subscribed to newsletter');
    } else {
        console.log('User unsubscribed from newsletter');
    }
});
```

13.5 Event Delegation

Understanding Event Bubbling

Event bubbling is the process where an event triggered on a child element bubbles up through its parent elements. This behavior enables event delegation, a powerful technique for handling events efficiently.

#javascript

```
// HTML structure:
// <div id="container">
//   <button id="child">Click me</button>
// </div>

const container = document.getElementById('container');
```

```
const childButton = document.getElementById('child');

// Event bubbling demonstration
childButton.addEventListener('click', function(event) {
    console.log('Child button clicked');
});

container.addEventListener('click', function(event) {
    console.log('Container clicked');
    console.log('Event target:', event.target.id);
    console.log('Current target:',
event.currentTarget.id);
});

// When child button is clicked, both handlers execute:
// "Child button clicked"
// "Container clicked"
```

Implementing Event Delegation

Event delegation attaches a single event listener to a parent element to handle events for multiple child elements:

#javascript

```
// Instead of adding listeners to each button
individually
const buttonContainer =
document.getElementById('buttonContainer');

// Single event listener handles all button clicks
buttonContainer.addEventListener('click', function(event)
{
```

```
    // Check if clicked element is a button
    if (event.target.tagName === 'BUTTON') {
        console.log('Button clicked:',
event.target.textContent);

        // Handle different button types
        if (event.target.classList.contains('delete-
btn')) {
            handleDelete(event.target);
        } else if (event.target.classList.contains('edit-
btn')) {
            handleEdit(event.target);
        }
    }
});

function handleDelete(button) {
    const listItem = button.closest('li');
    if (listItem) {
        listItem.remove();
    }
}

function handleEdit(button) {
    const listItem = button.closest('li');
    const textSpan = listItem.querySelector('.item-
text');
    const currentText = textSpan.textContent;

    const newText = prompt('Edit item:', currentText);
    if (newText !== null) {
        textSpan.textContent = newText;
```

```
    }
}
```

Dynamic Content Handling

Event delegation is particularly useful when dealing with dynamically added content:

#javascript

```
const todoList = document.getElementById('todoList');
const addButton = document.getElementById('addTodo');

// Event delegation for dynamically added todo items
todoList.addEventListener('click', function(event) {
    const target = event.target;

    if (target.classList.contains('complete-btn')) {
        // Toggle completion status
        const todoItem = target.closest('.todo-item');
        todoItem.classList.toggle('completed');

        if (todoItem.classList.contains('completed')) {
            target.textContent = 'Undo';
        } else {
            target.textContent = 'Complete';
        }
    }

    if (target.classList.contains('delete-btn')) {
        // Remove todo item
        const todoItem = target.closest('.todo-item');
```

```
        todoItem.remove();
    }
});

// Add new todo items dynamically
addButton.addEventListener('click', function() {
    const todoText = prompt('Enter todo item:');
    if (todoText) {
        const todoItem = createTodoElement(todoText);
        todoList.appendChild(todoItem);
    }
});

function createTodoElement(text) {
    const div = document.createElement('div');
    div.className = 'todo-item';
    div.innerHTML = `
        <span class="todo-text">${text}</span>
        <button class="complete-btn">Complete</button>
        <button class="delete-btn">Delete</button>
    `;
    return div;
}
```

Advanced Event Delegation Patterns

#javascript

```
// Table row selection with event delegation
const dataTable = document.getElementById('dataTable');
```

```
dataTable.addEventListener('click', function(event) {
    const clickedRow = event.target.closest('tr');

    if (clickedRow && clickedRow.parentElement.tagName
=== 'TBODY') {
        // Remove previous selection
        const previouslySelected =
this.querySelector('.selected');
        if (previouslySelected) {

previouslySelected.classList.remove('selected');
        }

        // Add selection to clicked row
        clickedRow.classList.add('selected');

        // Get row data
        const cells = clickedRow.querySelectorAll('td');
        const rowData = Array.from(cells).map(cell =>
cell.textContent);
        console.log('Selected row data:', rowData);
    }
});

// Form validation with event delegation
const formContainer =
document.getElementById('formContainer');

formContainer.addEventListener('input', function(event) {
    const target = event.target;

    if (target.type === 'email') {
```

```
        validateEmail(target);
    } else if (target.type === 'password') {
        validatePassword(target);
    } else if (target.type === 'text' && target.required)
{
        validateRequired(target);
    }
});

function validateEmail(input) {
    const isValid =
/^[^\s@]+@[^\s@]+\.[^\s@]+$/.test(input.value);
    updateFieldValidation(input, isValid);
}

function validatePassword(input) {
    const isValid = input.value.length >= 8;
    updateFieldValidation(input, isValid);
}

function validateRequired(input) {
    const isValid = input.value.trim().length > 0;
    updateFieldValidation(input, isValid);
}

function updateFieldValidation(input, isValid) {
    const errorMessage =
input.parentElement.querySelector('.error-message');

    if (isValid) {
        input.classList.remove('invalid');
```

```
        input.classList.add('valid');
        if (errorMessage) {
            errorMessage.style.display = 'none';
        }
    } else {
        input.classList.remove('valid');
        input.classList.add('invalid');
        if (errorMessage) {
            errorMessage.style.display = 'block';
        }
    }
}
```

Performance Benefits and Best Practices

Event delegation provides significant performance benefits, especially with large numbers of elements:

#javascript

```
// Performance comparison example
const itemList = document.getElementById('itemList');

// Method 1: Individual listeners (less efficient)
function addIndividualListeners() {
    const items = itemList.querySelectorAll('.item');
    items.forEach(function(item) {
        item.addEventListener('click', function() {
            console.log('Item clicked:',
this.textContent);
        });
    });
```

```
}

// Method 2: Event delegation (more efficient)
function addDelegatedListener() {
    itemList.addEventListener('click', function(event) {
        if (event.target.classList.contains('item')) {
            console.log('Item clicked:',
event.target.textContent);
        }
    });
}

// Best practices for event delegation
const smartContainer =
document.getElementById('smartContainer');

smartContainer.addEventListener('click', function(event)
{
    // Use closest() for more flexible matching
    const button = event.target.closest('.action-btn');
    if (!button) return;

    // Prevent multiple executions
    if (button.disabled) return;

    // Get action type from data attribute
    const action = button.dataset.action;

    switch (action) {
        case 'save':
            handleSave(button);
```

```
            break;
        case 'cancel':
            handleCancel(button);
            break;
        case 'edit':
            handleEdit(button);
            break;
        default:
            console.warn('Unknown action:', action);
    }
});

// Helper functions
function handleSave(button) {
    const form = button.closest('form');
    if (form && form.checkValidity()) {
        console.log('Saving form data...');
        button.disabled = true;

        // Simulate async operation
        setTimeout(() => {
            button.disabled = false;
            console.log('Save completed');
        }, 2000);
    }
}

function handleCancel(button) {
    const form = button.closest('form');
    if (form) {
        form.reset();
```

```
        console.log('Form cancelled');
    }
}

function handleEdit(button) {
    const editableElement =
button.parentElement.querySelector('.editable');
    if (editableElement) {
        editableElement.contentEditable = true;
        editableElement.focus();
        button.textContent = 'Save';
        button.dataset.action = 'save';
    }
}
```

Essential Tips

- Use semantic HTML elements with proper IDs and classes to make DOM selection more efficient and maintainable.
- Cache DOM selections when you need to access the same elements multiple times to improve performance.
- Always check if an element exists before trying to manipulate it to prevent runtime errors.
- Use event delegation for dynamic content and lists with many items to reduce memory usage and improve performance.
- Choose between `innerHTML`, `textContent`, and `innerText` based on your specific needs - `textContent` for plain text, `innerHTML` for HTML content.

Actionable Strategies

- Implement a consistent naming convention for IDs and classes that makes element selection predictable and maintainable.

- Create reusable event handler functions that can be attached to multiple elements instead of writing inline anonymous functions.
- Use the `dataset` API to store custom data attributes on elements for better event handling and state management.
- Implement proper form validation by combining multiple event types like `input`, `blur`, and `submit` for comprehensive user feedback.
- Leverage the event object properties like `preventDefault()` and `stopPropagation()` to control event behavior precisely.
- Build a library of common DOM manipulation functions that you can reuse across projects for consistent behavior.
- Practice debugging DOM events using browser developer tools to understand event flow and identify issues quickly.

Chapter 14: DOM Manipulation

The Document Object Model (DOM) represents the structure of HTML documents as a tree of objects that JavaScript can interact with dynamically. DOM manipulation forms the backbone of interactive web applications, allowing developers to modify content, styling, and structure in real-time based on user interactions or application logic.

14.1 Changing Element Text and HTML

Understanding Text and HTML Content

JavaScript provides multiple properties for accessing and modifying element content. The primary methods include `textContent`, `innerHTML`, and `innerText`, each serving different purposes and offering distinct advantages.

The textContent Property

The `textContent` property retrieves or sets the text content of an element and all its descendants. This property returns plain text without any HTML markup, making it safe for displaying user-generated content.

#javascript

```javascript
// HTML: <div id="myDiv">Hello
<strong>World</strong></div>
const element = document.getElementById('myDiv');
console.log(element.textContent); // Output: "Hello
World"


// Setting text content
element.textContent = 'New text content';
// Result: <div id="myDiv">New text content</div>
```

The innerHTML Property

The `innerHTML` property allows you to get or set the HTML content inside an element. This property interprets HTML tags and renders them accordingly, providing powerful formatting capabilities.

#javascript

```javascript
const container = document.getElementById('container');

// Setting HTML content
container.innerHTML = '<h2>Dynamic Title</h2><p>This is a paragraph.</p>';

// Getting HTML content
console.log(container.innerHTML);
// Output: "<h2>Dynamic Title</h2><p>This is a paragraph.</p>"
```

Security Considerations with innerHTML

When using `innerHTML` with user input, always sanitize the content to prevent Cross-Site Scripting (XSS) attacks. Never directly insert untrusted user input into `innerHTML`.

#javascript

```javascript
// Dangerous - don't do this with user input
const userInput = '<script>alert("XSS attack!")</script>';
element.innerHTML = userInput; // This could execute malicious code

// Safer approach for user input
element.textContent = userInput; // Treats everything as plain text
```

```
```

The innerText Property

The `innerText` property behaves similarly to `textContent` but respects styling. It won't return text from hidden elements and considers CSS styling when determining visible text.

#javascript

```
// HTML: <div>Visible text <span style="display:
none;">Hidden text</span></div>
const element = document.querySelector('div');

console.log(element.textContent); // "Visible text Hidden
text"
console.log(element.innerText);   // "Visible text"
```

Practical Examples of Text Manipulation

#javascript

```
// Dynamic content updates
function updateWelcomeMessage(username) {
    const welcomeElement =
document.getElementById('welcome');
    welcomeElement.textContent = `Welcome back,
${username}!`;
}

// Creating formatted content
function displayUserProfile(user) {
    const profileContainer =
document.getElementById('profile');
```

```
    profileContainer.innerHTML = `
        <h3>${user.name}</h3>
        <p>Email: ${user.email}</p>
        <p>Joined: ${user.joinDate}</p>
    `;
}

// Appending content
function addNotification(message) {
    const notificationArea =
document.getElementById('notifications');
    const currentContent = notificationArea.innerHTML;
    notificationArea.innerHTML = currentContent + `<div
class="notification">${message}</div>`;
}
```

14.2 Modifying Attributes and Styles

Working with Element Attributes

Attributes provide additional information about HTML elements and can be manipulated using JavaScript methods like `getAttribute()`, `setAttribute()`, `removeAttribute()`, and `hasAttribute()`.

Getting and Setting Attributes

#javascript

```
const image = document.getElementById('myImage');

// Getting attributes
const src = image.getAttribute('src');
```

```
const alt = image.getAttribute('alt');

// Setting attributes
image.setAttribute('src', 'new-image.jpg');
image.setAttribute('alt', 'New image description');
image.setAttribute('title', 'Hover tooltip text');

// Checking if attribute exists
if (image.hasAttribute('data-id')) {
    console.log('Element has data-id attribute');
}

// Removing attributes
image.removeAttribute('title');
```

Data Attributes

Data attributes provide a way to store custom data on HTML elements. They always begin with `data-` and can be accessed through the `dataset` property.

#javascript

```
// HTML: <div id="user" data-user-id="123" data-
role="admin"></div>
const userElement = document.getElementById('user');

// Accessing data attributes
console.log(userElement.dataset.userId); // "123"
console.log(userElement.dataset.role);   // "admin"

// Setting data attributes
userElement.dataset.lastLogin = '2024-01-15';
```

```
userElement.dataset.status = 'active';

// The HTML now becomes:
// <div id="user" data-user-id="123" data-role="admin"
data-last-login="2024-01-15" data-status="active"></div>
```

Modifying CSS Styles

JavaScript provides multiple ways to modify element styles, including the `style` property for inline styles and `className` for CSS classes.

The style Property

The `style` property allows direct manipulation of inline CSS styles. Property names follow camelCase convention instead of kebab-case.

#javascript

```
const element = document.getElementById('myElement');

// Setting individual styles
element.style.backgroundColor = 'blue';
element.style.fontSize = '18px';
element.style.marginTop = '20px';
element.style.borderRadius = '10px';

// Setting multiple styles
Object.assign(element.style, {
    color: 'white',
    padding: '15px',
    textAlign: 'center',
    boxShadow: '0 2px 5px rgba(0,0,0,0.3)'
```

```
});

// Getting computed styles
const computedStyle = window.getComputedStyle(element);
console.log(computedStyle.backgroundColor);
console.log(computedStyle.fontSize);
```

Dynamic Styling Based on Conditions

#javascript

```
function updateElementStyle(element, condition) {
    if (condition === 'success') {
        element.style.backgroundColor = '#4CAF50';
        element.style.color = 'white';
        element.style.border = '2px solid #45a049';
    } else if (condition === 'error') {
        element.style.backgroundColor = '#f44336';
        element.style.color = 'white';
        element.style.border = '2px solid #da190b';
    } else {
        element.style.backgroundColor = '#2196F3';
        element.style.color = 'white';
        element.style.border = '2px solid #0b7dda';
    }
}

// Usage
const statusElement = document.getElementById('status');
updateElementStyle(statusElement, 'success');
```

CSS Custom Properties (CSS Variables)

JavaScript can also manipulate CSS custom properties, allowing for dynamic theming and advanced styling techniques.

#javascript

```
// Setting CSS custom properties
document.documentElement.style.setProperty('--primary-
color', '#3498db');
document.documentElement.style.setProperty('--font-size',
'16px');

// Getting CSS custom properties
const primaryColor =
getComputedStyle(document.documentElement)
    .getPropertyValue('--primary-color');

// Creating a theme switcher
function switchTheme(theme) {
    const root = document.documentElement;

    if (theme === 'dark') {
        root.style.setProperty('--bg-color', '#2c3e50');
        root.style.setProperty('--text-color',
'#ecf0f1');
        root.style.setProperty('--accent-color',
'#e74c3c');
    } else {
        root.style.setProperty('--bg-color', '#ecf0f1');
        root.style.setProperty('--text-color',
'#2c3e50');
```

```
        root.style.setProperty('--accent-color',
'#3498db');
    }
}
```

14.3 Creating and Appending Elements

Creating New Elements

JavaScript provides several methods for creating new DOM elements dynamically. The most common approach uses `document.createElement()` to create elements programmatically.

Basic Element Creation

#javascript

```
// Creating a new paragraph element
const paragraph = document.createElement('p');
paragraph.textContent = 'This is a dynamically created
paragraph.';

// Creating a new image element
const image = document.createElement('img');
image.src = 'path/to/image.jpg';
image.alt = 'Dynamic image';
image.style.width = '200px';

// Creating a new div with multiple properties
const container = document.createElement('div');
container.className = 'dynamic-container';
container.id = 'newContainer';
```

```
container.style.backgroundColor = '#f0f0f0';
container.style.padding = '20px';
```

Complex Element Creation

#javascript

```
function createUserCard(user) {
    // Create main container
    const card = document.createElement('div');
    card.className = 'user-card';
    card.dataset.userId = user.id;

    // Create avatar image
    const avatar = document.createElement('img');
    avatar.src = user.avatarUrl;
    avatar.alt = `${user.name}'s avatar`;
    avatar.className = 'user-avatar';

    // Create name heading
    const name = document.createElement('h3');
    name.textContent = user.name;
    name.className = 'user-name';

    // Create email paragraph
    const email = document.createElement('p');
    email.textContent = user.email;
    email.className = 'user-email';

    // Create action button
    const button = document.createElement('button');
```

```
    button.textContent = 'View Profile';
    button.className = 'btn btn-primary';
    button.onclick = () => viewUserProfile(user.id);

    // Assemble the card
    card.appendChild(avatar);
    card.appendChild(name);
    card.appendChild(email);
    card.appendChild(button);

    return card;
}
```

Appending Elements to the DOM

Once elements are created, they need to be added to the DOM using various append methods.

appendChild() Method

#javascript

```
const container = document.getElementById('container');
const newElement = document.createElement('div');
newElement.textContent = 'New content';

// Append to the end of container's children
container.appendChild(newElement);
```

insertBefore() Method

#javascript

```javascript
const container = document.getElementById('container');
const newElement = document.createElement('div');
const referenceElement =
document.getElementById('reference');

// Insert newElement before referenceElement
container.insertBefore(newElement, referenceElement);
```

Modern Insertion Methods

#javascript

```javascript
const container = document.getElementById('container');
const newElement = document.createElement('div');

// Insert at the beginning
container.prepend(newElement);

// Insert at the end
container.append(newElement);

// Insert before the container
container.before(newElement);

// Insert after the container
container.after(newElement);
```

Creating Document Fragments

Document fragments provide an efficient way to batch DOM operations, reducing reflow and repaint operations.

#javascript

```
function createMultipleElements(items) {
    // Create a document fragment
    const fragment = document.createDocumentFragment();

    items.forEach(item => {
        const element = document.createElement('div');
        element.className = 'item';
        element.textContent = item.name;
        element.dataset.id = item.id;

        // Append to fragment instead of directly to DOM
        fragment.appendChild(element);
    });

    // Single DOM operation to append all elements

document.getElementById('container').appendChild(fragment
);
}

// Usage with array of items
const items = [
    { id: 1, name: 'Item 1' },
    { id: 2, name: 'Item 2' },
    { id: 3, name: 'Item 3' }
];

createMultipleElements(items);
```

Dynamic Form Creation

#javascript

```
function createContactForm() {
    const form = document.createElement('form');
    form.className = 'contact-form';
    form.method = 'POST';

    // Create form fields
    const fields = [
        { type: 'text', name: 'name', placeholder: 'Your
Name', required: true },
        { type: 'email', name: 'email', placeholder:
'Your Email', required: true },
        { type: 'textarea', name: 'message', placeholder:
'Your Message', required: true }
    ];

    fields.forEach(field => {
        const wrapper = document.createElement('div');
        wrapper.className = 'form-group';

        const label = document.createElement('label');
        label.textContent = field.placeholder;
        label.htmlFor = field.name;

        let input;
        if (field.type === 'textarea') {
            input = document.createElement('textarea');
            input.rows = 4;
        } else {
            input = document.createElement('input');
```

```
            input.type = field.type;
        }

        input.name = field.name;
        input.id = field.name;
        input.placeholder = field.placeholder;
        input.required = field.required;
        input.className = 'form-control';

        wrapper.appendChild(label);
        wrapper.appendChild(input);
        form.appendChild(wrapper);
    });

    // Create submit button
    const submitButton =
document.createElement('button');
    submitButton.type = 'submit';
    submitButton.textContent = 'Send Message';
    submitButton.className = 'btn btn-primary';

    form.appendChild(submitButton);

    return form;
}
```

14.4 Removing and Replacing Elements

Removing Elements from the DOM

JavaScript provides several methods for removing elements from the DOM, each with different use cases and browser compatibility considerations.

The remove() Method

The modern `remove()` method directly removes an element from its parent.

#javascript

```
const element =
document.getElementById('elementToRemove');
element.remove(); // Element is completely removed from
the DOM
```

The removeChild() Method

The traditional approach requires accessing the parent element first.

#javascript

```
const element =
document.getElementById('elementToRemove');
const parent = element.parentNode;
parent.removeChild(element);
```

Safe Removal Function

#javascript

```
function safeRemoveElement(elementId) {
    const element = document.getElementById(elementId);
    if (element) {
        // Check if remove method is supported
        if (element.remove) {
```

```
            element.remove();
        } else {
            // Fallback for older browsers
            element.parentNode.removeChild(element);
        }
        return true;
    }
    return false;
}

// Usage
if (safeRemoveElement('outdatedElement')) {
    console.log('Element removed successfully');
} else {
    console.log('Element not found');
}
```

Removing Multiple Elements

#javascript

```
function removeElementsByClass(className) {
    const elements =
document.querySelectorAll(`.${className}`);
    elements.forEach(element => element.remove());
}

function removeElementsBySelector(selector) {
    const elements = document.querySelectorAll(selector);
    elements.forEach(element => element.remove());
}
```

```
// Usage examples
removeElementsByClass('temporary-message');
removeElementsBySelector('.notification.read');
```

Conditional Removal

#javascript

```
function removeExpiredElements() {
    const elements = document.querySelectorAll('[data-
expires]');
    const now = new Date().getTime();

    elements.forEach(element => {
        const expirationTime =
parseInt(element.dataset.expires);
        if (now > expirationTime) {
            element.remove();
        }
    });
}

// Remove elements based on user interaction
function removeOnCondition(selector, condition) {
    const elements = document.querySelectorAll(selector);
    elements.forEach(element => {
        if (condition(element)) {
            element.remove();
        }
    });
```

```
}

// Usage
removeOnCondition('.user-post', (post) => {
    return post.dataset.score < 0; // Remove posts with
negative scores
});
```

Replacing Elements

JavaScript provides methods to replace existing elements with new content or elements entirely.

The replaceWith() Method

#javascript

```
const oldElement = document.getElementById('oldContent');
const newElement = document.createElement('div');
newElement.textContent = 'This is the new content';
newElement.className = 'new-content';

// Replace the old element with the new one
oldElement.replaceWith(newElement);
```

The replaceChild() Method

#javascript

```
const parent = document.getElementById('container');
const oldElement = document.getElementById('oldChild');
```

```
const newElement = document.createElement('div');
newElement.textContent = 'Replacement content';

parent.replaceChild(newElement, oldElement);
```

Advanced Replacement Techniques

#javascript

```
function replaceElementContent(targetId, newContent,
contentType = 'text') {
    const element = document.getElementById(targetId);
    if (!element) return false;

    if (contentType === 'html') {
        element.innerHTML = newContent;
    } else if (contentType === 'element') {
        element.innerHTML = '';
        element.appendChild(newContent);
    } else {
        element.textContent = newContent;
    }

    return true;
}

// Replace with new HTML content
replaceElementContent('status',
'<strong>Success!</strong>', 'html');

// Replace with new element
```

```
const newButton = document.createElement('button');
newButton.textContent = 'New Action';
replaceElementContent('buttonContainer', newButton,
'element');
```

Dynamic Content Replacement

#javascript

```
function createReplacementSystem() {
    const replacements = new Map();

    return {
        register: function(targetId, replacement) {
            replacements.set(targetId, replacement);
        },

        execute: function(targetId) {
            const replacement =
replacements.get(targetId);
            const target =
document.getElementById(targetId);

            if (target && replacement) {
                if (typeof replacement === 'function') {
                    const newElement = replacement();
                    target.replaceWith(newElement);
                } else {
                    target.replaceWith(replacement);
                }
                return true;
            }
```

```
            return false;
        },

        executeAll: function() {
            for (let [targetId] of replacements) {
                this.execute(targetId);
            }
        }
    };
}

// Usage
const replacer = createReplacementSystem();

// Register replacements
replacer.register('loading', () => {
    const success = document.createElement('div');
    success.className = 'success-message';
    success.textContent = 'Content loaded successfully!';
    return success;
});

// Execute replacement
replacer.execute('loading');
```

14.5 Working with Classes (classList)

Understanding the classList Property

The `classList` property provides a convenient way to manipulate CSS classes on elements. It returns a DOMTokenList object with methods for adding, removing, toggling, and checking classes.

Basic classList Methods

#javascript

```
const element = document.getElementById('myElement');

// Add classes
element.classList.add('active');
element.classList.add('highlighted', 'important'); // Add multiple classes

// Remove classes
element.classList.remove('inactive');
element.classList.remove('old-style', 'deprecated'); // Remove multiple classes

// Toggle classes
element.classList.toggle('visible'); // Adds if not present, removes if present

// Check if class exists
if (element.classList.contains('active')) {
    console.log('Element is active');
}

// Replace a class
element.classList.replace('old-class', 'new-class');
```

Advanced Class Manipulation

#javascript

```
function manageElementStates(element, state) {
    // Remove all state classes
    element.classList.remove('loading', 'success',
'error', 'pending');

    // Add the new state class
    element.classList.add(state);

    // Update content based on state
    switch(state) {
        case 'loading':
            element.textContent = 'Loading...';
            break;
        case 'success':
            element.textContent = 'Operation completed
successfully!';
            break;
        case 'error':
            element.textContent = 'An error occurred.
Please try again.';
            break;
        case 'pending':
            element.textContent = 'Please wait...';
            break;
    }
}

// Usage
const statusElement = document.getElementById('status');
```

```
manageElementStates(statusElement, 'loading');

// Simulate async operation
setTimeout(() => {
    manageElementStates(statusElement, 'success');
}, 2000);
```

Conditional Class Application

#javascript

```
function applyConditionalClasses(element, conditions) {
    Object.entries(conditions).forEach(([className,
condition]) => {
        if (condition) {
            element.classList.add(className);
        } else {
            element.classList.remove(className);
        }
    });
}

// Usage
const card = document.getElementById('userCard');
const user = { isActive: true, isPremium: false, isAdmin:
true };

applyConditionalClasses(card, {
    'user-active': user.isActive,
    'user-premium': user.isPremium,
    'user-admin': user.isAdmin,
```

```
    'user-inactive': !user.isActive
});
```

Creating a Class Manager

#javascript

```
class ClassManager {
    constructor(element) {
        this.element = element;
        this.initialClasses = new Set(element.classList);
    }

    addTemporary(className, duration = 3000) {
        this.element.classList.add(className);
        setTimeout(() => {
            this.element.classList.remove(className);
        }, duration);
    }

    addWithCallback(className, callback) {
        this.element.classList.add(className);
        if (typeof callback === 'function') {
            callback();
        }
    }

    toggleWithAnimation(className, animationClass =
'fade') {
        this.element.classList.add(animationClass);
```

```
        setTimeout(() => {
            this.element.classList.toggle(className);

this.element.classList.remove(animationClass);
        }, 150);
    }

    reset() {
        this.element.className = '';
        this.initialClasses.forEach(cls => {
            this.element.classList.add(cls);
        });
    }

    hasAny(classNames) {
        return classNames.some(className =>
            this.element.classList.contains(className)
        );
    }

    hasAll(classNames) {
        return classNames.every(className =>
            this.element.classList.contains(className)
        );
    }
}

// Usage
const button = document.getElementById('actionButton');
const manager = new ClassManager(button);
```

```
// Add temporary class
manager.addTemporary('processing', 2000);

// Toggle with animation
manager.toggleWithAnimation('expanded');

// Check multiple classes
if (manager.hasAny(['active', 'selected'])) {
    console.log('Button has active or selected state');
}
```

Theme and Style Management

#javascript

```
function createThemeManager() {
    const themes = {
        light: ['theme-light', 'bg-white', 'text-dark'],
        dark: ['theme-dark', 'bg-dark', 'text-light'],
        blue: ['theme-blue', 'bg-blue', 'text-white'],
        green: ['theme-green', 'bg-green', 'text-white']
    };

    let currentTheme = 'light';

    return {
        setTheme: function(themeName) {
            if (!themes[themeName]) return false;

            const body = document.body;
```

```
            // Remove all theme classes
            Object.values(themes).flat().forEach(cls => {
                body.classList.remove(cls);
            });

            // Add new theme classes
            themes[themeName].forEach(cls => {
                body.classList.add(cls);
            });

            currentTheme = themeName;
            return true;
        },

        getCurrentTheme: function() {
            return currentTheme;
        },

        toggleTheme: function() {
            const nextTheme = currentTheme === 'light' ?
'dark' : 'light';
            this.setTheme(nextTheme);
        },

        addTheme: function(name, classes) {
            themes[name] = classes;
        }
    };
}

// Usage
```

```
const themeManager = createThemeManager();

// Set theme
themeManager.setTheme('dark');

// Toggle between light and dark
themeManager.toggleTheme();

// Add custom theme
themeManager.addTheme('custom', ['theme-custom', 'bg-
gradient', 'text-shadow']);
```

Animation and Transition Classes

#javascript

```
function animateElement(element, animationClass, duration
= 1000) {
    return new Promise((resolve) => {
        element.classList.add(animationClass);

        setTimeout(() => {
            element.classList.remove(animationClass);
            resolve();
        }, duration);
    });
}

async function sequentialAnimations(element, animations)
{
    for (let animation of animations) {
```

```
        await animateElement(element, animation.class,
animation.duration);
    }
}

// Usage
const element =
document.getElementById('animatedElement');

// Single animation
animateElement(element, 'bounce', 500);

// Sequential animations
sequentialAnimations(element, [
    { class: 'fade-in', duration: 500 },
    { class: 'slide-up', duration: 300 },
    { class: 'pulse', duration: 200 }
]);
```

Essential Tips

- Cache DOM queries by storing element references in variables to avoid repeated lookups, especially inside loops or frequently called functions.
- Use Document Fragments when creating multiple elements to minimize DOM reflow and improve performance by batching all additions into a single operation.
- Always validate that elements exist before manipulating them to prevent runtime errors, especially when working with dynamically generated content.
- Prefer `textContent` over `innerHTML` when working with plain text to prevent potential XSS vulnerabilities and improve performance.
- Implement error handling around DOM manipulation operations to gracefully handle cases where elements might not exist or operations might fail.

Actionable Strategies

- Create reusable utility functions for common DOM operations like element creation, class management, and content updates to maintain consistency across your application.
- Implement a centralized event delegation system to handle events efficiently, especially for dynamically created elements that need event listeners.
- Build a component-based architecture where each UI component has its own DOM manipulation logic encapsulated in dedicated functions or classes.
- Use data attributes extensively to store metadata about elements, making it easier to query and manipulate elements based on their state or properties.
- Implement lazy loading for DOM-heavy operations by creating elements only when they're needed, reducing initial page load time and memory usage.
- Establish a clear naming convention for CSS classes and IDs that reflects their purpose and makes DOM manipulation code more readable and maintainable.
- Create debugging utilities that can visualize DOM changes in development, helping you track element creation, modification, and removal during testing.

Chapter 15: Error Handling

Error handling represents one of the most critical aspects of JavaScript development. Every application encounters unexpected situations, user input errors, network failures, and programming mistakes. Understanding how to anticipate, catch, and manage these errors transforms fragile code into robust, production-ready applications that provide meaningful feedback to users and developers alike.

15.1 Common JavaScript Errors

Understanding Error Types

JavaScript throws various types of errors, each indicating different problems in your code. Recognizing these error patterns helps you write more defensive code and debug issues more efficiently.

SyntaxError occurs when JavaScript cannot parse your code due to incorrect syntax. These errors prevent your script from running entirely.

#javascript

```
// SyntaxError examples
function broken( {
    console.log("Missing closing parenthesis");
}

let obj = {
    name: "John"
    age: 30  // Missing comma
};

if (condition {  // Missing closing parenthesis
    console.log("Syntax error");
```

```
}
```

ReferenceError happens when you try to access a variable or function that doesn't exist or isn't in scope.

javascript

```
// ReferenceError examples
console.log(undefinedVariable);  // ReferenceError: undefinedVariable is not defined

function example() {
    let localVar = "Hello";
}
console.log(localVar);  // ReferenceError: localVar is not defined

// Misspelled variable names
let userName = "Alice";
console.log(userNam);  // ReferenceError: userNam is not defined
```

TypeError occurs when you try to use a value in a way that's incompatible with its type.

javascript

```
// TypeError examples
let number = 42;
number();  // TypeError: number is not a function

let text = "Hello World";
```

```
text.push("!");  // TypeError: text.push is not a function

null.property;  // TypeError: Cannot read property 'property' of null

let arr = null;
arr.forEach(item => console.log(item));  // TypeError: Cannot read property 'forEach' of null
```

RangeError happens when a numeric value is outside its allowed range.

javascript

```
// RangeError examples
let arr = new Array(-1);  // RangeError: Invalid array length

function recursiveFunction() {
    return recursiveFunction();  // RangeError: Maximum call stack size exceeded
}
recursiveFunction();

let num = 123.456;
num.toFixed(-1);  // RangeError: toFixed() digits argument must be between 0 and 100
```

Runtime vs Compile-Time Errors

Compile-time errors (syntax errors) prevent your code from running at all. These are caught by the JavaScript engine before execution begins.

#javascript

```
// These will prevent the entire script from running
let obj = {
    name "John"  // Missing colon
};

function test() {
    return  // Missing semicolon and value
}
```

Runtime errors occur during code execution when everything appears syntactically correct but something goes wrong during operation.

javascript

```
// Runtime error - code runs until this point
let users = [
    { name: "John", age: 30 },
    { name: "Jane", age: 25 }
];

users.forEach(user => {
    console.log(user.name.toUpperCase());  // Works fine
});

// Later in the code...
users.push(null);
users.forEach(user => {
    console.log(user.name.toUpperCase());  // TypeError
when user is null
});
```

Logical Errors

Logical errors represent the most challenging category because they don't throw exceptions. Your code runs without errors but produces incorrect results.

#javascript

```
// Logical error - calculating total price
function calculateTotal(items) {
    let total = 0;
    for (let i = 0; i <= items.length; i++) {  // Should be i < items.length
        total += items[i].price;  // Will try to access undefined item
    }
    return total;
}

// Another logical error - age validation
function validateAge(age) {
    if (age = 18) {  // Assignment instead of comparison
        return "Adult";
    }
    return "Minor";
}
```

Asynchronous Errors

Asynchronous operations introduce additional complexity in error handling, especially with promises and async/await.

#javascript

```
// Promise rejection errors
fetch('/api/data')
    .then(response => response.json())
    .then(data => {
        // If this throws an error, it becomes a rejected
promise
        data.items.forEach(item => processItem(item));
    }); // Unhandled promise rejection if processItem
throws

// Async/await errors
async function fetchUserData(userId) {
    const response = await fetch(`/api/users/${userId}`);
    const userData = await response.json();

    // If response is not ok, this might still process
invalid data
    return userData.profile.settings; // Potential
TypeError
}
```

15.2 Using `try`, `catch`, and `finally`

Basic Try-Catch Structure

The try-catch statement provides a mechanism to handle errors gracefully without crashing your application. Code that might throw an error goes in the try block, while error handling logic goes in the catch block.

#javascript

```
// Basic try-catch structure
try {
```

```
    // Code that might throw an error
    let result = riskyOperation();
    console.log("Operation successful:", result);
} catch (error) {
    // Error handling code
    console.error("An error occurred:", error.message);
}

// Practical example - JSON parsing
function parseUserData(jsonString) {
    try {
        let userData = JSON.parse(jsonString);
        return {
            success: true,
            data: userData
        };
    } catch (error) {
        return {
            success: false,
            error: "Invalid JSON format"
        };
    }
}
```

Catching Specific Error Types

You can handle different types of errors differently by checking the error type within the catch block.

#javascript

```
function processUserInput(input) {
```

```
    try {
        // Attempt to process the input
        if (typeof input !== 'string') {
            throw new TypeError("Input must be a
string");
        }

        let data = JSON.parse(input);

        if (!data.hasOwnProperty('id')) {
            throw new ReferenceError("Missing required
'id' property");
        }

        return processData(data);

    } catch (error) {
        if (error instanceof TypeError) {
            console.error("Type error:", error.message);
            return { error: "Invalid input type" };
        } else if (error instanceof SyntaxError) {
            console.error("JSON parsing error:",
error.message);
            return { error: "Invalid JSON format" };
        } else if (error instanceof ReferenceError) {
            console.error("Missing data:",
error.message);
            return { error: "Required data missing" };
        } else {
            console.error("Unexpected error:", error);
            return { error: "Processing failed" };
        }
```

```
    }
}
```

The Finally Block

The finally block executes regardless of whether an error occurs, making it perfect for cleanup operations.

#javascript

```
function processFile(filename) {
    let fileHandle = null;

    try {
        fileHandle = openFile(filename);
        let content = readFile(fileHandle);
        let processedData = processContent(content);
        return processedData;

    } catch (error) {
        console.error("File processing failed:",
error.message);
        return null;

    } finally {
        // This always runs, whether there was an error
or not
        if (fileHandle) {
            closeFile(fileHandle);
            console.log("File handle closed");
        }
    }
```

```
}

// Database connection example
async function performDatabaseOperation() {
    let connection = null;

    try {
        connection = await database.connect();
        let result = await connection.query("SELECT *
FROM users");
        return result;

    } catch (error) {
        console.error("Database operation failed:",
error);
        throw error;  // Re-throw to let caller handle

    } finally {
        if (connection) {
            await connection.close();
            console.log("Database connection closed");
        }
    }
}
```

Nested Try-Catch Blocks

Sometimes you need multiple levels of error handling for different operations within the same function.

#javascript

```
function complexOperation(userData) {
    try {
        // First level - validate input format
        let parsedData;
        try {
            parsedData = JSON.parse(userData);
        } catch (parseError) {
            throw new Error("Invalid JSON input: " +
parseError.message);
        }

        // Second level - validate data structure
        try {
            validateUserSchema(parsedData);
        } catch (validationError) {
            throw new Error("Schema validation failed: "
+ validationError.message);
        }

        // Third level - process the data
        try {
            return processValidatedUser(parsedData);
        } catch (processingError) {
            throw new Error("Processing failed: " +
processingError.message);
        }

    } catch (error) {
        console.error("Complex operation failed:",
error.message);
        return {
```

```
            success: false,
            error: error.message,
            timestamp: new Date().toISOString()
        };
    }
}
```

Handling Asynchronous Errors

Try-catch works with async/await syntax, but requires careful attention to promise handling.

#javascript

```
// Async/await error handling
async function fetchAndProcessData(url) {
    try {
        let response = await fetch(url);

        if (!response.ok) {
            throw new Error(`HTTP error! status:
${response.status}`);
        }

        let data = await response.json();
        let processedData = await processApiData(data);

        return {
            success: true,
            data: processedData
        };
```

```
    } catch (error) {
        if (error.name === 'TypeError') {
            // Network error or fetch failure
            return {
                success: false,
                error: "Network connection failed"
            };
        } else if (error.message.includes('HTTP error'))
{
            // Server responded with error status
            return {
                success: false,
                error: "Server error occurred"
            };
        } else {
            // Other processing errors
            return {
                success: false,
                error: "Data processing failed"
            };
        }
    }
}

// Promise-based error handling
function fetchDataWithPromises(url) {
    return fetch(url)
        .then(response => {
            if (!response.ok) {
                throw new Error(`HTTP error! status:
${response.status}`);
```

```
            }
            return response.json();
        })
        .then(data => processApiData(data))
        .catch(error => {
            console.error("Fetch operation failed:",
error);
            throw error;  // Re-throw or return default
value
        });
}
```

15.3 Throwing Custom Errors

Creating Custom Error Classes

Custom errors provide more specific information about what went wrong and allow for more targeted error handling.

#javascript

```
// Basic custom error class
class ValidationError extends Error {
    constructor(message, field) {
        super(message);
        this.name = "ValidationError";
        this.field = field;
        this.timestamp = new Date().toISOString();
    }
}

class NetworkError extends Error {
```

```
    constructor(message, statusCode, url) {
        super(message);
        this.name = "NetworkError";
        this.statusCode = statusCode;
        this.url = url;
        this.timestamp = new Date().toISOString();
    }
}

class BusinessLogicError extends Error {
    constructor(message, errorCode, context) {
        super(message);
        this.name = "BusinessLogicError";
        this.errorCode = errorCode;
        this.context = context;
        this.timestamp = new Date().toISOString();
    }
}
```

Using Custom Errors in Practice

Custom errors make your code more maintainable and provide better debugging information.

#javascript

```
function validateUserRegistration(userData) {
    if (!userData.email) {
        throw new ValidationError("Email is required",
"email");
    }
```

```
    if (!isValidEmail(userData.email)) {
        throw new ValidationError("Invalid email format",
"email");
    }

    if (!userData.password || userData.password.length <
8) {
        throw new ValidationError("Password must be at
least 8 characters", "password");
    }

    if (userData.age && (userData.age < 13 ||
userData.age > 120)) {
        throw new ValidationError("Age must be between 13
and 120", "age");
    }
}

async function registerUser(userData) {
    try {
        // Validate input
        validateUserRegistration(userData);

        // Check if user already exists
        let existingUser = await
checkUserExists(userData.email);
        if (existingUser) {
            throw new BusinessLogicError(
                "User already exists",
                "USER_EXISTS",
                { email: userData.email }
            );
```

```
        }

        // Attempt to save user
        let newUser = await saveUser(userData);
        return { success: true, userId: newUser.id };

    } catch (error) {
        if (error instanceof ValidationError) {
            return {
                success: false,
                error: "Validation failed",
                field: error.field,
                message: error.message
            };
        } else if (error instanceof BusinessLogicError) {
            return {
                success: false,
                error: "Business rule violation",
                code: error.errorCode,
                message: error.message
            };
        } else {
            console.error("Unexpected registration
error:", error);
            return {
                success: false,
                error: "Registration failed due to system
error"
            };
        }
    }
```

```
}
```

Error Context and Stack Traces

Providing context with your custom errors helps with debugging and monitoring.

#javascript

```
class DetailedError extends Error {
    constructor(message, context = {}) {
        super(message);
        this.name = this.constructor.name;
        this.context = context;
        this.timestamp = new Date().toISOString();

        // Capture stack trace
        if (Error.captureStackTrace) {
            Error.captureStackTrace(this,
this.constructor);
        }
    }

    toJSON() {
        return {
            name: this.name,
            message: this.message,
            context: this.context,
            timestamp: this.timestamp,
            stack: this.stack
        };
    }
```

```
}

function processOrder(orderData) {
    try {
        if (!orderData.items || orderData.items.length
=== 0) {
            throw new DetailedError("Order must contain
at least one item", {
                orderId: orderData.id,
                customerEmail: orderData.customerEmail,
                attemptedAt: new Date().toISOString()
            });
        }

        let total = calculateOrderTotal(orderData.items);

        if (total > orderData.customerCreditLimit) {
            throw new DetailedError("Order exceeds
customer credit limit", {
                orderId: orderData.id,
                orderTotal: total,
                creditLimit:
orderData.customerCreditLimit,
                customerEmail: orderData.customerEmail
            });
        }

        return processPayment(orderData, total);

    } catch (error) {
        console.error("Order processing failed:",
error.toJSON());
```

```
        throw error;
    }
}
```

Throwing Errors for Flow Control

While not always recommended, throwing errors can be used for flow control in specific scenarios.

#javascript

```javascript
function findUserByEmail(email, users) {
    let user = users.find(u => u.email === email);

    if (!user) {
        throw new Error(`User not found: ${email}`);
    }

    return user;
}

function processUsers(emailList, userDatabase) {
    let results = [];
    let errors = [];

    for (let email of emailList) {
        try {
            let user = findUserByEmail(email,
userDatabase);
            let processedUser = processUserData(user);
            results.push(processedUser);
        } catch (error) {
```

```
            errors.push({
                email: email,
                error: error.message
            });
        }
    }

    return {
        successful: results,
        failed: errors,
        summary: {
            total: emailList.length,
            successful: results.length,
            failed: errors.length
        }
    };
}
```

15.4 Debugging with Developer Tools

Console Methods for Debugging

The browser's console provides various methods beyond `console.log()` for effective debugging and error tracking.

#javascript

```
// Different console methods for different purposes
function debuggingExample() {
    console.log("Regular log message");
    console.info("Informational message");
    console.warn("Warning message");
```

```
    console.error("Error message");

    // Group related console outputs
    console.group("User Processing");
    console.log("Processing user data...");
    console.log("Validating email...");
    console.log("Saving to database...");
    console.groupEnd();

    // Conditional logging
    let debugMode = true;
    console.assert(debugMode, "Debug mode should be
enabled");

    // Timing operations
    console.time("Database Query");
    // ... some operation
    console.timeEnd("Database Query");

    // Table format for objects
    let users = [
        { name: "John", age: 30, email:
"john@example.com" },
        { name: "Jane", age: 25, email:
"jane@example.com" }
    ];
    console.table(users);
}
```

Using Breakpoints and Step Debugging

Strategic placement of breakpoints and understanding step debugging helps identify issues quickly.

#javascript

```
function complexCalculation(data) {
    // Set breakpoint here to examine input data
    let processedData = data.map(item => {
        // Conditional breakpoint: item.value > 100
        if (item.value > 100) {
            debugger;  // Programmatic breakpoint
        }

        return {
            ...item,
            processed: true,
            calculatedValue: item.value * 2.5
        };
    });

    // Set breakpoint to examine processed results
    let filteredData = processedData.filter(item => {
        return item.calculatedValue < 1000;
    });

    return filteredData;
}

// Function to help with debugging async operations
async function debugAsyncOperation() {
    try {
        console.log("Starting async operation");
```

```
        let result1 = await firstAsyncCall();
        console.log("First call completed:", result1);

        let result2 = await secondAsyncCall(result1);
        console.log("Second call completed:", result2);

        return result2;
    } catch (error) {
        console.error("Async operation failed:", error);
        // Breakpoint here to examine error details
        debugger;
        throw error;
    }
}
```

Network Tab and API Debugging

Understanding how to debug network requests and API calls through developer tools.

#javascript

```
// Enhanced fetch function with debugging information
async function debuggableFetch(url, options = {}) {
    console.group(`API Call: ${options.method || 'GET'}
${url}`);
    console.log("Request options:", options);
    console.time("Request Duration");

    try {
        let response = await fetch(url, options);
```

```
        console.log("Response status:", response.status);
        console.log("Response headers:",
[...response.headers.entries()]);

        if (!response.ok) {
            throw new Error(`HTTP ${response.status}:
${response.statusText}`);
        }

        let data = await response.json();
        console.log("Response data:", data);
        console.timeEnd("Request Duration");
        console.groupEnd();

        return data;
    } catch (error) {
        console.error("Request failed:", error);
        console.timeEnd("Request Duration");
        console.groupEnd();
        throw error;
    }
}

// Usage with debugging
async function fetchUserProfile(userId) {
    try {
        let profile = await
debuggableFetch(`/api/users/${userId}`);
        let preferences = await
debuggableFetch(`/api/users/${userId}/preferences`);
```

```
        return {
            ...profile,
            preferences: preferences
        };
    } catch (error) {
        console.error("Failed to fetch user profile:",
error);
        return null;
    }
}
```

Performance Debugging

Identifying performance bottlenecks using console timing and performance monitoring.

#javascript

```
class PerformanceMonitor {
    constructor() {
        this.metrics = new Map();
    }

    startTimer(label) {
        this.metrics.set(label, {
            start: performance.now(),
            end: null,
            duration: null
        });
        console.time(label);
    }
```

```
    endTimer(label) {
        let metric = this.metrics.get(label);
        if (metric) {
            metric.end = performance.now();
            metric.duration = metric.end - metric.start;
            console.timeEnd(label);
            console.log(`${label} took
${metric.duration.toFixed(2)}ms`);
        }
    }

    getMetrics() {
        let results = {};
        for (let [label, metric] of this.metrics) {
            results[label] = metric.duration;
        }
        return results;
    }
}

// Usage example
let monitor = new PerformanceMonitor();

function processLargeDataset(data) {
    monitor.startTimer("Data Processing");

    monitor.startTimer("Filtering");
    let filtered = data.filter(item => item.active);
    monitor.endTimer("Filtering");

    monitor.startTimer("Transformation");
```

```
    let transformed = filtered.map(item => ({
        ...item,
        processedAt: new Date(),
        score: calculateScore(item)
    }));
    monitor.endTimer("Transformation");

    monitor.startTimer("Sorting");
    let sorted = transformed.sort((a, b) => b.score -
a.score);
    monitor.endTimer("Sorting");

    monitor.endTimer("Data Processing");

    console.log("Performance Summary:",
monitor.getMetrics());
    return sorted;
}
```

15.5 Defensive Programming Techniques

Input Validation and Sanitization

Defensive programming starts with never trusting input data and always validating what your functions receive.

#javascript

```
function sanitizeAndValidateInput(input, type, options =
{}) {
    // Handle null/undefined inputs
    if (input === null || input === undefined) {
```

```
        if (options.required) {
            throw new ValidationError("Required field
cannot be empty");
        }
        return options.defaultValue || null;
    }

    switch (type) {
        case 'string':
            if (typeof input !== 'string') {
                input = String(input);
            }

            // Trim whitespace
            input = input.trim();

            // Check length constraints
            if (options.minLength && input.length <
options.minLength) {
                throw new ValidationError(`String must be
at least ${options.minLength} characters`);
            }

            if (options.maxLength && input.length >
options.maxLength) {
                throw new ValidationError(`String cannot
exceed ${options.maxLength} characters`);
            }

            // Sanitize HTML if needed
            if (options.sanitizeHtml) {
                input = input.replace(/<[^>]*>/g, '');
```

```
            }

            return input;

        case 'number':
            let num = Number(input);

            if (isNaN(num)) {
                throw new ValidationError("Invalid number
format");
            }

            if (options.min !== undefined && num <
options.min) {
                throw new ValidationError(`Number must be
at least ${options.min}`);
            }

            if (options.max !== undefined && num >
options.max) {
                throw new ValidationError(`Number cannot
exceed ${options.max}`);
            }

            if (options.integer &&
!Number.isInteger(num)) {
                throw new ValidationError("Number must be
an integer");
            }

            return num;
```

```
        case 'email':
            let email = sanitizeAndValidateInput(input,
'string', options);
            let emailRegex =
/^[^\s@]+@[^\s@]+\.[^\s@]+$/;

            if (!emailRegex.test(email)) {
                throw new ValidationError("Invalid email
format");
            }

            return email.toLowerCase();

        case 'array':
            if (!Array.isArray(input)) {
                throw new ValidationError("Input must be
an array");
            }

            if (options.minItems && input.length <
options.minItems) {
                throw new ValidationError(`Array must
contain at least ${options.minItems} items`);
            }

            if (options.maxItems && input.length >
options.maxItems) {
                throw new ValidationError(`Array cannot
contain more than ${options.maxItems} items`);
            }

            return input;
```

```
        default:
            return input;
    }
}

// Usage example
function createUser(userData) {
    try {
        let user = {
            name: sanitizeAndValidateInput(userData.name,
'string', {
                required: true,
                minLength: 2,
                maxLength: 50,
                sanitizeHtml: true
            }),
            email:
sanitizeAndValidateInput(userData.email, 'email', {
                required: true
            }),
            age: sanitizeAndValidateInput(userData.age,
'number', {
                min: 13,
                max: 120,
                integer: true
            }),
            tags: sanitizeAndValidateInput(userData.tags,
'array', {
                maxItems: 10,
                defaultValue: []
            })
        };
```

```
        return saveUser(user);
    } catch (error) {
        console.error("User creation failed:",
error.message);
        throw error;
    }
}
```

Null and Undefined Checking

Implementing consistent strategies for handling null and undefined values prevents many runtime errors.

#javascript

```
// Utility functions for safe property access
function safeGet(obj, path, defaultValue = null) {
    if (!obj || typeof obj !== 'object') {
        return defaultValue;
    }

    let keys = path.split('.');
    let current = obj;

    for (let key of keys) {
        if (current === null || current === undefined ||
!(key in current)) {
            return defaultValue;
        }
        current = current[key];
    }
```

```
    return current;
}

function safeCall(fn, ...args) {
    if (typeof fn !== 'function') {
        console.warn("safeCall: Provided value is not a function");
        return null;
    }

    try {
        return fn(...args);
    } catch (error) {
        console.error("safeCall: Function execution failed:", error);
        return null;
    }
}

// Safe array operations
function safeArrayOperation(arr, operation, defaultValue = []) {
    if (!Array.isArray(arr)) {
        console.warn("Expected array but received:", typeof arr);
        return defaultValue;
    }

    try {
        return operation(arr);
    } catch (error) {
```

```
        console.error("Array operation failed:", error);
        return defaultValue;
    }
}

// Usage examples
function processUserProfile(userProfile) {
    // Safe property access
    let userName = safeGet(userProfile, 'personal.name', 
'Unknown User');
    let userEmail = safeGet(userProfile, 'contact.email', 
'');
    let preferences = safeGet(userProfile, 
'settings.preferences', {});

    // Safe array operations
    let hobbies = safeArrayOperation(
        safeGet(userProfile, 'personal.hobbies', []),
        arr => arr.filter(hobby => hobby && 
hobby.trim().length > 0),
        []
    );

    // Safe function calls
    let formattedName = safeCall(formatUserName, 
userName) || userName;

    return {
        name: formattedName,
        email: userEmail,
        hobbies: hobbies,
        preferences: preferences
```

```
    };
}
```

Type Checking and Guards

Implementing type guards and runtime type checking prevents type-related errors.

#javascript

```javascript
// Type checking utilities
function isString(value) {
    return typeof value === 'string';
}

function isNumber(value) {
    return typeof value === 'number' && !isNaN(value);
}

function isValidDate(value) {
    return value instanceof Date &&
!isNaN(value.getTime());
}

function isPlainObject(value) {
    return value !== null &&
           typeof value === 'object' &&
           value.constructor === Object;
}

function hasRequiredProperties(obj, requiredProps) {
    if (!isPlainObject(obj)) {
```

```
        return false;
    }

    return requiredProps.every(prop =>
obj.hasOwnProperty(prop));
}

// Type guard functions
function assertString(value, paramName) {
    if (!isString(value)) {
        throw new TypeError(`${paramName} must be a
string, received ${typeof value}`);
    }
}

function assertNumber(value, paramName) {
    if (!isNumber(value)) {
        throw new TypeError(`${paramName} must be a valid
number, received ${typeof value}`);
    }
}

function assertObject(value, paramName, requiredProps =
[]) {
    if (!isPlainObject(value)) {
        throw new TypeError(`${paramName} must be an
object, received ${typeof value}`);
    }

    if (!hasRequiredProperties(value, requiredProps)) {
        throw new TypeError(`${paramName} must have
properties: ${requiredProps.join(', ')}`);
```

```
    }
}

// Usage in functions
function calculateCompoundInterest(principal, rate, time,
compoundingFrequency) {
    // Type assertions
    assertNumber(principal, 'principal');
    assertNumber(rate, 'rate');
    assertNumber(time, 'time');
    assertNumber(compoundingFrequency,
'compoundingFrequency');

    // Value validations
    if (principal <= 0) {
        throw new RangeError("Principal must be
positive");
    }

    if (rate < 0) {
        throw new RangeError("Rate cannot be negative");
    }

    if (time <= 0) {
        throw new RangeError("Time must be positive");
    }

    if (compoundingFrequency <= 0) {
        throw new RangeError("Compounding frequency must
be positive");
    }
```

```
    // Perform calculation
    let amount = principal * Math.pow(
        (1 + rate / compoundingFrequency),
        compoundingFrequency * time
    );

    return {
        principal: principal,
        finalAmount: Math.round(amount * 100) / 100,
        interestEarned: Math.round((amount - principal) *
100) / 100
    };
}
```

Circuit Breaker Pattern

Implementing circuit breakers prevents cascading failures in systems with external dependencies.

#javascript

```
class CircuitBreaker {
    constructor(options = {}) {
        this.failureThreshold = options.failureThreshold
|| 5;
        this.recoveryTimeout = options.recoveryTimeout ||
30000;
        this.monitoringPeriod = options.monitoringPeriod
|| 60000;

        this.state = 'CLOSED';  // CLOSED, OPEN,
HALF_OPEN
        this.failureCount = 0;
```

```
        this.lastFailureTime = null;
        this.successCount = 0;
        this.requestCount = 0;
    }

    async execute(operation) {
        if (this.state === 'OPEN') {
            if (this.shouldAttemptReset()) {
                this.state = 'HALF_OPEN';
                console.log("Circuit breaker moving to
HALF_OPEN state");
            } else {
                throw new Error("Circuit breaker is OPEN
- request rejected");
            }
        }

        try {
            let result = await operation();
            this.onSuccess();
            return result;
        } catch (error) {
            this.onFailure();
            throw error;
        }
    }

    onSuccess() {
        this.failureCount = 0;
        this.successCount++;
```

```
        if (this.state === 'HALF_OPEN') {
            this.state = 'CLOSED';
            console.log("Circuit breaker CLOSED - service
recovered");
        }
    }

    onFailure() {
        this.failureCount++;
        this.lastFailureTime = Date.now();

        if (this.failureCount >= this.failureThreshold) {
            this.state = 'OPEN';
            console.log(`Circuit breaker OPEN -
${this.failureCount} failures detected`);
        }
    }

    shouldAttemptReset() {
        return Date.now() - this.lastFailureTime >=
this.recoveryTimeout;
    }

    getStats() {
        return {
            state: this.state,
            failureCount: this.failureCount,
            successCount: this.successCount,
            lastFailureTime: this.lastFailureTime
        };
    }
```

```
}

// Usage example with API calls
class ApiService {
    constructor() {
        this.circuitBreaker = new CircuitBreaker({
            failureThreshold: 3,
            recoveryTimeout: 30000
        });
    }

    async fetchUserData(userId) {
        return this.circuitBreaker.execute(async () => {
            let response = await
fetch(`/api/users/${userId}`);

            if (!response.ok) {
                throw new Error(`API request failed:
${response.status}`);
            }

            return response.json();
        });
    }

    async fetchUserDataWithFallback(userId) {
        try {
            return await this.fetchUserData(userId);
        } catch (error) {
            console.warn("Primary API failed, using
cached data:", error.message);
```

```javascript
            return this.getCachedUserData(userId);
        }
    }

    getCachedUserData(userId) {
        // Return cached or default user data
        return {
            id: userId,
            name: "Unknown User",
            email: "unknown@example.com",
            fromCache: true
        };
    }
}
```

Graceful Degradation

Building systems that continue functioning even when parts fail provides better user experience and system resilience.

```javascript
class FeatureManager {
    constructor() {
        this.features = new Map();
        this.fallbacks = new Map();
    }

    registerFeature(name, implementation, fallback = null) {
        this.features.set(name, implementation);
```

```
        if (fallback) {
            this.fallbacks.set(name, fallback);
        }
    }

    async executeFeature(name, ...args) {
        let feature = this.features.get(name);
        let fallback = this.fallbacks.get(name);

        if (!feature) {
            throw new Error(`Feature '${name}' not
registered`);
        }

        try {
            return await feature(...args);
        } catch (error) {
            console.warn(`Feature '${name}' failed,
attempting fallback:`, error.message);

            if (fallback) {
                try {
                    return await fallback(...args);
                } catch (fallbackError) {
                    console.error(`Fallback for '${name}'
also failed:`, fallbackError.message);
                    throw new Error(`Both primary and
fallback implementations failed for '${name}'`);
                }
            } else {
                throw error;
            }
```

```
        }
    }
}

// Example usage
let featureManager = new FeatureManager();

// Register features with fallbacks
featureManager.registerFeature(
    'imageOptimization',
    async (imageData) => {
        // Primary: Advanced AI-based optimization
        return await
advancedImageOptimization(imageData);
    },
    async (imageData) => {
        // Fallback: Basic compression
        return await basicImageCompression(imageData);
    }
);

featureManager.registerFeature(
    'userRecommendations',
    async (userId) => {
        // Primary: ML-based recommendations
        return await mlRecommendationService(userId);
    },
    async (userId) => {
        // Fallback: Popular items
        return await getPopularItems();
    }
```

```
);

featureManager.registerFeature(
    'searchResults',
    async (query) => {
        // Primary: Elasticsearch
        return await elasticsearchQuery(query);
    },
    async (query) => {
        // Fallback: Database LIKE search
        return await databaseSearch(query);
    }
);
```

Error Logging and Monitoring

Implementing comprehensive error logging helps track issues and improve system reliability.

#javascript

```
class ErrorLogger {
    constructor(options = {}) {
        this.environment = options.environment ||
'development';
        this.logLevel = options.logLevel || 'error';
        this.maxLogSize = options.maxLogSize || 1000;
        this.logs = [];
        this.errorCounts = new Map();
    }

    log(level, message, context = {}) {
```

```
        let logEntry = {
            timestamp: new Date().toISOString(),
            level: level,
            message: message,
            context: context,
            userAgent: typeof navigator !== 'undefined' ?
navigator.userAgent : 'Server',
            url: typeof window !== 'undefined' ?
window.location.href : 'N/A'
        };

        this.logs.push(logEntry);

        // Maintain log size limit
        if (this.logs.length > this.maxLogSize) {
            this.logs.shift();
        }

        // Track error frequency
        if (level === 'error') {
            let errorKey = this.generateErrorKey(message,
context);
            this.errorCounts.set(errorKey,
(this.errorCounts.get(errorKey) || 0) + 1);
        }

        // Console output in development
        if (this.environment === 'development') {
            console[level] ||
console.log(`[${level.toUpperCase()}]`, message,
context);
        }
```

```
        // Send to monitoring service in production
        if (this.environment === 'production' && level
=== 'error') {
            this.sendToMonitoringService(logEntry);
        }
    }

    error(message, context = {}) {
        this.log('error', message, context);
    }

    warn(message, context = {}) {
        this.log('warn', message, context);
    }

    info(message, context = {}) {
        this.log('info', message, context);
    }

    generateErrorKey(message, context) {
        return `${message}-${JSON.stringify(context)}`;
    }

    async sendToMonitoringService(logEntry) {
        try {
            await fetch('/api/logs', {
                method: 'POST',
                headers: { 'Content-Type':
'application/json' },
                body: JSON.stringify(logEntry)
```

```
        });
    } catch (error) {
        console.error('Failed to send log to
monitoring service:', error);
    }
  }

  getErrorSummary() {
    let summary = {};
    for (let [error, count] of this.errorCounts) {
        summary[error] = count;
    }
    return summary;
  }

  getRecentLogs(count = 50) {
    return this.logs.slice(-count);
  }
}

// Global error logger instance
let logger = new ErrorLogger({
  environment: 'production',
  logLevel: 'warn'
});

// Enhanced error handling with logging
class RobustApiClient {
  constructor(baseUrl) {
    this.baseUrl = baseUrl;
    this.retryAttempts = 3;
```

```
        this.retryDelay = 1000;
    }

    async makeRequest(endpoint, options = {}) {
        let url = `${this.baseUrl}${endpoint}`;
        let attempt = 1;

        while (attempt <= this.retryAttempts) {
            try {
                logger.info(`API request attempt
${attempt}`, {
                    url: url,
                    method: options.method || 'GET'
                });

                let response = await fetch(url, options);

                if (!response.ok) {
                    throw new Error(`HTTP
${response.status}: ${response.statusText}`);
                }

                let data = await response.json();

                logger.info('API request successful', {
                    url: url,
                    attempts: attempt
                });

                return data;
```

```
            } catch (error) {
                logger.error(`API request failed (attempt
${attempt})`, {
                    url: url,
                    error: error.message,
                    attempt: attempt,
                    maxAttempts: this.retryAttempts
                });

                if (attempt === this.retryAttempts) {
                    throw new Error(`API request failed
after ${this.retryAttempts} attempts: ${error.message}`);
                }

                // Wait before retry
                await new Promise(resolve =>
setTimeout(resolve, this.retryDelay * attempt));
                attempt++;
            }
        }
    }
}
```

Essential Tips

- Always validate input parameters at function boundaries, checking for null values, correct types, and valid ranges before processing begins.
- Create specific error types for different categories of failures, making it easier to handle different error scenarios appropriately and provide meaningful feedback to users.

- Implement fallback mechanisms and graceful degradation so your application continues functioning even when non-critical features fail, maintaining core functionality.
- Use descriptive error messages that help developers understand what went wrong and how to fix it, including relevant context information like parameter values or system state.
- Log errors consistently with appropriate detail levels, capturing enough information for debugging while avoiding sensitive data exposure in production environments.

Actionable Strategies

- Implement a centralized error handling system that captures all errors, categorizes them by severity, and routes them to appropriate logging and monitoring services for comprehensive oversight.
- Establish retry policies with exponential backoff for transient failures, distinguishing between recoverable errors that should be retried and permanent failures that should fail fast.
- Create comprehensive error boundaries in your application architecture that prevent errors in one component from crashing the entire system, isolating failures appropriately.
- Set up real-time monitoring and alerting for critical errors, with thresholds that trigger notifications when error rates exceed normal baselines or specific error types occur.
- Develop standardized error response formats for APIs that include error codes, human-readable messages, and additional context to help client applications handle errors gracefully.
- Implement proper error sanitization before displaying messages to end users, ensuring that technical details and sensitive information are not exposed while still providing helpful guidance.
- Build automated error recovery mechanisms where possible, such as cache fallbacks, service degradation modes, and automatic retry logic that can resolve common issues without manual intervention.